Housing and Social Justice

SOCIAL POLICY IN MODERN BRITAIN

General Editor: Jo Campling

HOUSING AND SOCIAL JUSTICE *Gill Burke*
VOLUNTARY ACTION AND THE SOCIAL SERVICES
  Roger Hadley
PENAL POLICY *Rod Morgan*
SOCIAL SECURITY AND INCOME MAINTENANCE *Mike Reddin*
FOUNDATIONS OF THE WELFARE STATE *Pat Thane*
THE ELDERLY IN MODERN SOCIETY *Anthea Tinker*
HELP FOR THE HANDICAPPED *Eda Topliss*

HOUSING AND SOCIAL JUSTICE

The role of policy in British housing

Gill Burke

LONGMAN
London and New York

LONGMAN GROUP LIMITED,
Longman House,
Burnt Mill, Harlow, Essex

Published in the United States of America by
Longman Inc., New York

© Longman Group Limited 1981

First published 1981

BRITISH LIBRARY CATALOGUING IN PUBLICATION DATA
Burke, Gill
  Housing and social justice. – (Social policy in modern Britain).
  1. Housing policy – Great Britain
  I. Title   II. Series
  301.5′4′0941   HD7333.A3   79-42624
  ISBN 0–582–29514–9

Set in 10/11 pt Linocomp Plantin
Printed in Great Britain by McCorquodale (Newton) Ltd, Lancashire

CONTENTS

Editor's preface   vii
Author's preface   viii
Acknowledgements   ix

PART ONE: THE BACKGROUND

1. Housing in Britain before 1945   2

PART TWO: THE HOUSING SECTORS

2. Council housing   16
3. Owner-occupation   35
4. The private rented sector   45

PART THREE: HOUSING PROBLEMS

5. Housing problems and housing sector relationships   62
6. Homelessness   64
7. Squatters   83
8. Rural life   92
9. Urban deprivation and the inner-city question   104

PART FOUR: HOUSING AND SOCIAL JUSTICE

10. Evaluation   148

PART FIVE: DOCUMENTS

Documents 1–30   166

Table of Statutes   213
Table of Reports   215
Select bibliography   218
Index   222

EDITOR'S PREFACE

This series, written by practising teachers in universities and polytechnics, is produced for students who are required to study social policy and administration, either as social science undergraduates or on the various professional courses. The books focus on essential topics in social policy and include new areas of discussion and research, to give students the opportunity to explore ideas and act as a basis of seminar work and further study. Each book combines an analysis of the selected theme, a critical narrative of the main developments and an assessment putting the topic into perspective as defined in the title. The supporting documents and comprehensive bibliography are an important aspect of the series.

Conventional footnotes are avoided and the following system of references is used: superior number (⁶) in the text refers the reader to the corresponding entry in the references at the end of the chapter. A number in square brackets, preceded by 'doc' [docs 6, 8], refers the reader to the corresponding items in the section of documents which follows the main text.

In *Housing and Social Justice* Gill Burke has provided an introduction to the development of housing policy in modern Britain. Her book combines an examination of the way in which the various housing sectors have developed, how they are structured today and the problems generated within and between them. The main emphasis is upon the effects of policy and the values, conflicts and ideologies which underlie housing policy. Problems such as homelessness, squatting and the rural and inner-city housing shortages are examined within the housing context and the broader context of British society. The final section evaluates recent housing policy with reference to theories of social justice and the role of social policy in achieving a fair distribution of resources is challenged.

Jo Campling

AUTHOR'S PREFACE

Housing offers so many different dimensions to study – social, economic, political, physical and spatial. It is this that makes it so interesting, and often so very difficult to come to grips with. This book is intended to be a beginning. It aims to provide a basic introduction to housing and housing policy in Britain. It examines how the various housing sectors have developed, what sort of problems this development has caused and what part has been played by policy. It also aims to raise issues about values and policies and the way housing, and other resources are distributed, since even a basic introduction should try to make people think and question. The bibliography at the end is quite a long one, but most of the books and journals referred to should be fairly easily accessible and will, I hope, provide the springboard for reading in depth.

Gill Burke

ACKNOWLEDGEMENTS

I would like to thank the following for their assistance in the preparation of this book: Campaign for the Homeless and Rootless; The Librarian, Department of the Environment Library; The Librarian, Environmental Studies Library, University College, London; Francis Beckett, Research Officer, National Union of Agricultural Workers; Shelter; Tom Corlett; Helen Moroney; my colleagues Irene Fox, Ray Lees and Alan Teague; and my neighbours and friends in the Fitzrovia district of central London, for whom housing problems are not theoretical issues.

We are grateful to the following for permission to reproduce copyright material:

George Allen and Unwin Publishers Ltd for an extract from pp. 78–80, *The Ministry of Housing and Local Government*, by Evelyn Sharpe; Faber and Faber Ltd for extracts from pp. 36 and 94, *The Radiant City*, by Le Corbusier, reprinted by Faber and Faber Ltd; the author, Professor Ruth Glass, for her letter 'The Rachman Affair: Story not new', in *The Times*, July 20th, 1963, reprinted by permission of the author; Her Majesty's Stationery Office for an extract from *Report of the Committee on Local Authority and Allied Personal Social Services*, Cmnd 3703, 1968; an extract from *Council Housing: Purposes, Procedures and Priorities*, by Housing Management Sub-Committee of Central Housing Advisory Committee, 1969; an extract from *Housing (Homeless Persons) Act 1977: Code of Guidance (England and Wales)*, by DOE/DHSS Welsh Office, 1978; an extract from 'Change and Decay', *Final Report of the Liverpool Inner Area Study*, by DOE, 1977; an extract from *Report of the Committee on New Towns Final Report*, Cmnd 6876, 1946, and an extract from *Policy for the Inner Cities*, Cmnd 6845, by DOE, 1977, reproduced with the permission of Her Majesty's Stationery Office; John Murray Publishers Ltd for an extract from the poem 'The Metropolitan Railway', by John Betjeman, from *Collected Poems*, John Murray Publishers Ltd and Houghton Mifflin Co; New Statesman for an extract from the article 'In the work-house', by Mary Cecil, in *New Statesman*, January 12th, 1962; Philag's Health Advisory Service for an extract from *Standards of Accommodation for Single People*, by D. Ormandy and A. Davies, published by Campaign for Homeless and Rootless; Shelter for an extract from *The Facts About Council House Sales*, Appendix, 1979; University of East Anglia for an extract from Table 3, p. 79, 'The Social Implications of Village Development', by J. M. Shaw, in *Social Issues in Rural Norfolk*, edited by N. Moseley, 1978.

Part one
THE BACKGROUND

Chapter one
HOUSING IN BRITAIN BEFORE 1945

During the eighteenth and nineteenth centuries Britain experienced a social and economic transformation. This period of change in industrial and financial organisation, in technological development, in labour relations, in increase of population, brought with it tremendous urban expansion. In 1801 the only town with a population of over 100,000 was London; by 1871 there were sixteen such towns, all save three of them in the Midlands or North of England. In 1801, the working people of Britain could still be fairly termed either agricultural workers or small craftsmen; by 1871 they had been transformed into an urban proletariat.

This immense urban expansion – what Engels termed the 'centralising tendency of Manufacture' – took place with little or no regulation or control. Local government as we know it today did not exist, 'town planning' was also non-existent. The result was appalling. The juxtaposition of dwellings and industry, the lack of ventilation and of adequate drainage or refuse collection, the lack of clean, fresh water, were all described by contemporary writers [doc 1]. Robert Owen's experiment at New Lanark, where a better standard of environment and amenity was shown not to be inconsistent with profit, did not convince his fellow entrepreneurs elsewhere. Other attempts at alternatives, such as the Chartist land schemes, did not last long.[1] But although the expansion of manufacturing and industrial towns greatly increased the amount of bad and slum housing, such housing conditions were by no means new. It is important to remember that bad housing predates the Industrial Revolution. It was the extent of the problem and the social and health threats that this industrial expansion posed that caught the attention of reformers.

THE DEVELOPMENT OF STATE INTERVENTION IN HOUSING

State intervention in housing can be said to have developed from two starting points.

Firstly, the 'sanitary idea'. This grew from Edwin Chadwick's concern with public health, and more especially from the devastating mortality of the cholera epidemics that raged during the nineteenth century. As the realisation grew that disease could spread from the crowded insanitary districts and attack the wealthier classes, so enthusiasm grew for measures to contain this. The policy emphasis was twofold – the introduction of piped water and drainage, plus slum clearance and demolition. Yet the main effect of policy based upon the sanitary idea was, as Steadman Jones has shown,[2] greatly to increase the housing shortage and those very conditions of over-crowding that it sought to assuage. Although the Citizens' and Labourers' Dwelling Act (the 'Torrens' Act) of 1868 introduced the principle of state control over the condition of houses and the right to demolish houses which were unsatisfactory, the net result was one of 'shovelling out the poor'. Many medical officers of health, when faced with overcrowding and migration into their districts from else-where, simply enforced the Torrens Act and demolished the buildings and forced the occupants to move elsewhere. Other medical officers were reluctant to undertake measures which might involve the demolition of property belonging to prominent local ratepayers. The demands of the labour market, especially for casual labour, meant that people had to live near their work. Thus what accommodation remained became more and more crowded.

Many sanitary reformers saw the conditions in which the poorer people lived as resulting less from overcrowding, lack of amenity and scarcity than from moral laxness by the people themselves. Cause and effect were often confused, especially where 'drink' was con-cerned. It was believed, however, that many of 'the poor' were reformable and that their housing problems could be solved by their being trained in the habits of thrift and household management. It was Octavia Hill who instituted the system whereby volunteer lady helpers 'trained' selected tenants in these wholesome principles [doc 2]. Kindly interest in the tenants' welfare, however, was combined with strict insistence upon regular payment of rents. Eviction was the consequence of falling into arrears. The Octavia Hill system can be said to have had more effect upon the develop-ment of social work and the welfare aspects of housing management than upon the housing problems of the nineteenth century.

The main impact of the sanitary idea resulted in demolition and increased overcrowding. But nonetheless it did establish the concept of minimum standards and the realisation of the health hazards of bad housing and overcrowding. It continued to play a major part in determining policy, and can still be seen in operation today.

The second starting point for the development of state intervention in housing was *market failure*. Once the concept of minimum standards had begun to be established this was inevitable. It was not possible to provide accommodation with adequate space, ventilation, water and drainage for the majority of working people because of the irreconcilable gap between the need to obtain a return on investment and the level of rents that people on low incomes could afford to pay. The realisation of market failure was slow in coming (indeed, it can be argued that some theorists and politicians still do not accept it) and attempts were made by philanthropists to stimulate investment in 'decent' rented housing by providing examples – models of what they felt was possible. Since nothing below a 5 per cent return would tempt a capitalist, the movement to provide model dwellings became termed 'five per cent philanthropy'. They did not, however, often succeed in achieving this level of return because costs, particularly the cost of land, rose steeply after 1859. Lord Shaftesbury's Society for Improving the Condition of the Labouring Classes, which was one of the most successful of the philanthropic housing associations, achieved only a $2\frac{3}{4}$ per cent yield after 1852. Nor were they able to house more than a section of the relatively prosperous working-class. There were two reasons for this. Firstly, the *rents were too high* for anyone not in secure regular employment. Even the Peabody Trust, whose funds had been 'specially appropriated to the poor of London and not to the artisans', and who under-cut the other model dwelling companies by 30 per cent, were charging rents of 5s. a week for three rooms and scullery in 1881. Very many of the 'poor of London' had weekly wages of less than 10s., many others who earned more did not have anything other than casual employment, whose fluctuations made savings or regular financial commitments impossible. Secondly, the model dwellings had *rules* that governed the behaviour of their tenants. Peabody tenants, for example, could not sublet, take in washing, undertake outwork, keep pets, paper their rooms, hang pictures on their walls or stay out after 11 p.m. (the front door was locked and the gas turned off each night to ensure this). Not only were these rules uncongenial, they effectively barred from tenancy all those who needed the income from washing, subletting or outwork as well as the many costermongers and street traders who needed room to stable their donkey or pony.

There was considerable opposition from among the working-class to the model dwellings; they saw them quite clearly as controlling and regulating mechanisms. In part, this opposition was generated by the design of many of the dwellings whose barrack-like appearance too closely resembled the 'model' workhouses and 'model' prisons also being erected at that time. Generally, though, public and Parliament welcomed the model dwellings societies and looked to them to offer a solution to the problems of housing for the poor. This was a solution the societies were unable to give. Landlords and builders simply did not take their 'models' from the societies. As Gauldie puts it, 'In spite of the interest of the Prince of Wales, and Lord Shaftesbury, the approval of Edwin Chadwick and George Godwin of "The Builder", the publicity gained at the Great Exhibition (where Prince Albert himself designed some model cottages) the invitation to imitate was not taken up commercially . . .'.[3]

What is important about the philanthropic housing associations is not their failure to 'solve' the problem of standards, costs and rents, but the fact that so much of their work, policy and outlook provided 'models' for the provision of later local council housing. In the 1880s and 1890s this was not surprising; there was, after all, a clear overlap between local government and housing association. These overlaps were in ideology, desire for sanitary reform and, in some cases, in personnel. This was particularly true in London, when after the passing of the 'Artisans' Dwellings Acts 1875 and 1882 (the Cross Acts) the Metropolitan Board of Works was established to clear overcrowded sites by demolition and sell these to the Trustees of the philanthropic societies for redevelopment. These new developments did try to match in dwellings provided the numbers of people displaced, but, as Steadman Jones has pointed out, it was not the same people who were rehoused in the new dwellings. 'Shovelling out the poor' continued more or less unchanged; the policy of the philanthropic associations of offering housing only to the 'better' class of artisan and workman was carried over into local government when rebuilding became their responsibility after the passing of the Housing of the Working Classes Acts 1890, 1894 and 1900.

The influence of the philanthropic societies on policy in the nineteenth century is understandable, but the extent to which the 'model dwelling ethic' can still be seen in policy for council housing in late twentieth-century Britain is perhaps a little surprising. The Peabody restrictions, for example, find parallels in the tenancy regulations of many of today's council dwellings. The 'block-and-gallery' design of so many model dwellings (of which the earliest, and perhaps most elegant example, designed by Henry Roberts for Lord Shaftesbury's society, can still be seen at Streatham Street in central London) provided a prototype for countless blocks of council flats. Above all, there carried through into the public sector what might almost be described as 'class-within-a-class' distinction in housing, a clear distinction between the deserving and the undeserving poor. It was the deserving poor – the steady artisans in regular employment – who were housed by the societies and later by the local councils [doc 3].

Uniting and underpinning the beliefs and policies of both sanitary and housing reformers lay fear. Fear of social unrest, fear of the 'contamination' of the slums. This was clearly articulated by contemporary writers. Pearson, in his analysis of the writings of Edwin Chadwick and others, shows how the symbolism of their language echoed their fear of the potentially explosive mob of slum dwellers.[4] Marx stated matters more bluntly – 'A spectre is haunting Europe, the spectre of revolution'.[5]

Many writers argued that the effect of having to live in slums might be to turn honest working men into criminals, revolutionaries, or both. The Rev. Thomas Beames, writing in 1852, after having discussed the fact that the Paris uprising of 1848 began in the slums of the St Antoine district, added: 'We have termed our rookeries plague spots; are they not indeed such? Where are our convicts nursed . . .? Do not such outcasts hide their heads in the rookeries . . .? And in close connection with such dregs of society the honest and hard-working labourer rests his weary head, his children play with felon's children, learning their habits, infected by their example.'[6] This view was echoed again and again. Lord Shaftesbury, in his evidence to the Royal Commission on the Housing of the Working Classes 1884, stressed the moral corruption that threatened children brought up in these slums. Other witnesses agreed. Slum-dwelling in noisome overcrowded cities, away from the uplifting example of social superiors (many of whom had moved away to the suburbs), might well lead to a pauperised and demoralised people who might cease to be industrious and rise up against their masters.

Much reforming effort was put into separating the 'honest hard-working labourer' from the feckless and undeserving 'residuum', albeit with little success. The model dwellings societies limited their activities mainly to London, and were unable to have any more than a marginal impact even there. The distinction the societies made between deserving workers and others, however, does help to explain how in Britain public sector housing developed as it did. Council housing can be said to be 'workers' housing'. It is not 'welfare housing' for the socially disadvantaged as it is, for example, in the United States. This is not to deny that many of the socially disadvantaged do get housed in the public sector – scarcity plus the allocation system ensures that they do – but the welfare function is still not the main policy objective.

The continued emphasis upon slum clearance, and the failure of both philanthropists and the market to provide adequate alternatives, continued the housing shortage and led to increasing working-class protest. By the early years of the twentieth century the response to absolute shortage of housing was showing itself in mass meetings and riots. But although these were on the whole sympathetically received by a British society rather more aware of the dimensions of poverty and rather less fearful of revolution than in earlier years, the emphasis for policy remained unchanged and still centred on the need to reduce overcrowding by demolishing the slums. Bad housing was seen as a problem that would solve itself once the problems of low income and bad health were solved rather than as a problem in its own right. Thus the attention of reformers was focused elsewhere – on the abolition of casual employment, upon the development of the insurance principle, upon the need for improved diet and improved maternity and child-care. The main social reform measures of the pre-war Liberal Government reflected this with legislation for school meals, old-age pension and health insurance. The implication for housing seemed to be that a healthier, better-off working-class might yet find its housing needs met by the private market. Thus, although the Liberal Government did pass housing legislation, the actual achievement in housing in the public sector remained small. The Housing and Town Planning Act 1909 was a far-sighted measure, but had little immediate effect. Although under the Act local authorities could retain rather than sell the homes they built, overall house building declined in the following years, while the problem of overcrowding and shortage in no way diminished. The 1911 census showed that in England and Wales 3,139,472 people were living in 430,000 tenements with more than two occupants per room. By 1914, out of all the local authorities in the country only 179 had applied for and obtained loans to build houses, 112 of these after 1909 largely as a result of 'prodding' by the local Government Board. By 1917, the overcrowding and shortage were at crisis point. Evidence to the Royal Commission on the Housing of the Industrial

Population of Scotland 1917 showed that nearly half the population of Scotland occupied dwellings of not more than two rooms. In London 17.8 per cent of the capital's population were families living more than two persons to a room.

The coming of war in 1914 concentrated labour in certain areas. This led to massively increased rents there. The working-class opposition to this, especially in Glasgow where there were riots, galvanised both housing reformers and government. Measures were introduced to *control* rents in the private sector, which were to have important implications for the public sector as well. The Rent and Mortgage Restriction Act 1915 can be said to have ensured that there could never again be market provision for adequate working-class housing at low rent, such provision necessarily developed as the task of the state.

The end of the First World War saw the acknowledgement of this in the drive to build council houses to provide 'Homes Fit for Heroes'. This was not simply a recognition by government of the war effort. Industrial unrest at home and the Bolshevik revolution abroad represented a very real threat.

The new housing drive constituted a move away from the purely sanitary approach, and involved a new means of financing – the government *subsidy*. Under the Housing and Town Planning Act 1919 (Addison's Act) the government proposed to subsidise the gap between the rent charged on the open market and that charged by local authorities. With this commitment to provide 'decent' housing at subsidised rents, 'council housing' arrived to stay. The intention was to build 500,000 new houses over three years. Yet Bowley suggests that the shortage of dwellings at the time of the Armistice was already about 600,000 and this estimate made no allowance for the replacing of insanitary dwellings or others that needed demolition.[7] Even had the estimates been correct, the rate of building required was impossible to achieve in the post-war situation of shortage of skilled labour and rising building costs. By 1920 subsidies were being offered to private builders as well – lump sums of £130–160 per house built for sale or rent. By 1921 the economic crisis and treasury anxiety over the 'open-ended' nature of the subsidies led to Lloyd George abandoning his commitments to Addison and the 'Homes for Heroes', and the subsidies were cut under the 'Geddes Axe'.

Despite the failure of the market and of central and local government to provide new dwellings to ease the housing shortage, the drive for slum clearance went on and by the 1930s had once more become the dominant policy in the housing field. Demolition was seen as the only solution for the slums. The Departmental Committee on Housing 1933 which recommended *compulsory purchase* powers for local authorities did not envisage these being used for rehabilitation of slum dwellings: 'We agree with the view that the first essential task is to clear the slums; we have made no proposals which would afford Local Authorities any excuse to slacken or reduce their efforts in this direction: and we have made it clear that we are definitely opposed to the policy of reconditioning as a cheap alternative to demolition and replacement.'

One trouble with the 'sanitary idea' approach to housing problems is the open-ended nature of what is defined as minimum standards. As a society's standards rise, so does the definition of the minimum. Thus, despite half a century of slum clearance, the slums were nowhere near eradicated, indeed they seemed to be increasing. The intention of the Housing Act 1930 had been to secure the demolition of *all* slums, and 145 local authorities had estimated then that this implied clearing 76,524 houses. By 1934 these same local authorities were putting forward programmes estimating clearing 172,261 houses, and there was still an immense gap between the amount of houses demolished and the number of new ones constructed. As well as this, rising costs meant that local authorities, despite government subsidy and the power to level a penny rate for housing, had increasingly to consider 'ability to pay' as a criterion for allocation. Not until 1934 was the criteria modified and special provision made for rehousing families, largely regardless of their means, and this was limited initially to families living in conditions of gross overcrowding or in the very worst slums.

Yet despite the difficulties, by the outbreak of the Second World War state intervention in the housing market had become established on a permanent basis to provide housing for the 'working-class' at below-market rents. Much of the effort was still concentrated upon slum clearance and motivated by the sanitary idea. There was some confusion as to just who counted as 'working-class' [doc 4]. The size of the public sector was not very large, less than 12 per cent, but the rôle of the state in housing had come a long way from the tentative public health interventions of the early nineteenth century.

CHANGES IN THE PRIVATE HOUSING MARKET: THE GROWTH OF THE BUILDING SOCIETIES

Until the middle of the twentieth century, relatively few people owned their own home. Renting was the established method of tenure, with an adequate supply of dwellings for those in the middle- and upper-income groups who could meet the market rent levels. Those who did buy their own homes tended to do so with a loan, most frequently from a building society.

The earliest societies began on the initiative of working people. They were building clubs, formed from the end of the eighteenth century by groups of tradesmen who clubbed together to build their own houses with their own hands, each exercising his trade – bricklayers, carpenters, painters – on a co-operative basis to the advantage of the group. From these developed the 'terminating societies' where members clubbed together with regular payments into a fund that terminated when the last member was housed. They were genuine self-help attempts, as Gauldie points out, 'not indeed by the poorest classes but by the respectable artisans',[3] begun in response to the bad housing conditions, insecurity of tenure, and housing shortage that became characteristic of urban Britain during and after its industrial transformation. Unlike the circumstances which had generated them, however, most of these societies did not survive the first part of the nineteenth century. There were three main reasons for this.

The first was financial; the margin available to working men for savings was insufficient to survive fluctuations in wages or periods of unemployment. As the purchasing power of their wages fell, so they were unable to keep up their payments. Gauldie gives the example of the Nottingham money clubs who 'employed builders to provide houses for their members from their savings as early as the 1790s, but this, a product of the prosperity of the independent knitters, could not survive the mechanisation of their trade'.[3] This narrowness of financial margin and the lack of capital reserves placed the societies at risk from inefficiencies and fraud, through unwise investment and through 'brick-on-edge' jerry-building [doc 5]. Secondly, this financial stringency made it essential to keep down costs and to economise on land and materials wherever possible. Thus it was that some of the first 'back-to-back houses' were built for working-men's building societies. Arguments concerning the advantages of such dwellings were countered by official statistics as to health and infant mortality risk, and the official view was enforced by *legislative* means. The Building Regulations that followed the Public Health Act of 1848, and more importantly the Metropolitan Building Act and the Labourers Dwellings Act of 1855, had a disastrous effect on the working-men's societies.

Finally, despite the desire of working-men for a healthy dwelling of their own, there was a *disincentive* to home ownership, which in its way could be said to have been a nineteenth-century form of 'poverty trap'. As owners of property they became liable for local rates and (if the value of their house surpassed £10 p.a.) for house tax. Added to their membership dues, plus the expense of maintenance and repairs, this meant a considerable increase in their outgoings. At the same time by virtue of their being property owners they were debarred from receiving Poor Relief and were also debarred by many local distress committees from receiving any form of relief during periods of unemployment. Although the working-men's societies failed, there was one important aspect that survived – the emphasis on *thrift and self-help among artisans*. This emphasis was carried through into the building societies that developed following the passing of the Building Societies Act of 1874. This Act gave building societies limited company status and brought them under the control of the Chief Registrar of Friendly Societies (whose supervision remains to this time). From the 1874 Act grew the 'permanent' building societies. In these, people might invest who were not themselves in need of housing, as well as providing a savings deposit for those hoping to own their home later. Many of the largest permanent societies had been formed before 1874 – the Leeds Permanent in 1848, the Abbey National in 1849, the Halifax in 1853 – but the Building Societies Act 1874 provided their consolidation and shaped their future development.

What characterised the permanent societies was the growing number of middle-class investors, middle-class managers, and gradually, over time, middle-class borrowers for house purchase. The wise investment of depositors' money and the housing of low-income groups frequently proved incompatible. Thus while some societies could claim to have been started by philanthropists and the medical men to benefit the 'provident working-man' others could claim their intention to be 'the erection of improved dwellings, chiefly but not exclusively for the working-classes'.[8] This continued to be the case from then on, not only because of the need for borrowers to have steady well-paid work to meet the repayment requirements, but also because increasingly the building societies focused on the need to keep their interest rates competitive to attract investors who might otherwise have sought other ways of getting return on their capital.

Although the building societies went from strength to strength in attracting funds and in lending – by 1890 they had nearly £50 million out on mortgage – they did not make any significant change in the *housing supply*. The impossibility of providing adequate artisans' housing to rent at a profit had, as we have seen, been acknowledged by government with policies to extend municipal involvement and to encourage philanthropic housing associations of the Peabody type. The need for workmen to be near their work also helped keep them in the rented sector since it was rented dwellings that were most to be found in the inner areas of towns. For the middle-classes there was an adequate supply of rented accommodation, since this was profitable at higher rents. The opportunity costs between renting and buying were not greatly different. By the time of the outbreak of the First World War only 10 per cent of houses were owner-occupied.

The first great increase in building-society activity came after the First World War. In 1920 there were 1,100 societies, most with surplus funds following the lull in lending during wartime. To these, the Housing Act 1923 gave the opportunity for expansion of activity not only with government blessing but with government financial support as well. Following the débâcle of the 'Homes for Heroes' policy, the new government of 1923, with Neville Chamberlain as Minister of Housing, turned to private enterprise to solve the housing shortage. Under Chamberlain's Housing Act 1923 local authorities were empowered to guarantee building-society mortgages which exceeded the (then usual) 70 per cent of valuation on all houses which cost less than £1,500. In addition, private builders were to receive a lump-sum subsidy of £75 per house. This could be added to by local authorities from the rates if they so chose. Although Chamberlain's Act itself was short-lived, the subsidy was not abolished and throughout the 1920s an unparalleled expansion of house building took place, matched by the rise in the number of borrowers with mortgages. In 1928 the amount advanced was £58.7 million, bringing the amount out on mortgage to £227 million. By 1937, when £136.9 million was advanced, the total amount out on mortgage was £656 million. Berry suggests that this expansion in house building may have been a major factor in Britain's comparatively rapid emergence from the depression.[9]

Yet for all this, a housing shortage remained, and it could be argued that but for the outbreak of the Second World War there might have been a shift back towards renting. The building boom was falling off, and private renting was still seen as a 'respectable' way to pay for accommodation.

In the years that followed the war, housing policy was to divide more clearly along party political lines, and the relationship between the sectors of the housing market was to change quite markedly, as owner-occupation and public-sector renting became the main forms of tenure and private renting declined almost to nothing. British society was also to change after the war. Memories of the depression and the war experience stimulated the building of a new 'welfare state', while later economic stimulus of consumption led to the belief that Britain was an 'affluent society'. Later still this view was to be questioned. In all these changes the housing situation played a part. By the late twentieth century it was clear that while the dark and noisome slums no longer existed on the scale they once had, they had not disappeared. The relativities of bad housing still continued.

REFERENCES

1. D. HARDY, *Alternative Communities in Nineteenth Century England*, Longman, London (1970).
2. G. STEADMAN JONES, *Outcast London: a study in the relationship between classes in Victorian Society*, Penguin, Harmondsworth (1976 paperback edn).
3. E. GAULDIE, *Cruel Habitations: a history of working-class housing 1780–1918*, Allen & Unwin, London (1974).
4. G. PEARSON, *The Deviant Imagination*, Ch. 6, 'King Mob', Macmillan, London (1974).
5. K. MARX and F. ENGELS, *The Communist Manifesto* (first published 1848); English paperback edn, Progress Publishers, Moscow (1977 edn).
6. T. BEAMES, *The Rookeries of London, Past, Present and Prospective* (first published 1852; facsimile, David & Charles, Newton Abbot, reprinted 1970).
7. M. BOWLEY, *Housing and the State*, Allen & Unwin, London (1945).
8. J. HOLE, *Homes for the Working Class*, Longmans, Green & Co., London (1866).
9. F. BERRY, *Housing: the great British failure*, Charles Knight, London (1974).

Part two
THE HOUSING SECTORS

Chapter two
COUNCIL HOUSING

Unlike owner-occupation, or the private rented sector, entry to the public-sector housing is not determined by ability to pay. Council housing is allocated according to 'housing need'. This is not necessarily a sign of poverty in money terms, and it is important to recall that poverty is a *relative* lack of command over resources:

A family may have an average income but be unable to obtain access to good housing at a reasonable rent: their position would be disadvantaged in comparison with a family in a low-rent council house. Indeed they may be solely 'housing poor'. A family living in a rural area may have resources and costs equivalent to an urban family but be cut off from access to a wide range of services, facilities and opportunities because they do not have a car and the bus service has been axed: they are 'transport poor'.[1]

To help them determine 'housing need' most local authorities operate a points system which takes into account social and environmental factors, such as the number of children in a family, any mental or physical disabilities, the number of rooms they at present occupy, the lack of amenities such as hot and cold water or own w.c., and so forth. Because there are more applicants than there are available council dwellings – except in a few areas – most local authorities also have a waiting list. The number of points a family is awarded, rather than the time they have spent on the list, usually determines the speed with which they are offered council accommodation. In addition, local authorities have a duty to rehouse people whose homes are demolished for local authority redevelopment, road building, slum-clearance schemes, or who are homeless. Many also include a 'quota' of families nominated by their Social Services department.

One of the main purposes of council housing has always been to meet the needs of lower income groups; indeed, until 1949 local authorities were restricted by law to providing houses for the 'working-classes' [doc 4]. Although this restriction was then abandoned and a more comprehensive, universalist policy introduced, the 1957 Housing Act subsequently placed a duty on local authorities to give 'reasonable preference' to persons occupying insanitary or overcrowded houses, or who had large families, or who were living under generally unsatisfactory housing conditions – those people, in fact, who could prove 'housing need'.

This implicit selectivity within a universalist, or almost universalist, policy can be said to have been introduced and to still operate for three main reasons: (*a*) *scarcity* both of low-rent, private-sector housing and of council housing itself; (*b*) the size and importance of the whole *private sector* which has an influence on public-sector policies in a far more direct and consequential way than in those other areas of social policy – health and education – where universalist policies also apply; (*c*) it is within the field of public-sector housing policies that clashes of *opposing ideologies* have been most apparent, and have shaped the nature and type of council housing and the way in which it has developed in Britain until today.

Today, approximately one-third of all housing tenures (32 per cent in 1977) are in the public sector. This involvement by the state in the provision of housing on any scale, is, however, comparatively recent. There were, of course, numerous legislative housing measures enacted during the nineteenth century; there was council house building by the London County Council after 1895 and by other County Councils after 1900, and there was a burst of activity following the First World War. Yet by 1947 only 12 per cent of housing tenures lay in the public sector. This slow growth can in part be explained by the reluctance of national and local government to sanction such direct interference in the workings of the market, but this in itself is an insufficient explanation. Throughout the nineteenth century there was considerable state intervention in almost all aspects of British life and industry. What needs to be borne in mind is the intention and effect of such intervention. The early measures, although achieving little at the time, did at least establish principles which could be acted upon later. '. . . nineteenth-century legislative activity insinuated into the statute book the principle of state responsibility for housing while at the same time ensuring, with all the outrage of which Parliament was capable, that such unwarrantable intrusion upon private rights would not be tolerated.'[2]

DEVELOPMENT OF STATE HOUSING POLICY SINCE 1945

It was after the Second World War that the real drive to build council houses began. Initially this was not surprising. Britain emerged from the war with 200,000 houses totally destroyed, another 250,000 so badly damaged they could not be lived in and as many more needing urgent repairs. In addition there was an enthusiasm for change, a determination that the misery of the depression of the 1920s and 1930s should never be repeated. This desire for change showed itself most clearly with the election, in 1945, of a Labour government with a massive majority. This government was committed to the extension of public-sector housing on ideological grounds, but also because the housing programmes of local authorities could be planned, regulated and controlled in a way that private-sector building could not. '. . . the speculative builder by his very nature is not a plannable instrument' stated the Minister of Housing, Aneurin Bevan. The post-war housing drive instituted by the Labour government included vastly increased powers for local authorities to compulsory purchase and requisition property, as well as increased subsidies both for new building and for slum clearance. But, for all this enthusiasm, there was no serious reappraisal of housing policy: 'The twin pillars of the whole programme – rent control and subsidised council housing – were devices that had been employed since the First World War.'[3] If the drive to build more council houses immediately after the war is not altogether surprising, the steady expansion of the public sector in the years that followed might well be. By 1961, after a decade of Conservative government, the public-sector share of housing tenures had risen to 26 per cent.

Most of this rapid increase took place in the early years of the new Conservative government. Completed dwellings rose from 150,000 for 1951 to 220,000 for 1954. But this increase in building masked the ideological divide between the Labour and Conservative administrations over housing.

Very soon the Conservative government's determination to foster and encourage private enterprise began to concentrate upon the ownership as well as the building of homes. As the White Paper *Housing the Next Step* (1953) put it, 'Her Majesty's Government believe that the people of this country prefer, in housing as in other matters, to help themselves as much as they can rather than rely wholly or mainly upon the efforts of Government, national or local.' These words heralded a shift of policy that was to have important long-term effects on the public sector, (*a*) because the emphasis upon owner occupation (encouraging the nation to become a 'property-owning democracy' as the then minister Harold Macmillan termed it) signalled the beginning not only of the rapid expansion of that sector but also the controversy that was to become increasingly fierce in the late 1970s regarding the rôle of council housing *per se*; (*b*) because if, in fact, most people were actually 'able to help themselves' then council housing could take on a residual function and change its nature quite dramatically from 'workers' housing' to 'welfare housing'. Subsequent Conservative administrations made it quite clear that these were the policies they continued to favour, while subsequent Labour ones, although pledging themselves to policies of municipalisation and the expansion of council-house building, also began in the early 1970s to encourage people to 'help themselves' into owner-occupation, without apparently feeling that there might be any contradictions in this.

The immediate result of these policy changes and the ideology underlying them was seen in the changing of the system of finance for council housing. Hitherto, local authorities had gone for finance for building to the Public Works Loans Board (PWLB) where interest rates had been kept at 3 per cent or lower. Now they were required to try to borrow first on the open market, turning to the PWLB only as a last resort. Public Works Loans Board interest rates were no longer to be pegged, but were to be fixed by reference to the credit of local authorities of 'good standing in the market', and by October 1956 this rate of interest had risen to $5\frac{3}{4}$ per cent.

This rise in interest rates, by greatly increasing the loan debt of local authorities, also greatly increased their housing costs. The increased costs of the earlier, expansionist period of the 1950s had at the time been largely offset by increased housing subsidies. Now, the general subsidy was replaced by specific subsidies, for slum clearance and special needs, and the government made it clear that increased costs must be met either by increased rate fund contributions or by increased rents. Council housing policy was 'clearly and explicitly to operate a "realistic rents" policy within a reduced building programme designed to meet special categories of need'.[4]

Despite the change in emphasis, there still did not appear to have been any serious attempt to rethink the objectives of housing policy in an integrated way; policy seemed much as it was during the 1920s. But there were important differences. Although it is possible to suggest that slum clearance, subsidy, rent control or rent increase are all intertwining threads of housing policy that can be historically traced and seemed to continue unchanged, Britain in the late 1950s–early 1960s was not the same society as it had earlier been, and the changes that had taken place in the social and economic structure must not be overlooked. No policy is ever quite identical to its earlier fellow, least of all in its implementation.

One aspect of social change that was highlighted during the debates on the 'realistic rents' proposals was that of the 'affluent worker'. It was argued that working-class incomes had risen to levels that made subsidising the rents of council houses an unnecessary waste. Those (few) families who could not meet the new rents would be entitled to rebates to alleviate any hardship, thus making for more efficient allocation of resources. The 'rediscovery of poverty' during the 1960s, particularly the poverty of large families,[5] offered evidence to question these assumptions of affluence. Indeed, further proposals to raise council rents in 1972 made, on the government's own estimates, about 40 per cent of council tenants eligible for rebates.[6] Yet the level of council house rents, and of tenants' ability to meet them, was to continue as a subject of fierce controversy, a controversy fuelled by changes within the other housing sectors. Mention was made of the rapidly expanding owner-occupied sector, and the 'injustice' of owner-occupiers who, struggling to 'help themselves', were also having to subsidise (as tax-payers) what were believed to be artificially low rents in the public sector. Less mention was made of council tenants who (as tax-payers) helped subsidise the owner-occupiers' relief on mortgage interest. Even less mention was made of the tenants in the rapidly shrinking private sector, who (as tax-payers) were helping to subsidise both the other sectors, with little or no apparent benefit to themselves. Nor did there seem to be much attention paid to the wide variations in rent levels and the implementation of rebate schemes among local authorities. For example, by 1972 the average weekly unrebated rent of a three-bedroomed council house built after 1964 was £1.79 in Wakefield, £5.26 in Portsmouth and £4.65 in Birmingham.[6] These variations reflected such factors as the proportion of older houses within a council's stock, whose costs would have been paid for by then; the political views of the council, the degree of scarcity and the extent of its building programme, as much as the vagueness of legislative terms like 'realistic'. Similarly, the level of income eligible for rebate varied widely from council to council as did the methods of administering rebate schemes.

The controversy over the level of council rents reached its height with the passing of the Housing Finance Act 1972, under which it was intended that 'fair rents' should be charged in the public sector – that is the estimated market rent a dwelling would command supposing supply and demand were broadly balanced in the area in which the dwelling was situated. The 'fair rent' system had developed from the 'realistic rents' policy of the 1950s and had been used to calculate rents in the private sector under the 1965 Rent Act (which will be discussed below); now it was to be applied nationally to the public sector through a series of phased increases. 'Fairness' was the principle adopted, the government claimed, as the means to obtain the policy objectives which underlay the 1972 Act. These were described in the White Paper *Fair Deal for Housing* (Cmnd 4728 1971):

(i) a decent home for every family at a price within their means;
(ii) a fairer choice between owning a home and renting one;
(iii) fairness between one citizen and another in giving and receiving help towards housing costs.

As Cullingworth noted, using terms such as 'realistic', 'fair' or 'decent' without clearly defining them make the administration of policies containing these terms open to variation and difficulty.[7] In order for an individual to be in a position to make a 'choice' between two items, all other variables must be equal. Thus it was argued that an increase in council rents did not make for a 'fairer choice' between council tenancy and owner-occupation if the council tenant could not pass the 'mortgage filter', or if there were increases in purchase prices due to scarcity; all that the increase could do was to make house purchase a more attractive option for the 'affluent worker' living in the public sector; it could not be termed 'fair' for the rest of council tenants. Many commentators were also doubtful as to the 'fairness' of the operation of the new rebate scheme proposed for council tenants unable to meet the increases in rents, compared with the continuation of tax relief to owner-occupiers. Put simply, the more an owner-occupier earned, and the more costly his mortgage, the higher his level of tax relief; the more a council tenant earned, the lower his level of rebate.

There were further dimensions to the rebate scheme, calling into question the 'fairness' of this way of giving help with housing costs, most of which centred on the question of 'take up'. The new rebate proposals did away with the proliferation of existing schemes and offered a national scheme that took account of factors such as family size as well as income; they were 'progressive with need' – that is, the rebate became larger as the applicant's income became smaller; but anxieties were expressed as to whether people entitled to this benefit would claim it for three reasons: (*a*) the method of calculating entitlement was so complicated that people might find it hard to tell whether they were eligible or not; (*b*) with so many potentially eligible persons (the government estimate was 40 per cent), there was an increased danger that many persons in need would be deterred from applying; (*c*) the onus was on the individual tenant to apply, thus making a public statement about his ability as a bread-winner, about his inability to meet his costs, about his 'poverty', in fact, which is always a problem with selective benefits based on calculations of ability to pay.

The main opposition to the 1972 Act came from Labour local authorities wholly unwilling to increase the rents of council housing to the levels proposed. Initially many of these authorities refused to implement the Act, but only one – Clay Cross Urban District Council – held out and defied the government until the election brought in a Labour administration that repealed the 'fair rent' clauses.

The Clay Cross defiance is of interest since it not only highlighted the issue of central control of local government and the conflict that lies there, but also because it drew attention to the rôle and powers of central-government servants with local-government spheres of activity, such as the District Auditor and the Housing Commissioner (appointed by the government to collect the rents from the Clay Cross council tenants). The District Auditor has power to levy a surcharge on members of the majority party of a local authority whose books are 'in the red' either by overspending or by failing to collect revenue such as rents. Since such a surcharge can well be of several thousand pounds, its existence is a real threat and a genuine curb on potential profligacy by local government. A notable earlier occasion when a surcharge had been levied was in 1956 when the St Pancras Borough Council had similarly defied government proposals to raise council rents and the tenants had staged a long and bitter rent strike.

Significantly, the incoming Labour government repealed only those parts of the 1972 Act which were clearly political hot potatoes. The national system of rebates continued, as did much of the frame-work of subsidies. But by now the need for a reappraisal of housing finance in both public and private sectors had begun to be appreciated by government. Pressure from groups such as 'Shelter' and the increasing costs of subsidies in a time of growing economic stringency had begun to force this reappraisal quite a while before the earlier Labour defeat in 1970; now, in the bitter aftermath of the repeal of the Housing Finance Act 1972, the new government promised a full and complete review of housing finance. Initiating the review, the then current Minister of Housing, Anthony Crosland, said that he sought for a new housing system that was 'more efficient and more equitable than the present dog's breakfast'. Yet despite initial enthusiasm, what finally emerged was a Green Paper that merely reviewed *housing policy* in public-sector housing finance.[8] This proposed no radical changes but urged local authorities and other public-sector bodies (new town corporations and housing associations) to develop 'more flexible' approaches to the problems of their areas. '. . . the real effectiveness of the public sector's contribution to the solution of our housing problems depends on the way in which national policies are applied "on the ground" – on the energy and foresight of the members who take local decisions.'[8] Hardly a clarion call for dynamic action from hard-pressed local authorities still grappling with the problems of bad housing, overcrowding, high building costs and shrinking budgets.

The Green Paper was greeted with disappointment. 'Those of us who were stimulated by the original enthusiasm of the late Tony Crosland (and who did not have to carry this over the political hurdles facing his successor Peter Shore. . . .) were distressed that the huge effort on the part of those within and without government should have produced such a poor creature as the "consultative document" for England and Wales.' Thus, commented Cullingworth bitterly, though disappointment did at least stimulate him to write a book.[7] Other commentators, while agreeing that the document was at best a damp squib, seemed to feel that this was more or less inevitable: '. . . housing has been a political football, a battleground for ideological initiatives and susceptible to populist bids by politicians ever eager to solve the "housing problem" by the imposition of yet another "solution".'

So far the public sector has been examined historically with most of the emphasis on the rôle and policies of successive governments. I have suggested that since the Second World War, housing policy, especially where the public sector was concerned, polarised along political lines. Yet it would be a mistake to see the major political parties' approach to housing too simply. Particularly important was the Labour party's – or at least the Labour government's – retreat from the quasi universalism of the Attlee days, and their espousal of alternative forms of tenure, particularly owner-occupation that took place during the late 1960s and early 1970s [doc 6]. It was a change of ideological perspective that was perhaps caused, as some cynics claimed, by the desire to gain votes, but which perhaps was also prompted by realisation that many local authorities were having tremendous difficulties meeting the demand for council housing from people in 'housing need'. These difficulties were particularly severe in towns and cities where there was overall scarcity of housing and severe competition for land use. The main causes were economic, in particular the combination of increasing costs of new building combined with increasing pressure on local authorities to curb expenditure. Whatever the reason, by the mid-1970s a sea change had taken place in the Labour government's attitude to owner-occupation that was bound to have consequences for the public sector.

CENTRAL GOVERNMENT AND LOCAL AUTHORITIES

If much of the initiation of policy is part of the political process, can the same be said of the actual administration of policy? Government, at central and local level, consists of two groups of people – the elected politicians and the paid employees. To some extent these two groups might be called 'amateurs' and 'professionals', although an amateur may occasionally have considerable specialist expertise. It is the 'amateurs' who are technically responsible for policy making, but it is the 'professionals' – the civil servants and the local government officers – who administer policy, and from them comes most of the data the politicians will use to formulate subsequent policies. This raises all sorts of interesting questions which can only be touched on here but need to be briefly examined, questions in particular about control, accountability and the effect of policy on the everyday lives of people.

The essential tool of central government for the control and regulation of local authorities is *finance*. The system of *Exchequer subsidies* and the *general Rate Support Grant* provide the means whereby a large part of the cost of local authority schemes can be met. Local authorities now finance the rest of their expenditure costs through borrowing on the open market, through issuing shares and through rate income. Government decision to cut funds – either generally through across-the-board cuts in rate support grants (as for example the £400 m. cut in the Budget of June 1979) or specifically – is obviously a powerful controlling mechanism. The degree of central control is more complex than that, however, and mechanisms such as 'loan sanction' and the 'cost yardstick' can also limit a local council's autonomy.

'Loan Sanction' is government permission to borrow money, and is only given for schemes approved within a local council's *capital expenditure programme*. This programme itself will have been drawn up within central government guidelines [doc 7]. A local council can decide whether it wishes to build on site A or site B, but what gets built and how much the cost will be is largely decided by central government – in the case of housing by the Department of the Environment.

The 'Housing Cost Yard Stick' was first introduced in the Housing Subsidies Act 1967. This Act was an *ad hoc* response to the problems local authorities were facing due to continuing rises in interest rates. Instead of reverting to the fixed low rate for the PWLB, the government introduced a general subsidy that made up the difference between current rates of interest and a rate of 4 per cent. Such a subsidy was far too open-ended to be introduced without controls of some sort. Local authorities had always had to submit their housing tenders for approval, under the 1967 Act the Ministry (of Housing and Local Government as it then was; it became part of the Department of the Environment (DOE) when the latter was created in 1971) took power to impose what upper cost limits should be on these tenders. The intention was to encourage cost-consciousness during the planning and designing stage of housing schemes.

The yardstick was based on housing standards originally laid down for the public sector by the Parker Morris Committee[9] and the 'allowable costs' were expressed in terms of building costs per person. The Parker Morris standards were intended to be minimum standards, so a 10 per cent tolerance was allowed for local authorities who wished to build above the minimum or to be innovative with building methods or materials. The Ministry, at that time, promised to review the level of allowable costs annually.

In fact the annual revision did not take place. The 10 per cent tolerance level almost at once became the means whereby local authorities absorbed rising building costs. As inflation began really to take hold, a 'market forces' allowance was introduced in 1972. The Ministry had always retained the power to grant exceptions and to agree to *ad hoc* yardsticks for special circumstances. The effect of the market forces allowance was to make every tender a candidate for *ad hoc* yardstick. By 1974 a 30 per cent tolerance level was allowed to enable local authorities to achieve Parker Morris standards.

Critics of the yardstick maintained that the requirement to keep within minimum levels in fact resulted in inferior buildings made of inferior materials, and that this was simply a means of postponing expenditure. Repair and maintenance costs would come home to roost later. Also, the fact that the building costs were calculated per person mitigated against low-rise, low-density schemes. On the other hand, supporters of the cost yardstick argued that the discipline of working within a framework of cost planning had long-term advantages for local authorities, and provided the opportunity for fruitful consultation between central and local government. What the yardstick certainly did do was provide a vehicle for control by central government of council house building.

THE LOCAL STATE

The conflict between central and local government can be said to have existed ever since the two institutions developed, but recent changes increased the tensions between them. The restructuring of local government in the early 1970s following the Royal Commission on Local Government in England (the Redcliffe Maud Commission)[10] resulted in the formation of much larger units of local administration with correspondingly larger budgets. Following the recommendation of the Baines Report[11] in 1972, these units were operated on a *corporate management* basis. Corporate management was very much the vogue of the early 1970s as the incoming Conservative government under Edward Heath introduced the concept that had already begun to be introduced into some British companies from the USA. At its most simple, corporate management means:

managing things as a whole, taking an overall view of an institution, whether it be a hospital, a company or a local authority, deciding what it should do and guiding its activities towards achieving these purposes, bearing in mind probable changes in the outside world . . . it can be sparked off by a recognition that an organisation has grown in size and complexity to the point where it has crossed a threshold and become unmanageable by existing methods.[12]

Certainly the local-government reforms made the new authorities more distant and remote from their local electorate, and gave them greatly increased bureaucracies. Cockburn has suggested that these changes made local authorities both more autonomous of central government and at the same time less accountable to local electorate; that they became a 'local state' within which the new corporate managers by defining a problem as 'technical' – in housing or planning for example – effectively limited non-expert participation in any attempt to seek solution.[12]

In their study of local-government housing policy in Birmingham, Lambert, Paris and Blackaby echoed this view.[13] They suggested that increasingly local councillors and their officers shared an 'ideological partnership' as to the goals of urban management and the administration of policy. They commented: 'The purpose and effect of management was to underline the dependency of people; there was little sign of their treatment as citizens with equal rights in relation to declared policies.'[13]

The changes in local-government structure did not appear to have much noticeable effect on housing policy as such. Despite local authorities' corporate strategies, housing policy frequently appeared to be formulated in the *ad hoc* way it always had been. It was in the day-to-day administration of policy that most people came to experience the growing bureaucratisation and distance that commentators pointed to. This was particularly important in the sensitive areas of access and allocation of council housing.

Access to council housing is, as said earlier, determined on the basis of 'housing need'. But not everyone who may 'need' a council house gets one. Although there was a tremendous burst of building in the mid-1960s, and council housing completions in 1967 reached 200,000 for the first time since 1955, there is still a housing shortage in very many areas. Also, in many areas there are thousands more applicants than there are vacant council dwellings. In some areas this may be a direct consequence of the historical legacy of slums and overcrowding; in others it may simply be that the local authority has not had a building programme on any scale for ideological reasons. Thus most local authorities have to determine what priorities they will give to families in housing need, and at this point the question of administration becomes very important. The Cullingworth Committee in 1969[14] expressed surprise that they had received so little evidence on the priorities issue: 'The bulk of our evidence was concerned with the relative claims of those in different types of housing need rather than the relative claims of different types of family with the same housing need.' They commented that the most thoughtful writing on the issue came from the Seebohm Committee[15] who were concerned with social services rather than with housing [doc 8] and stressed that 'policy should be directed towards helping people improve their housing situation.'

For anyone seeking access to council housing, the first step is to be registered on the *Waiting List*. At this point, and from then onwards, a system of filters operates which may at any point deny access. Right to register on waiting lists is restricted. Most local authorities have a 'residence' clause – two or three years' residence in the borough – before allowing registration. Many local authorities exclude specific categories such as single people, or owner-occupiers, or single-parent families from registration. The Cullingworth Committee recommended the abolition of the residence clause, so too did the more recent *Report of the Housing Services Advisory Group on 'The Allocation of Council Housing' (1978).*

Organisations such as the Single Homeless Action Campaign (SHAC) have campaigned for the right of single people to register for council housing, arguing that it would, if nothing else, make clear to some local authorities the true extent of 'housing need' in their districts. Shelter have pointed out that elderly owner-occupiers worried about rising repair costs might welcome an opportunity to 'retire' into council housing with all the support in terms of rent rebates, etc., this would bring.

An applicant who succeeds in getting on the waiting list has passed the first filter, but may still not obtain access to council housing. Rationing through the 'points' system has been mentioned earlier. An applicant may qualify for registration but may not be able to muster enough points *ever* to get rehoused. There are wide regional variations in waiting time, and in points allocation. Much depends on the amount of alternative housing available. In many areas the decline of the private rented sector has meant that those who are unable to buy their own home can have their housing needs met only by the public sector. In areas where demand for council housing outstrips supply only those families with maximum points will get access to council housing, together with people decanted through slum-clearance schemes. Other applicants, who may well be in bad housing themselves, may have to wait years before they are offered a council tenancy, if at all. Some inner-city authorities manage to house only a handful of applicants from the waiting list each year. In London, for example, in the borough of Lambeth, only 10 per cent of the families offered housing in 1978 came from the waiting list. Having to wait on the list a long time, and seeing others being offered council housing breeds resentment. This in turn filters back into the access and allocation process and is most clearly seen in the 'one-offer' policy adopted by many councils, where a tenancy is offered on a take-it-or-leave-it basis. The one-offer system is used mostly, but not exclusively, for homeless families, the more usual policy being to allow at least two refusals, thus giving some slight degree of choice.

Choice in the public sector is not quite the same as in the other housing sectors. People seeking to buy homes can shop around, within the limits of what they can afford. They can visit several estate agents and view all the flats and houses available within their price range. They can consider factors such as location, proximity of schools, conditions of the property, whether or not there is a garden, how near are the shops – all sorts of 'social' factors that add up and affect their decision to choose one property rather than another. People seeking to rent homes may find that in certain districts there is very little choice due to scarcity, and that this may also have increased prices. Potential tenants in the private sector may find their areas of choice more apparent than real if they have large families, or are black, or have low incomes. But above a certain level, and allowing for scarcity, the same sort of choices on a more limited scale are available to private-rented tenants as to owner-occupiers. For the person who has gained access to council housing the situation is different. A council dwelling is not chosen, it is *allocated*. Basic factors, such as the number and sex of the children in a family, will be taken into account, and council housing officers do often try to match needs and preferences to what property is available, but allocation policy does act as a filter and criticisms have been made of the way allocation works in practice.

There is at present no requirement for a council to publish the details of its allocation policy, nor to give applicants any information concerning their priority within the allocation scheme. This lack of any clear administrative framework can provide opportunities for subjectivity and discrimination, particularly where the assessment of applicants is concerned. Most (but not all) local authorities pay home visits to applicants – 'The objects of this visit are mainly to check the particulars the applicant has given about his accommodation, to assess the standards and capabilities of the family as tenants, and if an offer is imminent to discuss where accommodation is to be offered.'[16]

The Cullingworth Committee found wide variations in assessment practice and the way in which applicants were 'graded', and the reasons why grading was thought to be necessary [doc 9]. They argued for the need for more objective and clearly stated allocation methods than grading based on subjective assessment. Other studies of the housing process suggest that little has changed. Pat Niner's study of six local authorities in the West Midlands (1973) and the more recent examination of housing in Birmingham by

Lambert, Paris and Blackaby both draw attention to the continuation of subjective grading:

The rôle of the housing visitor was also unclear. When one did arrive eventually, many people became optimistic, hoping that the department would now appreciate their need, having actually sent one of its officers to see their housing conditions. Many believed that a lot depended on the visitor and that what he or she said counted; thus it was somehow necessary to convince him or her personally of their need for help. No small wonder, then, that they sometimes became confused and a little anxious when they saw the visitor inspect bedclothes and furniture . . .[13]

The first Housing Bill 1979 (it failed when the general election was called) had contained a measure requiring councils to publish allocation policies. But Nick Raynsford, of SHAC, argued that this measure of itself would not prevent councils from discriminating against certain categories of applicant.[17] This is not to say that housing officers are necessarily discriminatory or punitive, many are neither, but rather to draw attention to the difficulties that arise with subjective administration. *Discrimination* in allocation takes two main forms:

1. *Delay in getting housed*. In some cases amounting to virtual failure to get council housing. Some local authorities, for example, rarely house single-parent families since these do not contain sufficient adults to gain sufficient points. Some local authorities may discriminate almost by accident, when they give applicants the opportunity to state a preference about where, or in what type of housing, they would like to live:

   An applicant who requests a particularly attractive house type or estate, or a house in a part of town where there are very few council houses, may find himself waiting very much longer than one who is less particular. Sometimes this may not be a conscious choice, and one very valuable purpose of a home visit can be to explain to an applicant the implications of his request.[6]

A variant of this is the system, in Manchester, where points are allocated by need and the applicant is informed how long a wait is likely for different types of property. The applicant then is able to choose whether to wait possibly for a long while for better, newer, housing or to wait a shorter while for something less good. The dangers of this is that people in the most desperate housing need cannot wait. The delays that follow a housing visit can cause resentment, as can time spent on the waiting list. The feeling grows that 'they' are rehousing others rather than the applicant. Lambert, Paris and Blackaby found this in their Birmingham study; they quoted one middle-aged woman who commented 'They're not bothering with us. It's useless . . . I saw all these houses and flats being built down the road. I was waiting all that time while they built them but did they offer me one, not one of them.'[13]

2. *Who gets what housing?* The stock of housing of any one local authority will contain property of varying sorts and of various ages, in differing states of repair, some of it good and some of it less good. The judgement of the housing officer can determine what sort of property an applicant gets offered. In 1969 the Cullingworth Committee were commenting that for some local authorities 'Moral rectitude, social conformity, clean living and a "clear" rent book on occasion seemed to be essential quali-fications – at least for new houses.'[14] Since then there has been growing comment on the way in which some groups of people seem to be consistently allocated to the less good housing:

Housing in the increasingly large and varied public sector has been distributed amongst tenants through complicated procedures which have shifted people up and down the snakes and ladders of an administered market. The fortunate, the well organised and the articulate have climbed into the most popular estates; the unfortunate, the apathetic and the people who constantly get into debt drift down to the least popular estates.[18]

Housing procedure certainly seems a snakes-and-ladders business, but the existence of grading and the subjective nature of allocation appear to suggest that many 'unfortunate' people do not *drift* into the least popular estates but get *put* there. Also, bodies such as the Commission for Racial Equality point to areas where black council tenants are worse housed than most whites and suggest the existence of racial prejudice sometimes affects allocation. The keeping of 'ethnic' records by housing auth-orities might allow accurate monitoring of allocation policy, but is a highly contentious issue with many critics arguing that such a measure might well encourage racial discrimination.

The pitfalls and filters that thus exist in access to and allocation of council housing underline the importance of local government officers, who act as 'gatekeepers', and also of the rôle of the local state on a wider scale as controller and regulator of the urban environment and the people who live in it. Current policies for access and allocation and the assumptions that lie behind them 'tend to set queueing individual against queueing individual, neighbourhood against neighbourhood'[13] and to heighten and increase social and territorial inequality.

CHANGING CHARACTERISTICS OF TENANTS

I have discussed how council housing historically developed as 'workers' housing' rather than 'welfare housing' and how discussions about subsidies often include the use of the stereotype of the council tenant as an 'affluent worker'. There is some evidence to suggest that the social characteristics of council tenants have undergone some changes in the last twenty years.

In 1971, 81 per cent of council households could be classified as manual (as opposed to non-manual) workers. In this group, the number of households where the breadwinner was in *unskilled* manual work has subsequently risen, from 52 per cent in 1971 to 59 per cent in 1975. Murie suggested in 1977[19] that evidence on incomes indicated that 'the majority of low income families are in council housing', that 40 per cent of household heads with gross weekly incomes of less than £15 per week, 45 per cent with incomes between £15 and £30 per week, and 39 per cent of tenants with incomes of over £30 and up to £50 were council tenants. Only 9 per cent of those people who earned over £70 per week in 1975 were council tenants. The Family Expenditure Survey indicated that the percentage of council households with incomes within the lowest quarter of the income range for all households had increased from 20 per cent in 1954 to 33 per cent in 1976.

But, as Merrett points out, before we conclude that council housing has virtually ceased to be 'workers' housing' two important qualifications have to be made:

For various reasons, many of which are to do with local authority housing management, some groups of poor households, and particularly those without children and below retiring age, tend to be excluded from the council sector, and are, in consequence, pushed into very poor housing conditions in the private sector. Second . . . housing conditions within the council sector itself are not uniform . . . it is often the least well off and the most needy households who, once admitted to the council sector, are allocated the most inferior and inadequate dwellings.[20]

Possibly, then, these details tell us more about the demise of the affluent worker than of the possibly changed function of council housings. The conclusion that the majority of council tenants were workers with low wages raised important questions concerning the policy to force councils to sell their dwellings for owner-occupation. Since such a policy was clearly beset with problems and raised many broader issues, it will be discussed more fully.

REFERENCES

1. J. B. CULLINGWORTH, *Problems of an Urban Society*, Vol. 2. *The Social Content of Planning*, Allen & Unwin, London (1973).
2. E. GAULDIE, *op. cit.* (see ref. 3, Ch. 1).
3. D. DONNISON, *The Government of Housing*, Pelican, Harmondsworth (1967).
4. J. B. CULLINGWORTH, *Housing and Local Government*, Allen & Unwin, London (1966).
5. B. ABEL-SMITH and P. TOWNSEND, *The Poor and the Poorest*, Occasional Paper in Social Administration, No. 19, G. Bell & Sons, London (1965).
6. A. MURIE, P. NINER and C. WATSON, *Housing Policy and the Housing System*, Allen & Unwin, London (1976).
7. J. B. CULLINGWORTH, *Essays on Housing Policy*, Allen & Unwin, London (1979).
8. DEPT. OF THE ENVIRONMENT, *Housing Policy: a Consultative Document*, Cmnd 6851 (1977), and the *Technical Volume*, Parts 1, 2 and 3, HMSO (1977).
9. CENTRAL HOUSING ADVISORY COMMITTEE, *Homes for Today and Tomorrow* (Parker Morris Report), HMSO (1961).
10. *Royal Commission on Local Government in England* (Redcliffe Maud Report), Cmnd 4040, HMSO (1969).
11. STUDY GROUP ON LOCAL AUTHORITY MANAGEMENT STRUCTURE, *The New Local Authorities: Management and Structure* (Baines Report), HMSO (1972).
12. C. COCKBURN, *The Local State*, Pluto Press, London (1977).
13. J. LAMBERT, C. PARIS and B. BLACKABY, *Housing Policy and the State: allocation, access and control*, Macmillan, London (1979).
14. HOUSING MANAGEMENT SUB-COMMITTEE OF THE CENTRAL HOUSING ADVISORY COMMITTEE, Ninth Report. *Council Housing: Purposes, Procedures and Priorities* (Cullingworth Report), HMSO (1969).
15. *Report of the Committee on Local Authority and Allied Personal Social Services* (Seebohm Report), Cmnd 3703 (1968), HMSO.
16. INSTITUTE OF HOUSING MANAGERS, *The Allocation of Tenancies*, HMSO (1962).

17. SHELTER/HOUSING ACTION, *Housing: the next five years*, Report of Joint Conference, held June 1979.
18. D. DONNISON, 'The empty council houses', *New Society*, 14 June (1979).
19. A. MURIE, 'Council house sales mean Poor Law housing', *Roof*, February (1977).
20. S. MERRETT, *State Housing in Britain*, Routledge & Kegan Paul, London (1979).

Chapter three
OWNER-OCCUPATION. OWNERS AND MORTGAGEES

Today, owner-occupation is the largest of the housing sectors; 53 per cent of the total housing stock, that is 20.61 million dwellings, are owner-occupied. Government policy is aimed to encourage people's desire to own their own homes, although claiming that 'greater emphasis on home ownership does not mean less social emphasis in housing policy.'[1] For many people, home purchase is the largest single financial transaction of their lifetime, and the high capital cost of a house makes it a substantial capital investment. The price of housing is an important constraint on the ability of an individual household to gain access to owner-occupation, and the majority of those who do purchase their own homes do so by means of long-term loans. Nevitt has said that 'the nineteenth-century invention of the amortised loan was of such importance in housing economics it should rank with the steam engine in changing the face of Britain.'[2] Certainly today, 90 per cent of house purchases by first-time buyers, and 70–75 per cent of other house purchases are financed by such loans.

RÔLE OF THE BUILDING SOCIETIES

There are three main lending institutions to which an intending house purchaser can go – the building societies, local authorities and the insurance companies. Of these three it is the building societies that are the most important in that they provide between 80 and 90 per cent of all advances for house purchases by the three main lending institutions, both in terms of value and the number of advances. The lending policies of building societies, and the operation of the mortgage market, are important determinants as to who gets what within the owner-occupied housing sector, and are further important constraints on access to the sector by individual households.

Today, there are approximately 133 building societies. The continuing trend recently has been towards mergers between societies. Eighteen societies are particularly dominant, these accounted for 80 per cent of all building society mortgages granted in 1974 and operated 75 per cent of the branch offices in the United Kingdom. All these eighteen societies have assets of over £250 m. Four – the Halifax, the Abbey National, Leeds Permanent and the Woolwich Equitable – have assets exceeding £1,000 m. All offer a variety of ways of investing money, and though their primary task is still to fund mortgages for house purchase they also offer other forms of return. It is possible now to invest with a building society in order to receive annuity payment upon retirement and there are short-term savings schemes for holiday funding. Many of the 'high yield' investment schemes are precisely that – returns on capital invested over a fixed period. Thus the building societies have moved a long way from the 'terminating' societies of working men of the eighteenth and nineteenth centuries. They are now financial institutions in their own right, competing with others for investors' funds. The building societies are an attractive form of stable investment, although there is a ceiling on the amount that any one investor may place with any one society. They are also attractive to borrowers because there is the inducement of lower interest rates than elsewhere in the money market. This is because the building societies are allowed to pay income tax on behalf of their depositors at a 'composite rate' agreed with the Registrar General and the Inland Revenue. They also have a special low rate of corporation tax – 40 per cent, a recognition that their primary task is a different one from other financial institutions.

Naturally enough, the other financial institutions viewed the building societies as competitors, both for investment and for lending. The clearing banks in particular felt this keenly, even though they claimed to 'welcome the competition in financial markets because it fosters efficiency and benefits customers' [doc 10]. Membership of the financial markets, however, did pose some problems for the societies, the most acute being the need for stable funding. In order to be able to meet its mortgage requirements a society has to be reasonably sure that its assets will not fluctuate dramatically, and 'volatile' investors are not what it requires. The 'branch structure' of the societies, with what are almost 'shops' in the high street, emphasises the image of the building societies as 'purely the savings bank of the small investor', yet almost 80 per cent of funds invested come from 20 per cent of investors and these involve quite substantial individual investments.[3]

It was from investors such as these that the societies required stability, and who were the most responsive to changes in interest rates. When interest rates rose money poured into the building societies; when they fell, it poured out again. This resulted in alternating 'feasts and famines' for borrowers seeking mortgages. A 'feast' of borrowing subsequently caused a surge in house prices. A 'famine' cut back the number of new buildings started for sale and also contributed to the rise in price of existing buildings. The effect of the fluctuations of interest rate upon the building societies and upon the borrowing public caused enough government concern for a consultative body to be set up in 1973 between the societies and the relevant government departments. This body – the Joint Advisory Committee on Building Society Mortgage Finance – effected a *stabilisation arrangement*, whereby the building societies maintained a more or less constant interest rate, thus smoothing out the peaks and troughs in mortgage lending. However, this move led to the accusation that the building societies had begun to operate a 'price cartel in favour of the borrower and against the investor.'[4] The stabilisation arrangements certainly did work against any investor seeking a 'quick return' but these had never been the type of investor the societies sought to attract. However, by late 1979 rising interest rates were reaching levels where even investors interested in growth rather than income might be tempted elsewhere. Despite government pressure, the building societies had to consider raising their rates and making life financially harder for a formidably large and increasingly powerful section of the voting public, at a time when government policy was focused on massively increasing home ownership.

THE JOYS OF HOME-OWNERSHIP

There are at least two good reasons why people own their own homes. To begin with there is *security of tenure*. An owner-occupier, provided he or she keeps up the mortgage repayments, cannot be turned out. This is not entirely the case in the other housing sectors. Council tenants can be evicted for rent arrears. In the private-rented sector, although there has been legislation to give security of tenure, tenants are still sometimes 'winkled out', and under certain circumstances landlords can reclaim their property.

The second and most attractive reason is that there is a distinct *financial advantage* to home ownership. Not only is there the asset of the dwelling itself, which is a hedge against inflation and an investment which gains in value, but there is also a subsidy in the form of tax relief on mortgage interest. This is a very much larger subsidy than that given to the public sector: in 1976–77 tax relief on mortgage interest was £1,100 million (to 53 per cent of total housing stock), whereas housing subsidies to the public sector (32 per cent of total housing stock) was but £122 million. The steep rise in inflation which caused public-sector borrowing costs to increase during 1978–79 while building society rates were held steady temporarily reversed this, but not for long. Tax relief is payment forgone, and the money has to be raised elsewhere by the Exchequer and so falls upon the general body of taxpayers. As Berry comments acidly, 'Needless to say, there are still those, mainly house purchasers, who are still convinced that tax relief is not a subsidy but rather a matter of fiscal justice. No student of housing finance or for that matter any competent writer or commentator on housing still pretends that this is the case.'[5] Although this subsidy helps most at the time when it is needed most – that is at the beginning of the mortgage – it is an indiscriminate and regressive form of aid. The more affluent the purchaser, the more expensive the dwelling, the higher the tax relief. There are many occasions when it is social policy for groups to be funded by those who do not themselves benefit – childless tax-payers help fund education and child benefit, for example; but the regressive nature of mortgage relief makes it a policy where those in bad, or at least less desirable, housing, fund those in good, or more desirable, housing. In the wake of their first budget tax-cuts in 1979 it was rumoured that the new Conservative government would abolish mortgage relief, but no mention of this was made in the later Housing Bill.

Berry suggests that there may be a third reason for home ownership. This is that buying 'is so often the only way to get a house at all. No one in their right mind is going to invest in housing to let in present-day circumstances (except possibly the luxury end of the market).'[5] Certainly it is the case that one effect of the Rent Acts of 1957 and 1965 has been a shift of investment away from house renting, and a massive decrease in the supply of housing available to rent. The reasons for this will be discussed in the section on the Private Rented Sector but should be noted here since all sectors of the housing market interact and affect each other. The policy thinking behind the 1957 Rent Act aimed to introduce measures that would encourage landlords to repair and maintain their property, and would encourage private builders to increase their activities in the field of supplying buildings both for purchase as investment to rent and to purchase for owner-occupation. One way in which this was to be achieved was by winding up the system of cheap loans to the public sector. The 1965 Rent Act concentrated more on control of rent levels and security of tenure. The net effect of these policies, introduced as they were into a situation of already existing scarcity, was catastrophic. Following the passing of the 1957 Rent Act the number of houses going out of private-renting increased by perhaps as many as 100,000 a year. The Rent Act 1965 continued this trend. Such decreased supply did mean that for many, particularly new households, the only alternative form of housing available was owner-occupation with the prospect of beginning their housing career with what Pahl has termed 'the millstones of mortgage indebtedness' around their necks.[6]

It may be fairly commented, however, that many policy makers do not seem to consider mortgages as 'debts' but rather as examples of thrift and forethought – 'Of all forms of saving this one is the best.'[7] It would appear that the emphasis on the 'moral value' of housing is still as strong as it was in 1871, when a building society secretary commented: 'We are the greatest social reformers of the day.'[8] As the extension of owner-occupation is now the lynch-pin of housing policy for both major political parties, although there are differences of ideological emphasis, such underlying values become of considerable importance in the part they play, in particular because not everybody has access to the owner-occupied sector.

PROBLEMS OF ACCESS

Access to owner-occupation comes, as has been said, in the main through obtaining a loan with which to buy the dwelling. Meeting the requirements for this loan may not always be possible. The lending policies of the building societies and other financial institutions are crucial and there are several factors which may exclude a potential purchaser.

First, and simplest, there is the need for the potential purchaser to show that he or she has both sufficient *income* to meet repayments, and sufficient *savings* to make a deposit on a property. This leads inevitably to the second factor – *house price*. Building societies will not advance beyond what they feel a potential purchaser can afford to repay, usually not more than two-and-a-half times annual income. Potential purchasers must be able to find a dwelling within that range, and for those at the lower end of the income spectrum this may not be easy. In situations of shortage prices will rise.

Both the *age* and the *location* of a dwelling may place it outside the lending policy of a building society. Many first-time buyers can afford only older, cheaper houses, or flats in large, old houses which have been converted. Although the societies do lend on older property – 28 per cent of their loans on second-hand property in 1976 was on pre-1919 buildings – these tend to be 'of the more substantial kind of modernised older property in areas which are not declining.'[9] In those areas which the building societies see as poor security for their funds, or perhaps as poor investments for the house buyers themselves, they withdraw from lending. This policy by the building societies – termed 'redlining' (on the assumption that a red line is drawn on a map around those areas) – has only recently been openly acknowledged by the societies. It has been fiercely criticised by bodies such as Shelter [doc 11], who have attempted on many occasions to bring the practice to public attention. The 1977 Green Paper on Housing Policy[9] urged closer co-operation with local authorities to help reduce redlining: 'By working together at local level [these bodies] can assist in revitalising older urban areas including inner-city centres.'

A few of the major building societies appeared to at least be considering changing their policies by the late 1970s. The Provincial Building Society conducted a small experiment by lending on properties in inner-Bradford. The Abbey National went further than this, extending its lending in six selected areas, not only to owner-occupiers but also in co-operation with the local authority, lending to housing associations for renting property and to private landlords and tenants for repairs and improvements. This promised a revolutionary redefinition of the building societies' rôle. In an interview, the Chairman of Abbey National conceded that home ownership was what the building societies traditionally stood for, 'But it does make it harder for people to go where the work is – it's bad for mobility of labour. And if people want places to rent, they should have them.'[10]

These small beginnings represented important new developments, because, as must be clear from the discussion above, under most circumstances low-income families found it difficult if not impossible to purchase a dwelling with a building society loan. There were alternative forms of finance they might try and there were three of these:

1. There were alternative mortgage arrangements, such as an *Endowment Assurance Policy* or an *Option Mortgage*. Endowment

Assurance was more expensive than an 'ordinary' mortgage as the borrower paid both the interest on the loan and the insurance premium as well. Option Mortgages were more suitable to borrowers whose taxable income was too low to allow them much benefit from tax relief on mortgage interest. Under such schemes a lower rate of interest was paid and no tax relief claimed. Such mortgages seemed more often to be used by existing borrowers trying to lower their repayments when faced with rises in interest rates or by personal financial crises.

2.   There was the possibility of obtaining a *Bridging Loan* from a bank. In June 1979 the restriction on banks to provide loans pending the availability of building society funds was lifted. Bridging facilities were expensive, however. Charges were usually between 3–5 per cent above the base rate. Banks seemed willing to lend on older and on inner-city properties, but did require prospective borrowers to become banking customers by opening accounts.

3.   In fact, the only real method of access to owner-occupation for a low-income family was to obtain a mortgage from a *Local Authority*. Edwards has called local-authority mortgage schemes 'the only form of finance for house purchase which rests on an ideology of social responsibility rather than commercial enterprise'[11] because Local Authorities granted mortgages on older, or inner-city property to applicants with lower income levels than would building societies. The demand for these mortgages was already outstripping supply before the combination of rises in house prices and interest rates in the late 1960s, plus the cuts in public expenditure, effectively limited this form of activity by the public sector. Such was the effect of rising prices in urban areas, however, that even the alternative of a Local Authority mortgage was beyond the means of a low-income family. Borrowers needed to earn around the national average wage, and increasingly mortgages were being granted to young professional people who were able confidently to look forward to increased earnings in a few years.

It was this young, able group who benefited most from the *Homesteading* scheme introduced by the Greater London Council (GLC) in 1977. Under this scheme dilapidated and empty properties were offered rent-free on condition that the tenant renovated them. Once renovation was complete, rent payments or house purchase on easy terms would begin. The GLC claimed that so great was the demand for these properties that a lottery had to be run to draw names. By 1979, however, complaints were being heard from homesteaders in some properties that the amount of repair and renovation required was way beyond their financial and non-specialist capability to reach. Critics of the scheme also asked how it was the GLC came to have so many derelict properties on their hands in the first place, and how came these properties to be in such a state when they could have been used for short-life, licensed housing? Michael Harloe commented at the beginning of the scheme: 'It will be interesting to see whether homesteading is anything more than yet another way of evading the ultimate necessity for large-scale and effective public intervention.'[12] By 1979 the policy to sell off council houses for owner-occupation had rendered such intervention unlikely.

Thus far, this discussion of the owner-occupied sector has been mainly 'tenure' based, with the suggestion that there might be some inequalities in terms of financial benefit between this sector and the others in the housing market. An alternative approach would be to look at the owner-occupied sector in terms of the socio-economic groups within it. This approach shows quite a degree of class specificity. The General Household Survey found, in 1971, that of the occupational groups they examined, 85 per cent of the 'Professional' and 74 per cent of the 'Employers and Managers' groups were owner-occupiers, whereas only 21 per cent of 'Unskilled Manual Workers' owned their own homes. In contrast to this, 56 per cent of the 'Unskilled Manual Workers' rented their homes from public authorities, but only 10 per cent of the 'Employers and Managers' did and 3 per cent of the 'Professionals'. Of people buying with mortgages in 1976, 36 per cent had a weekly income of over £50 and up to £70 per week, while a further 44 per cent had weekly incomes of over £70. In the public sector only 9 per cent had weekly incomes of over £70. Private, unfurnished, rented tenants presented a different picture, 36 per cent having incomes of less than £25 per week. By 1979 this socio-economic profile of the sectors had hardly changed at all.

Since the mid-1960s government policy (regardless of political party) has been to extend the range of home ownership and access to owner-occupation. To help overcome the problem of funding first-time buyers, the 1977 Green Paper proposed a system of 'savings bonus' and 'loans' – the bonus would provide incentive to save and the loans would help those who could not raise a sufficient deposit. These, together with greater flexibility of lending and measures to ensure adequate mortgage funds from the building societies, would greatly stimulate demand and attract 'tens of thousands' of first-time purchasers. This demand would be met by the private house-building industry which, the Green Paper argued, had been under-utilised for some time due to uncertainties. The rationale for this was that builders needed an assurance that 'by the time the houses are ready – typically 6 to 12 months after starting – potential buyers will not be thwarted by shortage of mortgage funds'.[13] It could be argued, however, that such policies did not sufficiently emphasise the problem of scarcity of land or its high price, and that turning to the private builder to solve the problems of shortage would be no more likely to succeed than on previous occasions.

Critics such as Harvey, who put forward the view that the aim of home-ownership policies is to defuse class conflicts and give house-owners a vested interest in the *status quo*,[14] would certainly place these proposals in this category – of providing state aid for 'embourgeoisiement'. Other writers, like Berry, argue that there should be greater freedom of choice between buying and renting, which could be achieved by policies to equalise the subsidies between the sectors, starting with the abolition of tax relief on mortgage interest: 'Freedom of Choice,' says Berry, 'has been a housing catchphrase for many years; such policies might conceivably make this freedom a reality.'[15]

The great growth in owner-occupation is a phenomenon of the last fifty years. It has been fostered and encouraged by policies which laid great stress on the value of thrift, on the virtue of saving to own one's home. It has been financially supported at the expense of the other housing sectors, and made possible by the activities of the building societies. '. . . the case against owner-occupation rests on the fact that it has not solved or even helped to solve the major housing problems of the less affluent, nor is it possible for it to do so. This is not a failure of owner-occupation *per se*; within its limits house ownership has been a great success. It is a failure of policy on the part of those who . . . encourage owner-occupation at the expense of other tenures.'[14]

REFERENCES

1. DEPT. OF ENVIRONMENT, *op. cit.* (see ref. 8, Ch. 2).
2. A. A. NEVITT, *Housing, Taxation and Subsidies*, Nelson, London (1966).
3. P. WILLIAMS, *The Rôle of Financial Institutions and Estate Agents*

in the Private Housing Market, Centre for Urban and Regional Studies, Birmingham, Working Paper No. 39 (1976).

4. J. GOUGH and T. TAYLOR, *The Building Society Price Cartel*, Institute of Economic Affairs, London (1979).

5. F. BERRY, *op. cit.* (see ref. 9, Ch. 1).

6. R. PAHL, *Whose City?* (first published 1970; paperback edn, Penguin, Harmondsworth, 1975).

7. DEPT. OF ENVIRONMENT, *Widening the Choice: the next steps in housing*, Cmnd 5280, HMSO (1971).

8. E. GAULDIE, *op. cit.* (see ref. 3, Ch. 1).

9. DEPT. OF ENVIRONMENT, *op. cit.* (see ref. 8, Ch. 2).

10. K. WHITHORN, 'Breaking the habit', *The Observer*, 24 June (1979).

11. J. EDWARDS, *The Other Housing Problem: access and accountability*, CURS, Birmingham. Unpublished (1973).

12. M. HARLOE, 'Young and able gain from urban homesteading', *Roof*, May (1977).

13. DEPT. OF ENVIRONMENT, *op. cit.* (see ref. 8, Ch. 2).

14. D. HARVEY, *Social Justice and The City*, Edward Arnold (London) 1976.

15. F. BERRY, *op. cit.* (see ref. 9, Ch. 1).

Chapter four
THE PRIVATE RENTED SECTOR

Private renting of a house, a flat or a room, was the way most people lived up to and immediately after the Second World War. In 1947, 61 per cent of all housing tenures were in the private rented sector. Thereafter, with the growth of council dwellings and the encouragement of people to join the 'property-owning democracy', matters changed. By 1960 the proportion of private rented tenures had fallen to 31 per cent and by 1979 to a mere 12 per cent.

There are bad housing conditions in both public- and owner-occupied sectors. Councils have old housing needing renovation and badly built newer housing needing much repair. There are neglected owner-occupied homes, particularly in the inner-areas of cities where there has been industrial decline. But it is the private rented sector people generally have in mind when they talk about the 'problem' of bad housing, for it is there that the worst housing conditions are most concentrated. Over half the country's unfit houses are in the private rented sector, almost all its housing stock is old, 70 per cent of it being built before 1919. In 1976, 30 per cent of private rented dwellings lacked one or more standard amenities. That is, the households lacked the use of a fixed bath or shower, a washbasin, a sink (and lacked, too, the hot- and cold-water supply) and the exclusive use of a w.c. In other words, 30 per cent of dwellings in the private rented sector fell below minimum standards. It was to establish minimum standards that state intervention began in the housing market over a century before. Even allowing that our ideas of what constitutes a minimum standard change over time, the fact remained that in late twentieth-century Britain there were still dwellings, many dwellings, where a tenant's only water supply was a tap on the landing, and where he shared the outside w.c. with everyone else in the building. Thus the problems of providing minimum standards at a rent working people could afford – the very problems the philanthropic housing associations had focused on and failed to meet – were still only too real for some people, albeit a minority of the total housing population.

It has also been said that the 'problem' of the private rented sector is the problem of investment, or of lack of adequate return on capital invested. The investment income is the rent a landlord receives, and when rent levels are low there is insufficient to both make a profit and do repairs. Although for most landlords a building will have long since recovered its building costs, houses do need repair and housing depreciation cannot be set against tax in the way a piece of machinery can. Indeed, it could be said that there is an inbuilt disincentive to do repairs, maintain the property and charge a higher rent, since such an increase will count as taxable increased profits.

Most private landlords are relatively small investors. They own one or two properties, generally live in one as well as renting the rest of it out, are undercapitalised, and rely on their rents as their chief source of income. Only in London are financial institutions and companies involved in renting on any scale, where about half of all lettings are made by companies and the largest landlords are the Church Commissioners.

This apparent conflict between maintaining profit levels and maintaining the buildings does not, of course, apply to the upper end of the private rented market. Luxury rented accommodation is very much more likely to be part of an institution's portfolio, not least because of initial high-capital outlay. Much of this type of renting is short-lease to companies, wealthy overseas visitors and such like. Most of the legislative measures that will be discussed have little meaning for this part of the sector, which accounts for perhaps about one-third of all lettings. Today, the private rented sector has become almost completely polarised between this luxurious, high-rent, segment and the decidedly unluxurious relatively low-rental segment. 'Middle-level' rentals of the type characterised by the large blocks of purpose-built mansion flats now represent a residual amount. It was this segment of the private rented sector where the major shift to owner-occupation took place.

Housing policy for the private rented sector has tended to swing between 'pro-landlord' policies and 'pro-tenant' ones. 'Pro-landlord' policies were those concerned with raising rent levels and with improvement grants; 'pro-tenant' policies were aimed at providing security of tenure, regulating rent levels and rebate schemes. Neither set of policies appears to have achieved its declared objectives on any significant scale, and both had consequences other than those primarily intended. Meanwhile, housing policies directed at the other housing sectors also had consequences for the private sector. In the main it was these other sector policies that speeded its decline. The prevailing characteristic of the sector was *scarcity*, which worsened rather than improved over time.

RENT POLICIES

The post-war Labour government envisaged the withering away of the private sector before the onset of municipalisation, and thus paid little attention to its current needs. The first major policy moves came from the Conservative government of the 1950s. Their main aim was to stimulate the private-housing market, with policies that were both 'pro-landlord' and 'pro-owner-occupier'. Their intention was to overcome a landlord's disincentive to repair by *decontrolling rents*. This they did as part of the Rent Act 1957.

The purpose of rent decontrol was to create a free market in rented housing, which, the government believed, would stimulate supply by encouraging investment; would stimulate landlords to repair (both by increasing rents and by the introduction of 'disrepair procedures'); and stimulate the redistribution of housing on a more rational scale. In particular, it was felt that elderly households would thereby be encouraged to move to accommodation more suited to their needs rather than remain in housing too large for them but with a low-controlled rent. Two methods of decontrol were proposed – by *rateable value* and *vacant possession*. The first decontrolled all housing units over a certain level of rateable value – an estimated 750,000 dwellings; the second method decontrolled a unit as and when it became vacant.

In fact, as Joel-Barnett commented in his study of the 1957 Rent Act, 'Events proved the government's expectations as to the consequences of its own measures were quite inaccurate.'[1] This was not least because policy was based upon assumptions and 'guesstimates' rather than data and research. The assumptions about supply of housing underestimated the number of new households being formed (particularly among the young and the elderly) and ignored the timelags in construction and the already high degree of shortage in many areas, particularly London. The response of landlords to the incentives to repair was patchy and there were marked regional disparities; the 'disrepair' procedures proved unworkable. The number of units decontrolled by rateable value proved to be about half the estimated number, and these consisted mainly of purpose-built blocks and sub-divided, multi-occupied dwellings rather than the envisaged houses with gardens occupied by elderly couples. Above all, the government had seriously underestimated the rate of decontrol by vacant possession. It was the consequences of this that were to capture public attention rather than the fallacy of the government assumptions about the ability of the market to regulate private renting in a particular way.

The supply of private rented housing had already begun to diminish before the passing of the 1957 Rent Act, particularly in inner-city areas where slum-clearance programmes were being undertaken and where most rented accommodation was located. Between 1947 and 1961 the size of the private rented sector halved from 61 per cent to 31 per cent of all housing tenures. Decontrol hastened this decline, in particular decontrol through vacant possession. Property vacated by tenants increasingly became converted to owner-occupation as landlords capitalised upon their assets and shifted their investment elsewhere. In some cases, particularly in London, vacant possession was gained by harassment and force. While there is evidence to suggest that such pressure had frequently been put upon controlled tenants before the passing of the 1957 Rent Act, it was the 'decontrol with vacant possession' that provided the opportunity of high return with low overheads and opened the door to abuses. The forms of harassment were many and various – vindictive notices to quit, changing the lock on a front door, 'dumping on the floor of a tenant's room slimy cooked potatoes mixed with other filth and, for good measure, a dead rat'.[2] The activities of Perec Rachman in particular gained sufficient notoriety for his name to have become synonymous for exploitative landlords, even though he was 'not the only one to exploit the housing shortage, nor was he alone in his use of brutality'.[2] It was almost impossible for a tenant to prove a case against such a landlord, or to enrol police assistance.

At first, the 1957 Rent Act had little public impact (apart from among people experiencing the attentions of harassing landlords). Its broad objectives were not being met, but neither were they causing much public comment. In 1961, in their evaluation of *Housing Since the Rent Act*, Donnison, Cockburn and Corlett concluded that the whole measure had had little effect, particularly concerning repairs: 'The Act may have encouraged some landlords to repair their houses. If so, it only increased the proportion repaired to a figure similar to that for owner-occupied and council houses, and many of these repairs were done by the tenants themselves. Since private rented houses are older and in greater need of repair than other property, this is not an adequate achievement.'[3] They found that it was in the North of England, where rents were lowest, that landlords were most reluctant to repair.

It was in the South of England, particularly London, where rents were higher, but so too were opportunity costs, that the 1957 Rent Act had most effect. There the consequences of the Act became more and more noticeable, and housing – or at least those aspects of housing shortage manifest by harassment, eviction and homelessness – became a political issue. The revelation in 1963 that Christine Keeler, mistress of John Profumo, the Minister for War, had previously been kept by Rachman linked the government with a twilight world of hustlers, crime and housing harassment [doc 12]. By 1964 the pressure on private rented tenants had not diminished. The *Milner Holland Report* found that harassment and eviction continued. Seven hundred and fifty cases were reported to the Committee where a tenant had been subjected to actual ill-treatment during 1962–64, together with much general evidence of persuasion by means other than assault.[2] It was little wonder that 'security of tenure' became an election issue, and that the newly elected Labour government in 1964 hurriedly passed the Protection from Eviction Act while promising a fuller measure in due course.

The subsequent legislation – the Rent Act 1965 – could be called a 'pro-tenant' measure. It provided *security of tenure* for tenants in unfurnished rented dwellings together with a system of registered 'fair rents'. As the preceding White Paper put it, the intention was to 'lay the foundation for a better relationship between the landlord and the tenant of rented property by introducing a new and flexible system of rent regulation'.[4] The intention was to retain the existing supply of rented housing rather than attempt to increase supply through the market. If the 1957 Rent Act was based upon assumption rather than research, the 1965 Rent Act also lacked much research or wide debate in its formulation. The then Minister – Richard Crossman – adopted a more élitist approach [doc 13].

Under the 1965 Act a landlord or a tenant could apply to have the rent of a dwelling *registered*. This would be done by a Rent Officer, who in determining the fair-rent level took into account the size, condition and surrounding amenities enjoyed by the dwelling, but specifically excluded any consideration of the effect of scarcity, and the personal circumstances of landlord or tenant. Landlord and tenant could come to an agreement as to the rent level and call in the

Rent Officer only to adjudicate and register the agreed rent. The majority of registered rents were, in fact, 'agreed'. The fair-rent concept was intended to provide landlords with incentives to repair and to protect tenants from high scarcity rents. Security of tenure provisions removed almost all grounds for legal eviction save non-payment of rent. Those rents that had not been decontrolled under the 1957 Act stayed controlled – although 'creeping decontrol' was allowed when a dwelling became vacant.

During the decade 1961–71 the number of privately rented dwellings fell from 31.5 per cent of all tenures to 19.6 per cent. Opinions vary as to how direct a consequence of the 1965 Rent Act this was. There were strong pressures on landlords and those tenants who were able to pass the financial filters to switch out of renting. Subsidies made owner-occupation increasingly attractive for erstwhile tenants. The growth of demand for owner-occupation made selling increasingly attractive for erstwhile landlords. During the late 1960s, the 'break up' of many purpose-built blocks of flats, and the conversion of much rented housing from multi-occupation to single-owner occupation took place. The objective of maintaining existing supply failed to be achieved, largely as a consequence of these measures. Significantly, the 1965 Act, after a good start, failed to curb the number of illegal evictions, and homelessness continued to increase. Furthermore, some landlords discovered loopholes in the Act which enabled them to legally evict tenants. One such loophole lay in the grounds for eviction due to non-payment of rent, and worked as follows: a landlord would simply stop accepting the rent, and after three or four refusals tenants would often stop trying to offer it. Tenants with low incomes who tended to live hand-to-mouth soon stopped putting the rent money by. Several months later, when the unpaid rent had reached some hundred or so pounds, the landlord would apply for an eviction order on the grounds of non-payment. Lacking any proof of refusal to accept (such as a solicitor's letter) and lacking the lump sum to offer, the tenant often had no defence. John Greve, in his study of *Homelessness in London*,[5] found many cases where families had become homeless in this way. It can be fairly said that such actions would have been less likely to occur had there not been such strong incentives existing for landlords to empty their property for conversion to owner-occupation.

If supply was affected by policies other than the Rent Act, the Act itself worked less than effectively and could not be said to have really achieved its objective of 'laying a better foundation . . . by a new and flexible system of rent regulation'. Tenants and others criticised the high levels of 'fair rents' being set, especially in London. They also drew attention to the composition of many Rent Assessment Panels (who received Rent Officers' recommendations and who decided the fair rent when landlord or tenant disputed the Rent Officer's decision). These panels, critics argued, often were made up of surveyors, valuers, estate agents and other 'housing professionals' who could often be said to favour the landlord interest. On the other hand, landlords and others complained that the security of tenure measures unreasonably curtailed their autonomy of action regarding their own property, and made it nearly impossible to get rid of unsatisfactory tenants. They complained that the whole assessment machinery was cumbersome and that there were disparities between rents set by Rent Officers in adjoining districts. Increasingly, however, it was landlords and not tenants who applied to have fair rents set and registered. In the first year of the Act's operation, 1966, over half the applications had come from tenants and about one-third from landlords. By 1970, 68 per cent of applications were coming from landlords. In the majority of cases the fair-rent level was set above what the tenant was currently paying, yet there were few signs that increased rental income resulted in increased repairs.

Criticisms of the workings of the 1965 Act led to the inevitable examination by committee, in this case the Francis Committee who reported in 1971.[6] They drew attention to the marked differences in the workings of the Act, and in the private rented sector itself, between the country as a whole and areas of 'housing stress', particularly London and the West Midlands. They claimed that tenants on the whole were satisfied with their rent levels, and appeared largely to discount evidence that it was a desire to avoid trouble with the landlord and antagonise him from undertaking any repairs at all that prevented many tenants from applying to the Rent Officer: 'The grasping landlords who charge exorbitant rents are relatively few,' claimed the Committee, and went on to state, 'One of the things that has bedevilled the private sector of housing for a long time is the tendency among some persons – often people with deep social consciences who are rightly concerned about the housing conditions of the poor – to identify landlords as a class with a small minority of grasping landlords of the speculator type, and to assume or infer that any remedial action must be directed against landlords as such.'[6]

Octavia Hill could hardly have put it better. The economic trends which were making investment in middle- to low-income renting unattractive were generally ignored by the Committee, although they did recommend that new building should be excluded from the regulations altogether on the grounds that this would encourage 'massive investment'. Only one member dissented from this view, commenting, 'The demand for new accommodation to let at rent levels which might attract private capital is limited almost entirely to genuine transients such as visitors from abroad and people working away from their home areas on short-term contracts or elderly people unable to obtain a mortgage. This demand represents only a very small proportion of the demand for rented accommodation . . .'[6]

One of the problems that had concerned housing reformers and sundry 'people with deep social consciences' since the time of the Philanthropic Housing Association had been the gap between the rent level that would ensure minimum standards, as well as allow return on investment, and the rent levels that working people could afford to pay. The 1957 Rent Act had introduced decontrol on the assumption that rents were too low and people could pay more. By raising rents, the 1965 Rent Act in practice shared this assumption. While it was true that many controlled rents had been held at pre-war levels, it became increasingly clear that people's ability to pay higher rents did not always reach levels that would give an adequate return to the landlord and that many could not meet the new rents at all. The Housing Finance Act 1972 attempted to overcome this by allowing rents to rise to market level while introducing a subsidy for tenants unable to meet them. The Rent Rebate scheme applied to both public and private sectors, with rebates calculated on income, but also taking into account other factors such as the number of children in an applicant's family.

The problem with this, as with many similar schemes, was that success depended upon take-up, and take-up was low. The scheme was a selective one, with the onus on the tenant to claim. When added to other benefits and rebates that the tenant might be receiving there was a danger of landing in the 'poverty trap' of cumulative benefits reaching the tax threshold. The rebate scheme did represent an attempt to switch emphasis from the problems of landlords' disincentive to repair to the problems of low income, but as a measure for tackling low income, even together with others, it was inadequate.

The extension of security of tenure to furnished tenants with the Rent Act 1974 did slow the sector's decline, but did not halt it. The 1977 Green Paper commented, 'If the decline continues and no action were taken to compensate for the loss of accommodation, many people – particularly new or mobile households – might not be able to find the housing they need.'[7] But there were no strong recommendations other than speeding up possession-order proceedings, and establishing some form of publically accountable investment agency. The *Review of the Rent Acts* brought out by the DOE in the same year[8] showed a similar lack of vigour. The review placed its emphasis mainly on the need to maintain and repair the physical fabric of rented buildings within the context of security of tenure, while commenting that the government were willing to 'consider new ideas, or reconsider previously rejected ideas.'

The Conservative government in 1979 once again swung away from rent regulation and security of tenure. They proposed a 'pro-landlord' measure – 'Shortholding' within the context of market rents. 'Shortholds' were essentially short leaseholds of two or three years at an agreed rent, after which the landlord could, if he wished, repossess the property. The shorthold proposals were welcomed by many landlords, increasingly concerned at the effect of inflation upon income, and eager to charge market rents with the option of freedom to switch investment as and when they chose. Critics of the scheme, however, warned of the possibility of a return of the harassment episodes of the late 1950s and 1960s should some landlords seek to bring their properties within the scope of the shorthold provisions by evicting existing protected tenants.

In addition, the government sought to increase the supply of private rented housing by proposing that all new building to rent should be outside the scope of the Rent Acts. The Secretary of State commented that he hoped this would stimulate increased investment by financial institutions, including building societies, in private rented housing.

But little consideration seemed to have been given as to just who would rent these new properties or, indeed, take the market rent shortholds. Demand for rented housing had polarised between highly mobile members of the upper-income groups and those members of lower-income groups who could not gain access to the public sector nor buy – in particular young single people and new households. For almost everybody else the advantages of owner-occupation were immeasurably greater. The middle-income groups in particular would be unlikely to switch back to renting. Shortholding could really function effectively only where there was increased supply and thus increased choice, otherwise the problems of insecurity might well deter potential tenants.

The new policies did not represent a real attempt to increase supply of private rented housing. Neither, of course, had previous policies since the war. Rent decontrol, rent regulation and rent rebate schemes had all proved inadequate tools of policy in the face of pressures upon the private sector of investment disincentive, slum clearance, and especially the pressures of policies to stimulate the other housing sectors. Additional attempts to encourage the private landlord with the introduction of Improvement Grants by successive governments were also unsuccessful. These measures will be discussed again in the section on Inner Cities, but suffice it to say here that most improvement grants were taken up by owner-occupiers and public authorities rather than by private landlords. Even if, as the Francis Committee suggested, the majority of private landlords were not rapacious speculators, many of them did appear to be simply profit-takers. This was perhaps not surprising. The prior commitment of successive governments to the other housing sectors, and the location of so much rented property in the inner-city areas where land values were high and redevelopment likely, meant that the long-term future of much private rented property was problematic. It would have been easier to sympathise, however, had not profit-taking without maintenance of minimum standards so characterised the private landlords renting to the lower-income groups during the unregulated days of the mid-nineteenth century.

HOUSING ASSOCIATIONS

One form of semi-private sector renting encouraged by government during the 1960s and 1970s was that of housing associations. Heirs to the philanthropic housing associations of the nineteenth century, housing associations from 1974 were mainly funded by government. Although this part of the sector expanded rapidly, by 1979 housing association tenancies still amounted to less than 2 per cent of all housing tenures.

Apart from a few bodies, such as the Peabody Trust, the majority of the Victorian associations had long since handed over their dwellings to the local authorities. During the 1920s a new generation of housing associations came into being, registered under the Provident Societies Act 1893–94 (thus ensuring that investors received a return on capital but that the rate of interest was restricted by the Treasury and that the association was non-profit-making). One of the first, and possibly the most notable, of these housing associations of the 1920s was the St Pancras Housing Association, founded in 1924, with the specific intention of preventing 'shovelling out the poor':

The aim in every case was the rehousing of a given population from a slum area, either on the site of the demolished buildings or on a site adjacent to it, without disrupting the community; and in addition rehousing families from equally disgraceful conditions in the neighbourhood, including young marrieds who never had a home of their own and old people forced by the housing shortage to share accommodation with relatives.[9]

In addition to building flats and cottages, the Association also opened nursery schools and tenants' clubs. Although like similar associations it was operated upon paternalist principles, there was little of Octavia Hill apparent in its management. In terms of addition to the housing stock, and like similar associations, its output was small. Unlike many other associations, it stayed in business into the later part of the twentieth century. After the Second World War the majority of housing associations concentrated upon providing accommodation for special groups – the elderly or the handicapped, for example. Loans and subsidies were available for this through local authorities who often also attached conditions to the money, in particular the right to nominate some or all of the tenants.

After 1961 the types of housing association became much more varied. Some were specialist, some paternalistic, some 'democratic' and some purely commercial with committees consisting of estate agents and valuers. The voluntary housing movement was seen by the government as the 'third arm' of housing policy, offering an alternative between the increasingly monolithic public and owner-occupied sectors. Loans for building houses were made available on a larger scale, and by 1963 about 7,000 new dwellings had been built – not a great amount. In 1964 the government further enlarged and formalised the loans scheme, channelling all funds through a new established agency – the Housing Corporation. The Housing Corporation was also given the duty of promoting societies which would provide 'co-ownership' dwellings, where all the members of the society jointly owned the accommodation. This new development had many advantages in that a society could jointly benefit from the financial advantages of owner-occupation as well as obtaining a building loan to start off with. The majority of those benefiting from the first co-ownership schemes appeared to be young professional people without sufficient capital to pass the filter into ordinary owner-occupation. There were criticisms that this was simply subsidising owner-occupation without in any way relieving the pressures upon the private rented sector. The government had expressed the hope that the example of the Housing Corporation would tempt other forms of institutional finance, particularly building societies, to invest in rented housing. This proved to be a vain hope.

The initial enthusiasm for housing associations in the 1960s came from the Conservative government. Labour, as Cullingworth points out, had 'no heart in this funny little sector'.[10] But by the mid-1970s a more bipartisan approach had developed, with the Labour government introducing measures that had been largely drafted by the previous administration. The then Secretary of State justified this by claiming that housing associations had a rôle to play in extending social ownership into the private rented sector. The 1974 Housing Act 'transformed the Housing Corporation from a relatively modest organisation channelling Exchequer aid to the voluntary housing movement . . . to the dominant promotional supervisory and financial institution in the field. Its rôle was underpinned first by its financial strength and secondly by the new statutory requirement that before any association could borrow . . . it had to secure registration with the Corporation.'[10] Soon local authority areas were zoned to determine the spheres of action of the various associations. By 1977 the Housing Association Grant (HAG) was being paid to 2,400 registered associations, and some 16,000 new dwellings had been built.

There were two main criticisms of the new style Housing Corporation. The first concerned *Accountability*, the second its *Status* and the degree to which such a body could effect change within the private rented sector.

The Housing Corporation was a 'quango' (quasi-autonomous, non-governmental organisation) which received the bulk of its funds direct from central government. These funds it disbursed to housing associations registered with it. Yet neither the associations, nor the Corporation, opened their books to full public scrutiny. When accusations were made of mismanagement by an association, the Corporation would conduct an internal investigation but again did not publish details. By 1979 this was causing comment from the Public Accounts Committee of the House of Commons. Some commentators suggested that if the principle of public funds being publicly accounted for was to be complied with, far more detail needed to be available than that given in the Corporation's Annual Report.[11] To complicate matters, not all Housing Corporation money came from the state. In 1976–77, when faced with the possibility of decimation of its funds under the latest round of expenditure cuts, the Corporation had taken the unusual step (for a body of this kind) of raising a £35 m. loan on the private market through a syndicate of merchant banks.[12] While this perhaps provided a blueprint for action by similar bodies – especially after the change of government in 1979 – it also posed an interesting problem. The loan had been accepted at an above-market-level interest rate; repayment was to come out of housing association rental income. Yet how much of this income was generated by the use of public money? Indeed, could public and private funds be separated at this stage, or could it be said that public funds were also servicing the loan?

This ambivalence over funding reflected the ambivalent status of the Housing Corporation – a private-sector, public body. The housing associations it funded were totally private voluntary bodies, albeit with paid professional staff. While non-profit making, they were not necessarily offering a cheaper alternative to other private-sector property. Housing association rents were calculated on the 'fair rent' basis. As Cullingworth has shown, these tended to be significantly higher than their equivalent in the public sector, while the far better physical state of housing association housing also meant rents above private-sector equivalents. Despite the post-1974 expansion, the extent of voluntary housing activity in the private market overall was really not significant, and raised questions about the rôle and function of the associations and the Housing Corporation, particularly as to whether the task could have been better tackled by local authorities. Many commentators felt that local councils lacked both the flexibility and the will to undertake such activity. Local authority high building costs put small schemes out of the question; housing associations, it was argued, had lower overheads, could move faster, were not bogged down with bureaucracy. On the other hand, the Housing Act 1974, which reformed the Housing Corporation, had also introduced new measures for housing in the inner-cities in which local authorities were envisaged as playing a major part. These measures – which will be discussed later – certainly had little chance to prove their effectiveness, due to drastic cutting of their budgets. Whether the funds directed to the Housing Corporation could have been more effectively used as part of the inner-city housing action programme of local authorities must remain a matter for debate. Certainly much HAG money did go on housing association inner-city housing projects, and guaranteed the continuation of (some) private rented housing of reasonable condition at rents (some) working people could afford, but whether this was enough to stem the decline of the private rented sector was open to question.

Apart from the small proportion of people occupying the luxury end of private renting, the majority of tenants in the private sector can be termed 'housing poor'. They pay a higher proportion of their income in rent for lower standard accommodation than do members of their income or occupation groups in alternative forms of tenure. There still appears to be a limited number of small investors who are willing to offer housing in this sector – for which there is still demand – but who also appear to be willing only to take investment income rather than maintain, and who desire to repossess whenever they feel the opportunity is right. Despite demand, and inducements, finance-capital has not invested in private renting on any scale. Much of the condition of private rented housing reflects scarcity, particularly scarcity of land in the inner-city areas where most private renting is to be found. The Land Act 1975 had virtually no impact on this despite its declared objective of being 'to enable the community to control the development of land in accordance with needs and priorities'.[13] What development land there was in inner-city areas – and there was not much – was mainly taken by local authorities. Land scarcity simultaneously limited expansion while increasing the value of sites occupied by rented housing and thus increasing the opportunity cost of alternative forms of building investment. It may be that the building societies will play a larger rôle in the rented sector in the future, it may be that housing association activity will continue to increase. More probably the sector will continue its slow decline with worsening conditions, continued demand being met by minimum provision. As Shelter commented, 'The private landlord is dead, but he won't lie down.'

REFERENCES

1. M. JOEL-BARNETT, *The Politics of Legislation*, Weidenfeld & Nicolson, London (1969).
2. MINISTRY OF HOUSING AND LOCAL GOVERNMENT, *Report of the Committee on Housing in Greater London* (Milner Holland Report), Cmnd 2605, HMSO (1965).
3. D. DONNISON, C. COCKBURN and T. CORLETT, *Housing Since the Rent Act*, Occasional Paper in Social Administration, No. 3 (1961).
4. MINISTRY OF HOUSING AND LOCAL GOVERNMENT, *Rents and Security of Tenure: the Rent Bill*, Cmnd 2622, HMSO (1965).
5. J. GREVE, S. GREVE and D. PAGE, *Homelessness in London*, Scottish

Academic Press, Edinburgh (1971).

6. DEPT. OF ENVIRONMENT, *Report of the Committee on the Rent Acts* (Francis Report), Cmnd 4609, HMSO (1971).
7. DEPT. OF ENVIRONMENT, *op. cit.* (see ref. 8, Ch. 2).
8. DEPT. OF ENVIRONMENT, *Review of the Rent Acts: a consultative document*, HMSO (1977).
9. I. BARCLAY, *People Need Roots*, National Council for Social Services, London (1976).
10. J. B. CULLINGWORTH, *op. cit.* (see ref. 7, Ch. 2).
11. N. GINSBERG, *Class, Capital and Social Policy*, Macmillan, London (1979).
12. NATIONAL UNION OF PUBLIC EMPLOYEES/COMMUNITY ACTION, *Up Against a Brick Wall: the dead end of housing policy*, Community Action, London (1978).
13. DEPT. OF ENVIRONMENT, *Land*, Cmnd 5730, HMSO (1974).

Part three
HOUSING PROBLEMS

HOUSING PROBLEMS AND
HOUSING SECTOR RELATIONSHIPS

For nineteenth-century reformers the 'housing problem' was essentially the physical problem of 'bad' housing conditions – lack of ventilation, lack of running water, inadequate drainage and jerry-built, verminous structures. The economic implications of such a definition were not generally faced, but the implicit problem of providing physically adequate housing at rents working people could afford was faced, if not solved, by the growth of council housing, and the general growth of state intervention in the working of the housing market. As a society changes so its needs and expectations change, in housing as in all else. Since the Second World War, Britain has changed a great deal. Post-war policies of full employment and better health care led to many more people having higher disposable incomes, and to a growing population that married earlier and lived longer than had the generation before the war. These changes were reflected in the growing number of new households needing housing and the rising standard of expectation where housing standards were concerned. Housing policy concentrated on increasing the number of houses built, and encouraging people to own their own homes. Although living standards improved for many people, by the mid-1960s it had become clear that the fundamental inequalities had remained unaltered, and that a large part of the population were experiencing deprivation.

In housing, the physical problem of 'bad' housing remained in many areas despite the vast slum-clearance programmes, and many people continued to live in substandard and unfit dwellings. The problem of people who had nowhere to live at all became increasingly obvious. During the 1960s the 'housing problem' came to be seen as essentially a problem of the inner-cities – part of a cluster of problems termed 'urban deprivation'. Often these problems were discussed as though they were causes rather than effects, and it is important to remember that how a social issue is defined very much depends upon who is defining it. To talk of 'problems' is to talk about labelling. For example, Coates and Silburn, in their study of inner-Nottingham, found that people outside the area, particularly officials, saw the occupants of the St Ann's district as 'slum dwellers', as a 'different culture', whereas the people themselves felt they were part of British society as a whole – enjoying a pint of beer on a Saturday and with pictures of the Queen on their walls – but that they happened to live in houses needing repair.[1]

In the following section we are going to discuss some of the 'problem areas' of housing. These fall under two broad headings:

People: the problem of policies which result in people becoming homeless and the consequences of this;

Places: the problems of changes in rural areas, and in particular the growing deprivation in the inner-urban areas.

It is clear that policies adopted for one housing sector often have consequences – sometimes quite drastic ones – for other sectors. Policies for one sector can cause decline or expansion in another. Policies attempting to solve a problem in one sector may cause new problems to develop in another. The earlier section on the housing sectors will have provided many examples of this. Throughout this century, but particularly since the Second World War, the relationship between the housing sectors has become increasingly close and complex. One of the many disappointments of the 1977 Green Paper[2] was that it failed to grasp or do justice to this complexity in its overview of housing policy. A possible explanation for this may lie in many problems and conflicts that such a complex relationship must inevitably generate, conflicts beyond the scope of an incrementalist approach adopted by the writers of the Green Paper. It is important for us to bear in mind that the inequalities generated by the interrelationships of the housing sector are part of wider issues of command over resources.

REFERENCES

1. K. COATES and R. SILBURN, *Poverty: the forgotten Englishmen*, Pelican, Harmondsworth (1970).
2. DEPT. OF ENVIRONMENT, *op. cit.* (see ref. 8, Ch. 2).

Chapter six

HOMELESSNESS

From 1948–77 local authorities had a duty, under Part III Section 21 (1) of the National Assistance Act 1948, to provide temporary accommodation for 'persons who are in urgent need thereof'. The 1948 Act, stating boldly '. . . the existing Poor Law shall cease to have effect', took the relieving functions of the Poor Law and bifurcated them. 'Out Door Relief' became 'National Assistance' and 'In Door', or residential, relief became the responsibility of local-authority Welfare (later Social Services) Departments. The introduction of unemployment benefit in the early part of the twentieth century had already removed the 'able-bodied poor' from the Poor Law ambit; the Children's Act 1948 established a separate system of residential care for children. What 'In Door Relief' requirement remained was for the elderly, unable through age or infirmity to continue living in their own homes, for unmarried mothers and their babies, and for the 'persons in urgent need' mentioned above, who were, in fact, although the term was not used in the Act, homeless.

Part III accommodation (so called from Part III of the National Assistance Act that established it) for the homeless was intended to be temporary. Local authorities were given a degree of discretion but as the Ministry of Health pointed out, it was 'primarily intended to cover persons temporarily without accommodation as a result of such circumstances as fire, flood and eviction.'[1] Thus, because no one was expected to stay very long, there was little need for local authorities to provide much Part III accommodation for the homeless; indeed some authorities provided little if any. At the time the Act was passed there was still a problem of homelessness due to wartime bomb damage, but essentially homelessness was seen as a diminishing and residual problem. It was assumed that families coming into Part III would soon be able to make alternative arrangements. Stays of any length of time were in any case discouraged by policies of 'deterrence' and 'less eligibility' reminiscent of the Poor Law. Husbands were often not admitted, and the standard of accommodation, in terms of privacy, basic comfort and facilities for cooking and washing, was poor. Indeed, for at least fifteen years after the passing of the 1948 Act most homeless family accommodation was situated in what had previously been workhouses [doc 14].

Part III accommodation for the homeless was intended for families – that is, one or more parents with children under sixteen. This made, and still does to some extent, accurate assessment of the actual numbers of homeless people impossible. Official figures represented only those families who had actually gained admission to Part III. People who had applied but failed to get admitted; people who had not applied at all; childless couples; expectant mothers; the single homeless both old and young – were all missing from the statistics. As well as all these people, who were actually houseless, there were also those who, Shelter argued, were homeless in the real sense of the word in that the conditions they had to live in simply could not be termed 'homes': '. . . the home is the central part of the social fabric of our society, and not just bricks and mortar. Above all else the home is the basis of family life. . . . Thus, any family is actually homeless if it is split up because the home is too small, or if it is living in housing conditions so unfit or overcrowded that it cannot lead a civilised family life.'[2] Even after 1977, when the categories entitled to accommodation for the homeless were extended, estimates were still arguable. What is not arguable is that what was intended as a residual measure in 1948 had become severely strained due to increased demand from the late 1950s onward.

THE INCREASE IN HOMELESSNESS

Homelessness, as measured by admittance to Part III, began to increase in the 1950s, some while before the 1957 Rent Act provided Rachman and his ilk with incentives to evict their tenants. This increase was largely a consequence of the renewed expansion of slum-clearance programmes and road-building schemes, both of which had the same effect of 'shovelling out the poor' as they had had in the nineteenth century. These pressures continued with increasing severity as the property boom of the 1960s got under way.

It was, however, the evictions and harassment that followed the 1957 Rent Act that first drew public attention to the homeless, and subsequently to the condition of homeless family accommodation. The Profumo scandal and the political storms of the last days of the Macmillan government kept housing (or lack of it) to the forefront of debate, subsequently emphasised by the publication of the Milner Holland Report.[3] Then, in 1966, the TV play *Cathy Come Home* portrayed in quasi-documentary fashion the grim descent into helplessness, despair and family break-up that lack of housing created, together with the punitive attitudes of many who had dealings with the homeless. Brandon claims that *Cathy Come Home* did 'more than anything to raise public consciousness and alter the map of homelessness.'[4] One result, at least, was that five organisations involved in housing aid – both in London and other major cities – launched a national joint fund-raising campaign. To do this they established a charitable trust – Shelter – which at once embarked upon a skilfully designed advertising and publicity campaign for donations in a manner quite unlike that normally used by charities. Seyd has illustrated how Shelter has developed over the years since its foundation, from being 'a Christian Charity group devoted entirely to raising money, to being a housing pressure group commenting on all aspects of policy . . .'[5]

The increase in homelessness continued through the 1960s into the 1970s. In 1966 there were 2,558 households in temporary accommodation, by 1970 there were 4,926 and by 1976 there were 10,270 – some 50,000 people. Although only recently brought to public notice, this was clearly not a temporary phenomenon, but the product of trends in the housing market established over time and continuing in force. The shrinking of the private rented sector through the switch of investment to commercial development or to selling for owner-occupation, the continuation of illegal evictions, the growth of public-sector activity in slum clearance and redevelopment, and the continued rise in the cost of renting or buying due to scarcity were all contributing factors.

Although homelessness occurred all over the country, in rural as well as urban areas, the highest number of families in Part III accommodation were to be found in London. How much this reflected a possible greater responsiveness and flexibility in admissions policy among London, as opposed to other local authorities, or how much this was simply a matter of size and employment possibilities is difficult to say: 'From the individual's point of view the London housing market is an unusually difficult one. To a great extent this is due to the extraordinarily persistent demand, and to the exceptionally high rent and price levels, but there is another factor –

size. . . . The combination of high costs and a huge market means that the lower a person's income the less likely he is to be able to fulfil his housing needs.'[6]

CONSEQUENCES OF THE INCREASE

One consequence of the increase in homelessness and increased admissions to Part III was increased pressure on a limited supply. Many local authorities enlarged their Part III provision to include blocks of flats. These, although frequently built pre-1914, lacking facilities and due in the long term for redevelopment, were an improvement on the hostel provision of the old workhouses. Some authorities modernised and improved the flats to a degree that made them superior to 'the poor-quality housing in the private sector from which most homeless families come.'[6] As Greve commented, 'There can be no doubt, however, that by and large living conditions in temporary accommodation have improved considerably in recent years. It is important to put this on record. It has to be recognised, however, that the improvement has been so dramatic only because there was so much room for improvement in the first place.'[6]

The expansion of local-authority temporary accommodation was not a large one, and the emphasis upon short-stay remained. Both Greve and Glastonbury[7] found wide variations in policy and practice between boroughs as to length of stay – indeed to almost all aspects of homelessness. Some boroughs moved families through temporary accommodation, into 'halfway houses' and then into permanent council tenancies; some boroughs operated a time-limit, after which the family had to leave and find their own solution; many operated the 'one-offer' policy. A family's progress through temporary accommodation and the length of time they stayed varied from borough to borough, but also often from family to family. Much depended upon the relationship of a family to the social worker involved, who as the person who recommended rehousing played a key 'gatekeeper' rôle. 'Cleanliness', 'Good Behaviour', together with regular payment of rent (temporary accommodation was, and is, not free), were the factors that most often seemed to be 'rewarded' by rehousing, while families who 'resisted' attempts to 'help' them were not. As Greve commented, 'The danger of merit-reward systems is that personal prejudices can introduce considerations beyond the proper province of a public service.'[6] Some families appeared to become 'trapped' in temporary accommodation for years. Greve found a 'small minority' of families in his sample had been in temporary accommodation for five years or more. In the long run, however, '. . . throughout the whole process, from application through to permanent rehousing, the controlling factor is the amount of accommodation, temporary and permanent, which the particular council has decided to allocate to the homeless. The amount of temporary accommodation determines how many applicants can be accepted and also, therefore, the priorities which govern selection procedures. The amount of permanent housing affects the rate at which families are discharged. The process clearly depends upon a smooth flow and any increase in pressure will tend to have repercussions throughout.'[6]

This last sentence was to prove only too true, as cutbacks in council building came with cuts in public expenditure. Council-house 'starts' began to decrease after 1968 and the supply of available council housing slowly stopped growing. Urban authorities, already under pressure with long waiting lists of people in bad housing, increasingly found the 'smooth-flow' of families through homeless family accommodation difficult to achieve. Bottlenecks occurred as homeless family accommodation became filled, and applications still increased. The deterrent effect of the Protection from Eviction Act 1964 and the Rent Act 1965 had proved shortlived and the actions of private landlords had increased as a cause of homelessness. In this situation, local authorities found themselves dealing with large numbers of homeless families but with nowhere to put them. One result of this was the adoption of even more rigorous screening of applicants, and of offering travel warrants to any place where a family might have friends or relatives who might accommodate them, or of simply offering the bus fare to travel over the borough boundary.

Another result was the increased use by local authorities of bed-and-breakfast hotels for homeless families. What Bailey terms 'this utterly disastrous situation'[8] began in London in 1971 and had soon spread to other parts of the country. By the end of 1973 there were a total of 673 homeless families in bed-and-breakfast accommodation in the Inner London boroughs, and 379 families in the Outer London boroughs. By 1976, during the six months from 30 June to 31 December, 1,500 families in the whole of London occupied such accommodation, at a cost of about £1,045,305. Bailey estimated that for 1975–76 Manchester spent £196,829 on bed-and-breakfast accommodation, Avon £159,000 and Liverpool £100,000, while more rural areas such as Dorset spent £25,000 and Norfolk £17,689.[8]

This course of action was immensely costly for the local

authorities, immensely unsatisfactory for the homeless families [doc 15], and immensely profitable for the owners of the hotels. Soon many of these small hotels began to take only homeless families. In some areas blocks of houses were purchased and turned into bed-and-breakfast hotels (making the previous tenants 'homeless' in the process). Companies were established that specialised solely in that form of provision. Shelter drew attention to one company in particular – Southside Investment Co. – who between April and October 1974 were paid £13,013 by the London Boroughs of Tower Hamlets and Lambeth to accommodate homeless families in conditions which were often overcrowded and in an establishment that had insufficient sanitary facilities to comply with the standards for multi-occupied dwellings.

The local-authority response to the growth of bed-and-breakfast expenditure by 1976 was to cut it back. In some cases they bought up the hotels and used them as hostel accommodation themselves, which did, at least, mean that the families could stay indoors during the day. Some authorities, faced with still further cuts in expenditure demanded by the government at the behest of the International Monetary Fund, saw bed-and-breakfast as an area where savings could be made and drastically cut their expenditure. Bailey claimed that overall the reduction in expenditure had been achieved by councils adopting a 'get tough policy . . . in other words the numbers of families applying for homeless family accommodation has continued to increase but the percentage of families actually given accommodation has decreased.'[8]

REASONS AND CAUSE OF HOMELESSNESS, AND HOMELESS FAMILIES

The reasons for a family losing their accommodation have stayed remarkably static over the past fifteen to twenty years. 'Rent arrears', 'landlord requiring accommodation', 'unauthorised occupancy' and 'family disputes' have stayed as the main reasons for families being admitted to temporary accommodation. In 1977 the DOE calculated that 52 per cent of families lost their previous accommodation through disputes either with family or friends. But, as Greve pointed out, these reasons do not disentangle cause from effect.[6] The reasons as recorded by local authorities and the DOE do not tell us 'how far the housing shortage, high rents and low incomes lead to rent arrears and subsequently homelessness; (or) how far the tenant's behaviour is the precipitating cause.'[6] The high incidence of 'family dispute' should perhaps be seen as an effect of overcrowding, or of the stress arising from families having to live with their in-laws, rather than as a causal explanation. Not all families evicted for rent arrears come from the private sector; local authorities also evict, despite the evidence that shows the majority of tenants get into arrears only as a result of sudden crisis plus low income.

Homeless families themselves have been frequently categorised as 'the feckless', 'irresponsible', 'problem' families who often falsely represent themselves as homeless in order to 'jump the queue' into council housing. Greve's study found that although the families he studied in temporary accommodation were predominantly young, with larger than average families and lower than average incomes, they nonetheless were 'ordinary decent Londoners' rather than the socially pathological. Among the Commonwealth immigrant families, the same conclusion applied. Almost all the Commonwealth-born men were in full employment, and, although their earnings were even lower on the whole than the white families, very few were evicted for rent arrears.[6] Certainly, both Glastonbury in his study of homelessness in Wales and the West of England[7] and Greve in London found that homeless families had personal and social problems, but as Greve commented:

. . . even so, it is the lack of adequate and secure accommodation at rents that can be paid out of average and below-average earnings that renders most people homeless. Were it not for the growing shortage of rented housing in Inner London many of the families who do not display conventional standards of behaviour would still find room in the housing stock. Were it not for rising rents – particularly in the expanding furnished sector – many of those evicted for rent arrears would still be paying their way.[6]

CONSEQUENCES OF HOMELESSNESS

A homeless family is a family 'at risk'; due to the stress of the situation it may break-up and cease being a family unit. There is the risk of desertion by one or either parent, the risk of mental breakdown, the risk of the wage-earner losing his or her job, the risks of losing all local contacts and support, the risk of the children being received into care of the local authority. These risks do not significantly decrease when a family obtains temporary accommodation, and the longer the family remains in hostel or bed-and-breakfast accommodation the greater will be the added strain imposed upon it.[9] It is possible to suggest that some families could be said to have a 'homeless family career', whereby they move from being 'ordinary decent Londoners' (or Mancunians, Liverpudlians or whatever) and become 'problem families', and 'social casualties' as a consequence of being homeless. Certainly it could be suggested that there might be what Wilkins termed 'reaction to reaction' as the family responded to the treatment it received, and to its 'labelling' as deviant.[10]

What happens to those families who fail to obtain admission to temporary accommodation? I have painted such a black picture of what writers have had to say about local-authority provision that it might easily be felt that those who failed to get admitted had a lucky escape. But, of course, their situation is much worse and they are every bit as much 'at risk' if not more so. We have no way of knowing accurately how many people are involved; the number of unsuccessful applicants (33,820 in 1976) tells us nothing beyond the fact that they were unsuccessful. No follow-up work has been done. Nor can anything much be known or guessed about those families who do not apply. One possible indicator is the number of children received into care due to homelessness, but this does not give a completely clear measure. Over recent years the numbers of children coming into care through eviction, or through the family becoming homeless through some other cause, has fallen; in 1971 there were 2,900 such children, by 1976 there were 1,200. The number received into care due to unsatisfactory home conditions, however, has risen from 3,000 in 1971 to 5,000 in 1976. It is not possible to say in how many cases of reception into care under other categories (for example 'long-term illness of parent or guardian', or 'child abandoned') bad housing or homelessness was the precipitating factor, but much of what we know about the effects of housing stress and urban deprivation suggests the likelihood of such cases. The most that can be said with any certainty is that the number of children received into care due to homelessness or bad housing conditions has remained at around 6,000 since 1971, with consequent adverse effects upon the family unit.

In circumstances such as these, reception into care of the children further alienates and demoralises parents already under stress and 'at risk' themselves. Many writers have drawn attention to the fact that 'the longer a child remains in care the more difficult maintaining links with parents become and the more remote the likelihood of re-establishing the family again.'[11] Also, most of the cost, despite possible parental contributions, is borne by all of us through taxation. It is very costly (about £100 per week in 1978) to keep a child in local-authority care. Moreover, 'Taking children into care does not resolve a family's housing problems; it tends rather to have the opposite effect and make them worse, even though relieving parents of their children usually enables these adults to find accommodation – usually of poor quality and often insecure – for themselves and without their children. Until accommodation suitable for parents and children can be found children necessarily remain in care.'[6]

THE SINGLE HOMELESS

So far this discussion on homelessness has dealt solely with homeless families, but there is another group of homeless people – the single homeless. Jane Morton suggests that 'single adults are the largest outstanding crag of unsatisfied housing need in Britain.'[12] This is possibly because these needs are hidden from public view and the attention of the media and public opinion focus on the minority. There were an estimated 11 million single adults in England and Wales at the time of the 1971 Census, yet only 3 million were recorded as having a place of their own to live. A further 700,000 shared with other single adults. Not all the remainder were necessarily 'homeless'; many lived in other people's households as relatives or as (grown-up) children or because they had a 'living-in' job. In fact we do not know just how many single homeless people there are, and estimates can be made only about those of the group who are 'visible' enough to be counted, and even that is difficult, as will be explained.

The single homeless are not a homogeneous group. There are the 'young', almost all of whom are squatters of one sort or another and who will be discussed more fully later. In 1971 there were virtually no single people squatting, by 1976 the number was estimated to be around 10,000. Then there are what I will term the 'hidden' single homeless, who have jobs and live in bed-and-breakfast small hotels or houses in multi-occupation where they are, in effect, licensees and have no security of tenure, or who have 'living-in jobs' and no other home to go to should they lose their position. Then there are the groups of single homeless, all of whose definitions have their beginnings in the old idea of vagrancy – the people living in common lodging houses; the people who live either regularly or irregularly in hostels; the people who visit the night shelters and reception centres and the people who sleep rough. In these groups there must

obviously be an overlap of personnel since an important characteristic is that these are people – as the Supplementary Benefit
Commission puts it – 'without a settled way of life'.[13] Brandon puts
it more dramatically:

They are covered by a wide variety of terms – vagrant, hobo, tramp,
wayfarer, down-and-out, and more recently social drop-out and non-citizen.
Such words tell us very little. . . . Many of these single men and women live
in a condition of homelessness which in terms of both isolation and physical
squalor far exceeds that of most homeless families. They are found in a
tremendous number of holes and burrows. . . . Their life expectancy is
short.[14]

These groups of people without a settled way of life can also be
called 'hidden people' since there are no accurate figures as to just
how many of them there are. Wingfield Digby's survey for the Office
of Population Census and Surveys in 1972 found 26,823 people
being accommodated in the hostels and lodging houses he examined,
but his survey excluded the small, unlicensed lodging houses and the
many beds in mental hospitals occupied by (potentially) homeless
single people.[15] The St Mungo Trust attempted to count the number
of people sleeping rough in inner-London and in two outer-London
boroughs on one night in 1972. They found 1,415 people, but
admitted there might be many more they missed. They also
estimated that on that same night a further 1,048 single-homeless
people were in the hospitals, police cells and reception centres in the
areas they examined; about 500 more were in Brixton Prison and
about 9,000 in common lodging houses, making a total of 11,963
people altogether.[16]

Among the single homeless there are many suffering from mental
illness, many who have recently been discharged from psychiatric
hospital or prison, many who have drink problems or who are
alcoholic and many who fit the term 'social inadequates'.[16] Most are
middle-aged or elderly. Despite this, a high proportion of the single
homeless keep working, although the drift into homelessness almost
inevitably means working at casual jobs. These are usually in the
catering trade, and the wages received are far below the legal
minimum.[17] The OPCS survey found 43 per cent of the men and
40 per cent of the women interviewed were in work.

The accommodation available to the single homeless has been
declining over the past fifteen years. The number of beds available in
hostels and lodgings had fallen by 17 per cent between 1965 and
1972. There has also been a decline in the number of beds in

psychiatric hospitals following the shift of policy towards community care in 1960. Many of the large old houses that had previously been let as bed-sitters or small hotels have been acquired by local authorities for conversion to family flats or demolished. Many small hotels and hostels could not afford to implement the regulations of the Fire Precautions Act 1971 and so closed down (of those that did not close, many remain an appalling fire risk). Of the commercial firms that had run lodging houses, many ceased to exist, while others – especially the Rowton House group in London – up-graded some of their buildings to hotels beyond the price range of most of the previous users and closed the rest, selling off the sites for redevelopment. Overall, redevelopment meant the demolition of city centres where the low-rent housing and lodging houses had been situated, and also the cheap shops and cafés that had helped make an unsettled low-income way of life supportable. As Fox and Fogg commented, 'One effect of redevelopment has often been to remove the last rung of the social ladder – the point at which people may not be doing too well but where they can maintain some contact with the rest of society and thereby the potential for self-rehabilitation.'[18]

The conditions in reception centres, hostels, common lodging houses and most other accommodation for the single homeless have been described as at best spartan and at worst disgusting. In the case of hostels, the OPCS survey found that 85 per cent of the buildings used had been built before 1914 and a very high proportion lacked adequate washing or toilet facilities. Very few new hostels have been built since 1965. Apart from Glasgow, where new hostels of 240 and 61 beds opened in 1970, the OPCS survey found that only five hostels with 58 beds between them had been opened in the whole of Great Britain.[15] The closure, or even the improvement, of the existing sub-standard hostels has proved hard to achieve, not least because of the wide range of bodies who run them – the Department of Health and Social Security; local authorities; large voluntary bodies such as the Salvation Army; small voluntary bodies and private and commercial organisations.

The Campaign for the Homeless and Rootless (CHAR) have argued that the voluntary sector can no longer adequately provide for the single homeless. They have urged that all hostels together with the DHSS reception centres should be transferred to local authorities with the long-term aim of these having statutory housing obligations for the single homeless. It has sometimes been argued that accommodation for the single homeless must be spartan lest it deter those who have embraced a rough and self-destructive mode of life; also, more pragmatically, that there is little point in providing amenities that will be abused. But this does not excuse the lack of facilities for basic hygiene. Furthermore, the single homeless themselves, when questioned in the OPCS survey, clearly would have preferred something better [doc 16]. One CHAR worker stayed overnight at the Camberwell Reception Centre in South London and concluded that the appallingly low standard of accommodation in what had been an old Poor Law Institution was a major cause of the 'disturbing pattern of violence' which had been reported there.[19]

Similarly with common lodging houses and houses in multiple occupation. Standards have almost always been found to be below the minimum standard for any other form of housing. Common lodging houses are licensed and regulated by local authorities, yet these on the whole have proved unwilling to enforce the regulations. Partly there was the problem of finding unregistered lodging houses, but more important was the implicit threat that an owner, if pressed, might close the house and evict the residents, leaving the rehousing problem to the local authority. Few authorities were willing to accept such a housing commitment. Where houses in multiple occupation were concerned the same threat applied, although in that case local authorities had greater powers and could issue a Control Order and manage the house themselves for five years if they so wished. The threat of eviction was a real fear for the inhabitants too. A CHAR report on standards of accommodation contained this warning:

We would sound a strong cautionary note to anyone pressing for improvements in single-person accommodation: be prepared for the possibility that your attempt to improve standards might result in an owner closing the premises altogether or in reducing the number of beds. This must be guarded against and alternative accommodation lined up in case. Invariably residents of hostels are licensees not tenants, and as such they have no security and little protection in law. Many hostel users put up with appalling standards of accommodation. There is a very genuine fear that hostel managers or owners will throw out 'trouble-makers' and make it difficult for them to find a place in the future.[20]

With regard to the single homeless, the question has been asked, 'Which do they need, housing or case-work by social workers?' Tidmarsh has argued that, in fact, the matter should not be looked at as an either/or alternative.[21] But the posing of the question in those terms did highlight the ambivalence of much social policy where the single homeless, and indeed where homeless families, were concerned. Similarly – since the way a problem is defined affects how people respond to it – it served to highlight the ambivalence of 'public opinion'. After their examination of the problems of the single homeless, Wilkinson, Galley and Dobkin had commented, 'On undertaking this study we found an appalling lack of public awareness, or interest in the question, a general attitude which seemed to imply that with disinterest the problem would go away.'[16] This 'disinterest' was perhaps consequential on seeing homelessness as a 'social' problem, that is a problem of individual personal circumstances and failings, rather than a 'housing' problem consequent upon the decline of low-rent housing.

THE HOUSING (HOMELESS PERSONS) ACT 1977

This ambivalence as to whether homelessness is a social or a housing problem was highlighted but was not resolved either with the passing or the administration of the Housing (Homeless Persons) Act 1977. The Act was the first major change in the statutory provision for the homeless for thirty years, and the first-ever piece of legislation dealing specifically with homelessness. Yet it had a stormy passage into the statute book, and within a year of its becoming law criticisms were being voiced as to its effectiveness.

Since late 1973, a group of voluntary organisations working with and for the homeless had been pressing the case for new legislation that would clearly define the responsibilities of local authorities where both the single homeless and homeless families were concerned. The group consisted of CHAR; the Catholic Housing Aid Society; Shelter/Shelter Housing Action Campaign; Child Poverty Action Group; the National Women's Aid Federation and the National Council for One Parent Families. The government's response to this pressure was initially to issue a circular which made recommendations, in a purely advisory way, to local authorities on how to tackle the problems of homelessness. In particular, the circular stressed that homelessness ought to be tackled by local authority housing departments rather than by social services. This view had already been expressed by the Seebohm report[22] and echoed by the Cullingworth Committee in 1969[23] who argued that if there was evidence to suggest that homelessness was a housing problem rather than a problem of the personal inadequacies of the homeless, then responsibility should lie with the housing departments throughout. Some local authorities, notably those in urban areas most concerned with homelessness, implemented all or some of the recommendations, but many local authorities did not. In many parts of the country homeless people were still refused accommodation, families were still split up and children taken into care because of homelessness.

Proposals for legislative reform were introduced to Parliament in a Private Member's Bill. This had tacit government backing as government proposals had been drafted and subsequently dropped. It is interesting to note how many 'social-reform' measures, where opinions for and against may cut across party political boundaries, have reached the statute book in this way. The reform of the laws concerning divorce, homosexuality and abortion are all examples of this.

Opposition to the Bill came particularly from those local councils who had done least for the homeless to date, and who resented the clear (and as they saw it possibly costly) obligations the Bill would impose on them if it became law. Their lobby gained the support of several MPs. Despite the research that had been done in the field, the debates and committee sessions appeared to be dominated more by the rehearsal of opinion than by fact. The stereotype of the homeless person as a feckless inadequate 'jumping the queue' into council housing was raised yet again. William Rees Davies, the Conservative MP for Thanet, went so far as to describe the Bill as 'a charter for the rent-dodger, the scrounger, and for the encouragement of the homeleaver'. The Bill was much amended. Nonetheless the Act that emerged did considerably widen the scope of local authorities' responsibilities for the homeless, even if many commentators felt it fell short of what might have been achieved.

The Act defined homeless persons as 'those without accommodation they were entitled to occupy'. This definition specifically included such groups as 'battered wives' – who might have a home but who ran the risk of violence if they returned to it. As well as the homeless, temporary – and subsequently permanent – housing was to be given to those in need who fell into 'Priority Groups'. It was under this heading that for the first time many of the single homeless became entitled to housing [doc 17].

Local-authority housing departments were required under the Act to investigate and establish:

(*a*) whether an applicant was homeless or threatened with homelessness under the Act;
(*b*) whether he or she fell into any of the priority groups;
(*c*) once satisfied that a person was homeless or in priority need, temporary refuge had to be offered while investigations were

made to see whether they had become homeless intentionally. This concept of *intentional homelessness* was one of the most serious amendments inserted during the Bill's passage through Parliament. Persons deemed to have made themselves homeless intentionally had to find his or her own accommodation, and would not be rehoused temporarily or permanently.

Councils had further duties under the Act, and the government issued a *Code of Guidance* (to which they were obliged under the Act to 'have regard') to assist them in carrying out these duties. But as Shelter commented, 'The most important aspect of the Act is that the first port of call for anyone who is likely to lose their home or has literally nowhere to stay today is the local housing department.'[24] It appeared that the homeless had been squarely defined as having 'housing' rather than 'social' problems.

The new legislation meant that a great many more people applied to councils for help. Some 12,000 households were accepted as homeless by local authorities in England during the first quarter of 1978, compared with 8,000 in the same period the previous year. But from the beginning it was clear that there were wide variations as to how the clauses of the Act were being interpreted. The wording of the Act itself was loose enough to allow councils to make widely different levels of provision. The *Code of Guidance* was also 'regarded' differently by different authorities, and its legal standing was far from clear.

The clause that caused the most controversy, and where there were the widest variations of interpretation, was that concerning 'intentional homelessness'. Many councils appeared to make their own definition of intentionality and ignored the *Code of Guidance* altogether. Afan District Council, for example, included 'family dispute' cases, thereby setting outside the full provision of the Act the category which accounted for the largest single reason for homelessness.[25] Many authorities included 'rent arrears' among their 'intentional' categories. The *Code of Guidance* had stated that 'the numbers of those to be regarded as having become homeless intentionally are expected to be small'[26] and certainly the numbers for the first half year of the Act's operation were not great – about 600 households, or 4 per cent of those accepted as homeless. However, 500 of these cases were outside London and 320 of them in non-metropolitan areas, thus suggesting that rural and semi-urban areas were taking a much harder line than the cities and the capital put together. An amusing comment on the interpretation of intentionality came from Shelter: their magazine *Roof* (Sept. 1978) portrayed on the cover a family sitting amidst the ruins of their home which had been demolished by a large oak tree falling on it. On the tree was standing an official from the local housing department, saying '. . . and as it was you that planted the acorn twenty-eight years ago, I must classify you as intentionally homeless.' More seriously, it was clear that a households' chances of obtaining temporary accommodation and subsequent rehousing depended more upon the *area* in which they became homeless than upon the *circumstances*.

Those local authorities that had opposed the passage of the Act had expressed fears that when the Act came into force they would experience a flood of applicants coming from outside their areas seeking a desirable place to live. This was not entirely new. Some London authorities had been complaining for years that the existence of main-line termini in their boroughs made them the first port of call for homeless families getting off the trains, despite evidence that the majority of families accepted as homeless by them had lived in their boroughs for a year or more. Now other authorities expressed similar fears in forthright terms. The mayor of Slough was reported as describing the 1977 Act as forcing Slough to provide a home for 'pillocks from anywhere'.[27] Councils in seaside towns and holiday areas where there was much seasonal letting felt particularly vulnerable. For example, Tendring Council in Essex declared one whole area – Jaywick Sands on the outskirts of Clacton – to be 'holiday accommodation' from which they would not rehouse people, despite the fact that the district contained 5,000 permanent residents. The Chairman of the Housing Selection Committee (himself a Jaywick resident) was quoted as saying, 'The people who belong here don't want council houses – what we have done is to ensure that work-shy labourers don't move their families into holiday homes and then expect us to house them.'[28] In many cases there appeared to be attempts to link statements about 'feckless' homeless 'queue-jumpers' with implications that these 'outsiders' were also foreign and/or black.

Statements and actions such as these obviously made a mockery of the *Code of Guidance*'s advice that 'careful and sensitive inquiries will be important in establishing the facts of the case'.[26] But they do tell us important things about the way in which the homeless are perceived, despite all the evidence to the contrary. The research evidence suggests that homeless families are not 'work-shy labourers'; indeed, Greve's term was 'ordinary decent Londoners' whose problems of low income were exacerbated by the shortage of low-rent housing. The OPCS examination of single people in hostels and lodgings found almost half of them trying to keep at work of some sort and wishing they could have a 'place of their own'. The Association of Metropolitan Authorities, reporting on the first six months of the working of the 1977 Act, found no evidence that reduced fear of eviction had led to increased rent arrears. CHAR reported that some metropolitan authorities with immense housing pressures had decided to ignore the requirement to decide whether an applicant was intentionally homeless, arguing that it was unworkable in practice. The homelessness statistics showed 80 per cent of households accepted as homeless during the first half of 1978 had been resident in the area in which they were applying for over a year; many of these would also have been on council waiting lists as well and could hardly be described as 'queue-jumpers'.

Increased housing responsibility for the homeless does, of course, mean increased costs. The AMA found that costs to metropolitan authorities had increased in the range of £1,500 to £3,000 a month since the Act became operative. But many of these authorities had already been incurring far higher homeless family expenditure than those smaller councils who were now complaining. Shelter suggested that councils opposed to the Housing (Homeless Persons) Act 1977 had more fundamental fears than 'invasions of mythical swarms of outsiders'. 'The Act embodies the basic principle that housing should be available for all, a concept which grates on those brought up with the attitude that housing has to be earned at the very least by serving time on a waiting list.'[27] Put another way, the responsibilities placed upon local authorities by the Housing (Homeless Persons) Act implied that homelessness was a housing problem to be dealt with by housing provision from the public sector; those local authorities that opposed the Act still defined homelessness as a social problem of individual failing to be dealt with, if at all, by means other than housing. Since the Act did not include any enforcement clauses, nor procedures for redress of grievance, an individual applicant could not demand that he or she had a 'right' to be treated as a 'housing problem', and the ambivalence remained. For students of social policy the question also remains as to the worth of legislation that is open to such wide variations in practice. On the one hand it can be argued that the 1977 Act has brought about important reforms, and for all its loopholes represents a step in the right direction, particularly where the single homeless are concerned. On the other hand the existence of the Act may well mean that homelessness will 'go to the bottom of the queue for legislative change for a good many years to come, the existing inequalities will continue and possibly the very tensions which legislation is attempting to ameliorate may well, in fact, be exacerbated.'[29]

The variations in implementation and the clear flouting by a significant minority of the intention of the Housing (Homeless Persons) Act 1977 should perhaps be contrasted with the administration of policy in other sectors. Berry has drawn attention to the minority of local authorities who flouted the intention of the Housing Finance Act 1972 – 'They were universally condemned and the whole panoply of law was invoked to coerce them into obedience.' He also commented, 'Where are the Housing Commissioners hastening to intervene so as to secure the homeless their rights? Which of Her Majesty's ministers . . . is preparing to redress the balance by exercise of default powers? There is none and there will be none. There will be none because the homeless cut no ice politically. The poor have never counted for much but those who have no home have no vote either.'[30] While this last point may not be true in every case, since long-stay hostel dwellers may succeed in getting on the electoral register, it is nonetheless an interesting comment. Disenfranchisement was, of course, one of the consequences of reception into the workhouse under the old Poor Law.

REFERENCES

1. MINISTRY OF HEALTH, *Circular 87/48*, HMSO (1948).
2. SHELTER, *Who are the Homeless? Face the Facts* (1969).
3. MINISTRY OF HOUSING AND LOCAL GOVERNMENT, *op. cit.* (see ref. 2, Ch. 4).
4. D. BRANDON, *Homelessness*, Sheldon Press, London (1971).
5. P. SEYD, 'Shelter: the National Campaign for the Homeless', *Political Quarterly*, vol. 46 (1975).
6. J. GREVE, S. GREVE and D. PAGE, *op. cit.* (see ref. 5, Ch. 4).
7. B. GLASTONBURY, *Homeless near a Thousand Homes: a study of homeless families in South Wales and the West of England*, Allen & Unwin, London (1971).
8. R. BAILEY, *The Homeless and the Empty Houses*, Pelican, Harmondsworth (1971).
9. SHELTER, *Bed and Breakfast Report* (1974).
10. L. WILKINS, *Social Deviance, Social Policy, Action and Research*, Tavistock, London (1964).
11. J. HEYWOOD, *Children in Care*, Routledge & Kegan Paul,

London (1965).

12. J. MORTON, 'Who'll house the single?', *New Society*, 25 March (1976).

13. SUPPLEMENTARY BENEFITS COMMISSION, *Annual Report for 1976*, Ch. 5, HMSO (1977).

14. D. BRANDON, *The Treadmill: a report on common lodging houses*, Christian Action, London (1969).

15. OFFICE OF POPULATION, CENSUS AND SURVEYS, P. WINGFIELD-DIGBY, *Hostels and Lodgings for Single People*, HMSO (1976).

16. A. WILKINSON, R. GALLEY and L. DOBKIN, *Down and Out: the problems of the single homeless*, Appendix 1, National Advisory Committee of the Young Conservatives, London (1973).

17. P. ERLAM and G. BROWN, *Catering for Single People? A report by the Low Pay Unit and CHAR on homeless workers in the catering trade*, Campaign for the Homeless and Rootless, London (1977).

18. J. FOX and N. FOGG, *Sunday Times Magazine*, 24 June (1973).

19. CAMPAIGN FOR THE HOMELESS AND ROOTLESS, *Annual Report for 1978-9*, London (1979).

20. D. ORMANDY and A. DAVIES, *Standards of Accommodation for Single People*, CHAR (1977).

21. D. TIDMARSH, *The Needs of Homeless Men – Casework or Housing?* Paper given to the National Cyrenians Conference, unpublished. March (1974).

22. *Report of the Committee on Local Authority and Allied Personal Social Services*. Cmnd 3703, 1968.

23. HOUSING MANAGEMENT SUB-COMMITTEE OF THE CENTRAL HOUSING ADVISORY COMMITTEE, *op. cit.* (see ref. 14, Ch. 2).

24. SHELTER, *Where Homelessness Means Hopelessness* (1978).

25. L. WOODCOCK, *Rent Arrears and Eviction Survey*, for Shelter/Housing Action Campaign. Unpublished (1978).

26. DOE/DHSS/WELSH OFFICE, *Housing (Homeless Persons) Act 1977: Code of Guidance (England and Wales)*, HMSO (1978).

27. SHELTER, 'Law of the letter beats the letter of the law', *Roof*, November (1978).

28. 'Homeless in a holiday town', in *The Guardian*, 2 March (1979).

29. D. YATES, *Homelessness: the translation of social policy into legal rules*, paper given to the Social Administration Association Conference. Unpublished (1979).

30. F. BERRY, 'Anomalous treatment of the homeless', *Roof*, January (1979).

Chapter seven
SQUATTERS

'What is a squatter? He is one who without any colour of right enters an unoccupied house or land intending to stay there as long as he can. He may seek to justify or excuse his conduct. He may say that he was homeless and that this house or land was standing empty doing nothing. But this plea is of no avail in Law.'[1]

Squatting is not a new phenomenon. In the seventeenth century, for example, Gerrard Winstanley provided a cogent argument as to why the Diggers should have the 'freedom' to establish a community on unused land.[2] More recently, squatting movements started spontaneously after both world wars. In 1919 returning servicemen found there was a shortage of homes for heroes and for a lot of other people as well. After the Second World War, in 1945, the squatting movement began as a protest against large houses in the south coast resorts of Brighton and Hastings being left empty for most of the year and then let (at very high rents) during the holiday season. 'Vigilante' groups of ex-servicemen installed homeless families in these properties by night. Following this, the government gave local authorities increased powers of requisition and compulsory purchase, but the requisition powers were temporary only for what was seen as an abnormal post-war situation.

The following year (1946) a family squatted in the officers' mess of a disused anti-aircraft camp in Lincolnshire, thus drawing attention to the many hundreds of similar camps standing empty. By October 1946 there were 39,535 people squatting in 1,038 camps in England and Wales, with a further 4,000 in Scotland.[3] Meanwhile, in London, squatters had occupied a block of luxury flats in Kensington and subsequently other flats and hotels in central London that were empty. The Kensington squat – at Duchess of Bedford Buildings – possibly had 'political' undertones. At least, when five of the organisers were arrested and charged (under the

Forcible Entry Act of 1381) much play was made of the fact that they were members of the Communist Party.[3] The actual squatting campaign really lasted only for 1945–46, but 850 of the disused camps were handed over by the Ministry of Works to the new occupants, many of whom remained in them for several years, while in London the majority of the squatters were rehoused by local authorities. Attention had been most forcibly drawn to the problem of post-war homelessness, but it was nonetheless seen as purely a post-war phenomenon, and the reality of the housing shortage which had already existed before the war went unnoticed.

But as homelessness grew rather than diminished during the 1950s and 1960s, so squatting as a reaction and protest against this returned. There were three factors that could be said to have provided the impetus for this:

The first was the 'husbands' revolt' at King Hill Hostel in Kent, during 1965–66. At this ex-workhouse, used as a homeless family hostel, husbands were allowed to visit their wives and families only 'during the daytime at week-ends; at all other times they were forbidden to be in the hostel.'[3] Several husbands refused to accept the ruling and moved in. The conflict lasted for a year, with Kent County Council taking out injunctions restraining the husbands from entering, and jailing one husband (who visited his wife because the children were ill and she was on the verge of a nervous breakdown) for contempt of court. In the end Kent modified their rules, as did twenty-two other local authorities.[3]

Secondly there were the growing number of empty houses all over the country but especially in London. The 1971 Census showed that there were 675,000 empty dwellings in England and Wales. At least 100,000 of these were in London and nearly half of them were owned by the Greater London Council and the London Boroughs. Many of these houses would, of course, be vacant only for a short time as they were being sold or re-let. The majority of the houses in local-authority ownership, however, had been purchased and cleared of tenants for redevelopment programmes, while in the private sector many owners appeared to be keeping their property empty. The London Boroughs Association reported 40,000 private residential properties in London had been empty for at least a year, and a further 9,400 had been empty for more than two years.[4] Of all these empty homes, those cleared for local-authority redevelopment were perhaps the most noticeable. Large areas, of several streets at a time, would be cleared and the houses boarded up. Increasingly, as the number of 'starts' in local-authority housebuilding declined, as funds were cut after 1968, these desolate areas stood empty awaiting demolition and redevelopment for increasingly long times – several years in many instances. In the centre of London itself, 'partnerships' between local authorities and speculative developers, or simply government departments and institutions, added subtle variations on the 'redevelopment blight' as the 'property boom' turned homes and industrial premises into potential office developments.[5] As private housing became scarcer and scarcer, especially for those with low incomes and families, and as bottlenecks developing in council accommodation made councils even more rigorous in their allocation of housing to the homeless, these empty houses and redevelopment areas assumed a 'political' visibility.

The third factor was the third showing of *Cathy Come Home* on TV in 1969. This had the effect of galvanising a small group of housing-rights activists into deciding that 'something must be done'. They were led by Ron Bailey, who described, in his book *The Squatters*[3] how, having woken his friends up at three in the morning to discuss initial proposals, the 'London Squatters Campaign' was formed. It was felt that action by government and local authorities on the one hand, and Shelter's fund-raising on the other had both failed to cause any significant alteration in the housing crisis. Bailey and some members of the founding group had been involved in the King Hill Hostel protest, and from their experiences there had grown their belief in the efficacy of direct action. They decided that 'Squatting should be the movement of ordinary people to challenge the authorities on the whole issue. It must become the living demonstration that ordinary people will no longer accept the intolerable housing shortage. It must become the threat that will compel government, national and local, to change its priorities.'[3]

The campaign began with two token squats of four and twenty-four hours. Following this the group took the decision to squat in empty council property, since 'it was the councils who statutorily ought to be housing people',[3] and began to move homeless families into various houses due for redevelopment by Redbridge Council. It is interesting to note that the redevelopment proposals – which had caused Redbridge to clear the area some while previous to the beginning of the squatting campaign in 1969 – had still not been approved by the Secretary of State when the whole affair ended two years later and, indeed, were finally rejected. During the early part of 1969 the squatters 'played a game of musical chairs' with Redbridge – as one squatting family would leave in response to a court order evicting them, another would move in. The council's response to this was to hire a firm of professional bailiffs who attempted to evict the squatting families by force and without a court order, culminating in a violent attack on two houses simultaneously in June. The actions of the bailiffs received considerable publicity both locally and nationally. Pictures appeared in the papers of helmeted men attacking the squatted houses and hurling bricks and other missiles. The squatters received a generally sympathetic press, but Redbridge Council remained unsympathetic.

Possibly the most important direct consequence of the early squatting campaign was the issuing of a government circular in July 1969, recommending to all local authorities that they utilise their empty property on a short-life basis, by letting to licensed tenants. Many councils began to make such use of dwellings – due for demolition in the long term – arranging the repair, maintenance and lettings through recognised housing associations. In some cases, as squatting spread throughout Britain, councils recognised the *fait accompli* by making squatters into licensed tenants. Not all empty property was used in this way, however, and many local authorities continued with a policy of 'brick-up and demolish' in redevelopment areas.

Back in Redbridge, one consequence of the bailiffs' violent behaviour was that 'defenders' began to move in with the families in the squatted houses. As the strain of the bailiffs' harassment, and of being barricaded in and constantly on the watch, began to tell on them, the families began to move out. Bailey has described how, with the families gone, the 'defenders' began to turn inwards and develop different objectives from those of the original squatting group. These newcomers '. . . thought they had established a free society at "their" house. The interests of the squatting families became subordinate to "the revolution".'[3] A split developed (which continued to characterise the squatting movement) between those seeking a solution to the immediate housing problems of homeless families and others in 'housing need' and those seeking to make a wider political statement. Finally, in 1971, the squatting families were rehoused, and the houses rehabilitated – some by Redbridge and others through housing associations.

The next phase of squatting was to receive a far more hostile reception generally. In part, this reflected the spread of the movement nationally – there were more local authorities involved; in part it reflected the split in the movement mentioned above; and in part (possibly in particular) it reflected the much more hostile media coverage the movement received. This culminated in the summer of

1975 with a series of newspaper articles that made exaggerated and quite misleading claims, and the spreading of a scare story that contributed towards later legislative changes. These made squatting a criminal rather than a civil offence. Paris and Poppleton have suggested that squatting 'provides a case study of media involvement in the creation of stereotypes.'[6] They argue that the media coverage helped create a stereotype of the squatters as 'folk devils' and created a 'moral panic' as defined by Cohen in his work on Mods and Rockers.[7] Stereotypes of any group both reinforce and determine the way that group gets treated, as has been discussed with reference to homeless families above. With squatters, as with homeless families, there was considerable ambivalence in the way in which their actions were viewed.

Factors other than media coverage also played a part in creating the public image of squatters. Numerous court decisions established that a squatter was a person with no rights in law. As Lord Denning, the Master of the Rolls, commented, 'The courts must for the sake of law and order take a firm stand. They must refuse to admit the plea of necessity to the hungry and homeless and trust that their distress will be relieved by the charitable and the good.'[8]

The stereotype of the squatter that became established by the mid-1970s was of a person 'outside' society, having no rights in law and posing a threat. Paris and Poppleton quote the *Sunday People* as saying, 'Squatting in 1975 is highly organised nationwide, spreading rapidly and DANGEROUS.'[6] Increasingly, squatters were perceived not only as outside society but also as outside the housing problem, and attention was drawn away from the housing shortage which had precipitated them. Myths about squatters became firmly established, in particular that they would seize and squat in owner-occupied property while the owner was away.

The source of this myth, a letter to *The Times* of 11 July 1975, claimed that squatters had broken into a house in Kensington while the owner was on holiday, '. . . to sleep in our beds, in our sheets, to daub crude drawings in black on our walls, to use our food, light and telephone, to steal £300 worth of antique furniture . . .' A subsequent letter from the solicitor to the Metropolitan Police cast considerable doubts on the veracity of the claims, 'which were not in accordance with the facts on police records.' Nonetheless more was made of the letter than of its refutation. Hugh Rossi, MP, tabled a motion in the House asking the government to introduce legislation to make such a situation a criminal offence; a Private Member's Bill – The Empty Houses (Prevention of Squatting) Bill – was introduced;

the Automobile Association offered its members a special holiday insurance scheme to protect them against such eventualities. The result of all this was the passing of the Criminal Law Act 1977 which made it a criminal offence to trespass and to fail to leave a property when required to do so by 'a displaced residential occupier', the penalty being a fine of up to £1,000 or six months' imprisonment. Eviction no longer required a court order, and a police constable in uniform could arrest without warrant anyone he suspected, with reasonable cause, to be guilty of the offence.

One result of the new law was that the police, rather than firms of private bailiffs, could now be used to evict squatters. This was almost immediately demonstrated in 1978 when several hundred police with riot shields and bulldozers evicted the 'defenders' squatting a block of flats in Huntley Street, Central London. The conflict between police and 'folk devils' received considerable publicity, in the course of which the reasons why the flats were empty and squatted in the first place became lost from view.

By its nature, squatting is immeasurable, and any statements about the numbers or types of people squatting cannot be authoritative, but we can try to form a general picture. What studies have been made suggest that squatters come from the same groups as the homeless, subject to the same sorts of pressures and housing opportunities. Kingham's report on unofficial squatters in six London boroughs showed them to be the sort of people who would normally be found in the private rented sector. They were predominantly young and on average their educational attainments were high; almost half the sample had children with them, and about a quarter of the group were black.[9] Waugh, examining the various estimates, concluded that in 1976 there were between 10,000 and 50,000 squats in the country as a whole. Many of these were unlicensed and illegal and offered only an insecure refuge.[10]

It is possible to suggest that many squatters can be classified as young single homeless, that is, young people who are squatting because they can find nowhere to live rather than those who have chosen squatting 'as a way of life', although it is the latter who most closely fit the 'folk devil' stereotype. Karn's study, *No Place That's Home*, reviewed the employment, financial and housing opportunities for young people in Birmingham, and concluded that young working people and students there found accommodation very difficult to obtain with their low incomes. Young people with the lowest incomes, those with unstable employment and those whom private landlords rejected out of prejudice, became homeless, forced out by the fierce competition for increasingly scarce private rented housing.[11]

As a group the young single homeless vary widely in needs, age and maturity, although all share the basic housing need that makes them turn to squatting. Many of them do perhaps try to develop 'alternative' life-styles. Chippendale's study of young people in multi-occupied dwellings[12] and Hands's comments on student housing[13] both stressed the importance to the young people there of large communal cooking and eating facilities and the social interaction that came from the use of these. Wates also drew attention to the development of 'community spirit' within a large squat:

Squatters did not merely provide housing for themselves: they also gave a boost to the whole area. Derelict buildings, which were previously a fire-and-damp hazard as well as being an eyesore, were now inhabited and in many cases cleaned up. The squatters also revived the faltering trade of many of the small shops and businesses. Above all, perhaps, they re-established Tolmers as a place with a 'community', albeit a very different kind of community from the one of the past.[5]

Other young squatters may well be experiencing crises of some sort. A particularly vulnerable group are the young people who leave home following family disputes, or simply to look for work in a city away from home. This is not entirely an urban phenomenon, as studies in Lancashire,[14] Surrey[15] and Essex[16] make clear, but the risk to vulnerable young people is possibly greater in the city areas, particularly when, as Karn noted above, low-income and low-employment skills are matched with severe shortage of low-rent housing. Deakin and Willis, in *Johnny Go Home*, provided examples of the risks awaiting runaway adolescents homeless and soon penniless in London.[17] The Community Relations Commission, in a survey of unemployment and homelessness among young blacks, identified as some of the causes – the poor housing conditions in which many immigrant families have to live; parents who cannot understand the difficulties their children face; and unemployment which itself caused conflict between parent and child and in some cases led to rejection from the family home.[18] Kingham, in his survey of squatters, found that many of the squatters had been under some sort of pressure and crisis before they finally took up squatting.[9]

Squatters are not a homogenous group, nor do they on the whole fit the stereotype that had developed as squatting developed during the 1970s. It seems clear that the dividing line between squatters and the homeless, either single people or families, is a very slight one, and that both are overwhelmingly a consequence of the shortage of low-rent housing and cutbacks in the public sector. Squatting can be said to be a 'political' act, not least since on occasion such acts flout the law, and squatting in an area scheduled for redevelopment may well 'politicise' a squatter who simply started out looking for somewhere to live, as Wates has shown.[5] Frequently squatters end up as licensed tenants of local authorities and many eventually get rehoused and thus 'jump the queue', but as Richard Balfe commented when he was Chairman of the Greater London Council Housing Development Committee in 1975, 'Waiting list families can fume at the "queue-jumping" squatters despite the fact that the fastest way to get a council house is to be fortunate enough to live in a clearance area. While they fume, they do not question a system which condemns them to years on a list [and] which tolerates homelessness.'[19]

REFERENCES

1. LORD DENNING, *McPhail* v. *Persons Unknown*. 3WLR at P73. The Incorporated Council for Law Reporting for England & Wales, London (1973).
2. G. WINSTANLEY, *The Laws of Freedom* (first published 1652), in *Winstanley: The Laws of Freedom and Other Writings*, with Introduction by C. Hill, Pelican, Harmondsworth (1973).
3. R. BAILEY, *The Squatters*, Penguin, Harmondsworth (1973).
4. D. WATKINSON and M. READ, *Squatting and Civil Liberties*, National Council for Civil Liberties, London (1976).
5. N. WATES, *The Battle for Tolmers Square*, Routledge & Kegan Paul, London (1976).
6. C. PARIS and C. POPPLETON, *Squatting: a bibliography*, Centre for Environmental Studies Occasional Paper 3 (1978).
7. S. COHEN, *Folk Devils and Moral Panics* (first edn 1972; second edn Martin Robertson, Oxford, 1980).
8. LORD DENNING, *London Borough of Southwark* v. *Williams*, in *Law Reports: Chancery Division 734*, The Incorporated Council for Law Reporting for England & Wales, London (1973).
9. M. KINGHAM, *Squatters in London*, Shelter, London (1977).
10. S. WAUGH, *Needs and Provisions for Young Single Homeless People*, CHAR, London (1976).
11. V. KARN, *No Place That's Home: a report on accommodation for homeless young people in Birmingham*, Centre for Urban and Environmental Studies. Birmingham Research Memorandum No. 32 (1974).

12. A. CHIPPENDALE, *Housing for Single Young People*, Institute for Advanced Architectural Studies. York. Unpublished (1976).
13. J. HANDS, *The Homeless of the 1980s*, paper given to the Student Community Housing Association Conference. Unpublished (1971).
14. LANCASHIRE SOCIAL SERVICES DEPARTMENT, Research Section, *Report on the Single Homeless Project* (1973).
15. M. NORRIS, *Report on the Single Homeless in Surrey*, Surrey Community Development Trust, Research Paper No. 8 (1974).
16. ESSEX SOCIAL SERVICES DEPARTMENT, *Survey of Single Homeless* (1975).
17. J. DEAKIN and N. WILLIS, *Johnny Go Home*, Futura/Quartet Books, London (1976).
18. COMMUNITY RELATIONS COMMISSION, *Unemployment and Homelessness: a report*, HMSO (1974).
19. R. BALFE, *The Sunday Times*, 2 November (1975).

Chapter eight
RURAL LIFE

Modern Britain is an urban society. Indeed, Hall and others suggest that 19,600 square miles of Britain could be defined as being a 'megalopolis' – that is 'the zone where functional urban areas, in terms of commuting fields or urban service areas, grow and merge and overlap in increasing ways.'[1]

Even outside the area of megalopolis, rural land and rural life might seem under such pressure from encroaching urban and suburbanism as to be scarcely distinguishable as a separate entity – at least as far as housing policy is concerned. There are distinctive problems concerning rural housing, however, although these, like urban housing problems, link into and have relationships with wider issues than simply housing. Although these rural housing issues will be discussed under their 'problem' headings it is important to keep in mind that these may represent symptoms rather than causes. Today's rural housing problems have their causes in the social and economic changes that predated the Industrial Revolution and the growth of manufacturing towns, in what Blythe terms the 'long abandonment' of the land,[2] as well as in the depression in agriculture of the nineteenth century and the 'transport revolution' of the twentieth.

There is still some dispute as to whether agricultural workers were 'pushed' off the land in the eighteenth century by the process of enclosures, technological improvements and new farming methods, or whether they were 'pulled' away, having lost their land, by the prospect of becoming wage-labourers in the new growing industrial towns. Either way, by the mid-nineteenth century only a minority of people – about one-fifth of the total occupied population – were employed on the land. The opening up of cheap overseas sources of supply of grain and meat and wool led to sharp reductions in price and severe depression in British agriculture from the 1870s onwards.

The steps taken by farmers and landowners to counteract these price falls – increased mechanisation and decreased use of skilled labour – further increased the impoverishment of the agricultural population and further hastened the migration from the countryside either into the towns or as emigrants overseas. This process continued into the twentieth century, albeit with conflict. By 1971 less than 10 per cent of the population of Great Britain lived in rural areas, and even fewer people actually worked there as well.

COMMUTER VILLAGES

This change in the pattern of living and working in different places was not, of course, simply a rural phenomenon. For most of the twentieth century, people had been moving away from their places of work in towns and cities to the suburbs. Cheap transport helped first the white-collar workers and later the skilled artisans to travel daily to and from their homes. Villages on the fringes of towns and cities gradually became incorporated into them as the rows of suburbs spread out to link them. Small towns and villages further away from the main employment areas also experienced an influx of population who 'commuted' to work first by train, and then from the late 1950s, increasingly by car. The towns and villages of the South-east had long had railway commuter links with London. The relaxation of credit and hire-purchase restrictions in the 1950s and the subsequent growth in car ownership, followed by the vast expansion of road building, especially motorways, all helped put the remoter rural areas within commuting range of many towns and cities. By the early 1960s the population of many rural areas began to increase.

Other factors were involved as well. Pahl has described the process in the rural area of Hertfordshire he studied:

Not only has population increased, but so has employment in the towns, particularly in the factories manufacturing engineering and electrical goods and vehicles. There have been consistently more jobs on offer than workers unemployed, even though the numbers employed in agriculture declined by some 5,000, well above the national average during the decade. Hence the rural areas have become more dormitory in character. . . .[3]

The earlier decline in rural population had, however, been matched by a similar decline in vital support services such as schools, doctors' surgeries and shops. In many rural areas the influx of incomers had not yet reversed this trend, even where it reversed the population decline. In rural Norfolk, for example, the population began to increase again from the early 1960s, but in 1978, of the 340 parishes in the area, 45 per cent did not contain a primary school, and twenty-five schools had shut since 1964. Similarly the number of doctors' surgeries declined, as did the numbers of child health clinics. Seventeen of the parishes that lost these clinics were more than three miles from the nearest alternative. The County Planning Officer for Norfolk calculated that there had been a 40 per cent decline in village foodshops between 1950 and 1960.[4] Yet in many parishes, although the population grew, facilities continued to be lost [doc 18]. The growth of commuter villages and decline in services and facilities available to the inhabitants raised issues in social and in planning policy. Firstly, in what way, if any, had the social structure of the rural areas changed as a result of in-migration, and what were the consequences? Secondly, in what way, if any, should housing development be planned and resources allocated?

WHO WERE THE COMMUTER VILLAGERS?

To examine change in the social structure of the commuter villages we need to be able to categorise the groups of people living there. Pahl has attempted to define the social elements within commuter villages while at the same time stressing, 'To consider "the village" as a sort of average of all such groups is extremely misleading . . . There is no village population as such; rather there are specific populations which for various, but identifiable reasons find themselves in a village.'[5]

Some of these specific populations were of long standing. These were the large land and property owners; the tenants in tied cottages; the local tradesmen and small businessmen; and the council house tenants. These last lived but did not necessarily work within the village; they were 'simply manual workers living on a small estate surrounded by fields because they were either born there or lived there long enough to qualify for a council house.'

Then there were the incomers, whom Pahl placed in four different categories:

1. '*Salaried immigrants with capital*' who aspired to a style of life that included a 'period property' – an expensive house that might give the impression that the owner's wealth was part of a deeply rooted heritage.

2. '*Spiralists*' – people whose career patterns involved them in frequently moving house as they moved up the status hierarchy

of their organisations. These were people in professional and managerial occupations – local government officers, managers in industry, etc.

3. *'Reluctant commuters'* who had limited income and little capital and simply wanted a house at a price they could afford. Scarcity and high price in towns, plus the difficulties of getting a mortgage on older property, brought them out to new housing estates with lower prices.

4. *'The retired.'* Pahl suggests that this is a very mixed group. Some may come for the environmental qualities in the area, or for supposed advantages of climate. Others may move because they want to purchase a bungalow, which may be more easily available, and possibly cheaper, than in more urban areas. The retired group posed most problems when it came to issues such as access to shops and on their long-term increasing need for support from health and social services.

Pahl found that the most important factor in promoting change in the social structure of commuting villages was 'social class' rather than simply commuting characteristics alone. The in-migrants were predominantly 'middle-class' who brought with them a different package of life-style and expectation, and thus by making the (established) working-class villagers aware of national class divisions effectively polarised the village. This is ironic since the middle-class people Pahl studied had come to the villages to enjoy 'rural life' and participate in the 'village community', and by their presence they helped to destroy what 'community' there was, that is if we accept Pahl's suggestion that 'part of the basis of the local village community was the sharing of deprivation due to the isolation of country life and the sharing of the limited world of families within the village.'[4] The incomers were less isolated (apart from the retired) than settled villagers, and maintained a whole range of contacts with the outside world because of their mobility; they 'participated' but they did not 'share'.

HOUSING POLICY AND COMMUTER VILLAGES

All the groups of incomers were owner-occupiers, the majority of them buying newly built houses on estates on the outskirts of the village. It was only the salaried immigrants, some upper-echelon spiralists and some better-off retired people who could afford, or desired, to buy older property within the village itself. 'Most spiralists chose something that could be quickly and easily sold again when the time came for the next career move. The reluctant commuters, who might well have desired a country cottage, were faced by the joint problems of price and mortgage difficulties on older property. The retired people frequently chose the greater convenience and lower repair bills of bungalows.

The new housing developments posed something of a 'catch 22' for local-authority planners seeking to arrange and control development. Concentration of housing in 'selected' villages would make services easier to provide, but might swamp the 'character' of these villages. Concentration would also have undesirable consequences for those villages not 'selected' for growth and development since their available services would inevitably diminish still further. On the other hand, allowing new housing piecemeal might be economically inefficient where the provision of services was concerned by stretching resources over too wide a field. Central government policy aimed to limit the amount of new building that could be undertaken. *Circular 122/73* issued by the Department of the Environment in 1973 emphasised that the bulk of housing development in future was to take place in towns, either by rebuilding or expansion. It did suggest that although some villages had reached the limits of their natural growth, 'a good deal of housing land can be found by infilling of villages, and by modest expansion, including expansion outside (but not divorced from) village envelopes . . . where this is consistent with community capacity.' Like many government circulars this was at once both specific and vague, laying down planning guidelines yet leaving it to local authorities to define 'modest expansion' and 'community capacity', and leaving to the free market the price of land and of housing.

SECOND HOMES AND HOLIDAY LETS

The commuter villages developed on the rural-urban fringes of metropolitan areas and then, as improved transport networks brought new areas within reach, developed further afield. Their development posed problems of polarisation within the village class structure and for the provision of support services and facilities. They were, however, permanent settlements. The main characteristic of second homes and holiday lets was that they were not permanent settlements but, especially second homes, left empty for long periods each year.

Second homes, while also benefiting from the transport revolution, are to be found in the more distant rural areas, giving their owners the advantage of empty space and fine scenery. Often they double-up as holiday lets, but their function is less a source of income than a rural retreat. Like the commuter villages, they are a symptom rather than a cause of rural decline. Out-migration of population from an area in response to lack of employment, following changes in agriculture or the decline of a traditional industry, is followed by in-movement of people employed and living elsewhere, using the housing for leisure purposes. As the proportion of second homes in the local housing stock increases and all-the-year-round population declines, the problems for the remaining population increase. In Denbighshire, Jacobs estimated that a level of second-home ownership of over 12 per cent in any one parish was saturation point, after which social problems and declining services for the native population became acute.[6] Hardly surprisingly, second-home owners tend to be among the better-off. Like the incomers to the commuter villages they appear to seek 'meaningful community' in country life. Bell and Newby suggest that incomers had an idealised view, a 'village in the mind' which was essentially paternalistic and which demanded a deferential response from the local native people. This deference was frequently withheld since the incomers lacked traditional authority or a meaningful place within the village hierarchy.[7]

Unlike the incomer to the commuter villages, however, the second-home owners' opportunities for participation in village events were more limited, and might thus lessen the possibility of hostility from the locals. Bollom found, in a study of five Welsh villages, that the majority of village activities took place during the winter, when there was less work on the land, and that the majority of village-based organisations conducted their operations in the Welsh language – two fairly major factors in limiting possible participation by summer-visiting English speakers.[8] In these villages there seemed few 'symbolic occasions' to provide opportunities for interaction between the two groups and what hostility was expressed was more towards the *concept* of second-home ownership than towards individual owners. In general, where an incomer/native divide was apparent it was couched in ethnic rather than class terms. Emmet suggests that this may amount to the same thing: 'The English take the place of the upper-, upper-middle or ruling-class, and nationalism is the dress in which class antagonism is expressed.'[9]

How much the growth of second-home ownership has contributed to the increased sense of national identity and the growth of nationalism in Wales, Cornwall or Scotland is hard to say. Certainly the phenomenon has been criticised by Plaid Cymry in Wales, and Mebyon Kernow in Cornwall [doc 19]. But whether the relationship between second-home owners and local people is of ethnic hostility, or whether it is, as Downing and Dower have suggested, simply the natural instinct of the human group to fear and to feel threatened by the incursion of aliens,[10] the growth of second-home ownership does take housing out of local use.

Holiday lets share many of the characteristics of second homes, although they are more likely to be locally owned. They are a response to the national increase of leisure and the increase in price of hotel and guest-house accommodation in areas of high tourist demand. Intending purchasers of property for second homes or for holiday lets compete with local people seeking homes for themselves. In this competition local home-seekers are at a disadvantage unless they have capital and/or a high income.

The market in holiday property has developed in three main stages: in the initial stage the property was cheap. Much had been empty for years, reflecting the decline in the rural population and of the small local fishing industries at the seaside. While not necessarily sub-standard in construction, the buildings were old and lacked amenities. Although the House Purchase and Housing Act 1959 encouraged building societies to lend on pre-1919 property and introduced standard grants for the installation of basic amenities, in practice it proved more difficult for local home-seekers to obtain a mortgage on an old cottage than on a newly built dwelling. Those with capital to purchase outright and repair beyond the basics were in a more advantageous position. As the growth of car ownership and improved road networks put even the remotest farm building on a mountainside within reach of the holiday maker, so increasingly those with capital entered the rural property market. In the second stage the price rose as a consequence of increased demand. The increase effectively excluded all local home-seekers without a high income as well as those without capital. In the more popular seaside towns and villages, as the amount of empty property declined and tourism grew, there was a shift of investment out of permanent renting into selling for holiday lets and second homes. The third stage is that in many rural areas there is an acute shortage of housing to rent. This is masked by the growth of 'winter lets', whereby families who have spent the summer in overcrowded sharing arrangements or split up between parents and friends avail themselves of a temporary and insecure housing resource. Not only holiday cottages but also caravans on the many permanent sites in holiday areas provide winter accommodation. Facilities are not always good and overcharging is common. Larkin has commented that 'caravan sites can be the true ghettoes of the rural poor, since, however inadequate this accommodation may be . . . it is easier of access than any other form of housing tenure.'[11]

The difficulties come at the end of the winter. We have already examined the way many District Councils reacted to the Housing (Homeless Persons) Act 1977. Their reaction to the winter-let situation was, in many cases, to refuse to rehouse families evicted from holiday lets or holiday caravan sites even when these were local families and not 'pillocks from everywhere'.

It is the shortage of private rented housing for people unable to obtain mortgages in the face of rising prices and unable to obtain access to the limited supply of council housing that is the most serious problem of the rural areas. It affects the districts of the commuter villages as well as those under pressure from tourism, because the designation of villages for 'modest growth' drives up the price of land, and the restriction of growth in non-designated villages drives up the price of existing dwellings. It is more serious because it is more deep-rooted and structural than the problem of allocation of support-service resources. The housing shortage forces people, especially young families, away from their local area, thus continuing the 'abandonment of the land'. In holiday districts this increases the reliance on seasonal migrant labour to service the tourist industry, thereby making other forms of economic regeneration more difficult and helping to perpetuate the industrial decline and structural unemployment of these areas. This in turn forces more people to leave. To comment upon the 'abandonment of the land' is not to propose a romantic view of rural life. Contemporary accounts by those who worked the land make it quite clear to us that rural life was, and often still is, a life of unremitting toil.[12] It is more an observation on the social and cost implications of the loss to an area of so many young people and an increasing number of elderly who remain; and on the increased social polarity between the remaining local people – council tenants and those in tied cottages on the one hand and their new (richer) neighbours on the other.

TIED COTTAGES

Housing provided by an employer for his employee is not a purely rural phenomenon. Tied housing exists for nurses, teachers, *au pairs*, domestic servants, servicemen, hotel and bar staff, care-takers, prison officers, firemen, policemen, ambulancemen, clergymen, coalminers, council gravediggers and some employees of the British Steel Corporation, as well as agricultural and Forestry Commission workers. In 1974, for example, 70,000 hotel and restaurant staff 'lived in'.

Agricultural workers in tied accommodation received security of tenure under the Rent (Agriculture) Act 1976. The National Coal Board, with a surplus of miners' cottages in many areas, allow retired miners and miners' widows to stay in their cottages as licensed tenants. The other occupational groups have to leave their accommodation if they cease working for that employer or retire.

It is the agricultural worker's tied cottage that is probably the best-known form of tied housing. It is one of the oldest examples, and has been termed 'the last remnant of feudalism', although the image of the lowly farmworker utterly dependent on his master's goodwill is now anachronistic in most cases. There are three advantages for the farmworker living in a tied cottage:

1. The accommodation is low-rent, virtually free, often with sufficient land or garden on which to grow his own food.
2. There is no expense or travelling time needed to get to work.
3. It is often the only housing to which he has access.

But these advantages must be matched against the disadvantages, and these attach to the job as much as to the tied housing:

1. Low wages, among the lowest in the country as a whole.
2. Isolation, and therefore travelling time and expense to shops and school for his wife and family.

The main problem for tenants in tied accommodation is that they have to leave their home should they leave their job. Some employers may use the threat of losing the accommodation as an employment sanction. Since the wages of those in tied accommodation tend to be low – because of the free/cheap accommodation – there is little opportunity for the worker to amass sufficient savings to enter the owner-occupied sector, and the shrinkage of the private rented sector makes other accommodation difficult to find. For many people this limits their employment mobility and they become 'trapped' in low-paid living-in jobs. Others who have spent their working lives in tied accommodation find themselves homeless upon retirement. Illness or accident also puts people in tied accommodation at risk of homelessness. What happens to them then depends very much on which local-authority area they find themselves in. Some local authorities refuse to allow people in tied accommodation to register on their waiting lists, claiming they are already adequately housed. Some (often the same ones) categorise eviction from tied accommodation as being 'intentionally' homeless.

Agricultural workers, as mentioned above, now have security of tenure. Once a farmworker's employment ceases he becomes a protected tenant under the Rent Act. Initially this seemed to be working well; the problems of bottleneck and staff shortage the farmers anticipated did not materialise. One reason for this was that a mechanism existed under the 1976 Act for the farmworker to be rehoused by the local authority should it be absolutely necessary that the farmer had the tied cottage back. The farmer/landlord can go to the local Agricultural Dwelling Housing Advisory Panel (ADHAP) and claim:

(*a*) that he requires the accommodation for another employee;
(*b*) that he cannot reasonably supply suitable alternative accommodation;
(*c*) the local authority ought, 'in the interests of efficient agriculture', to provide alternative accommodation. The ADHAP advises the local authority as to whether or not they consider the claim is justified; if it is, the local authority has a statutory duty to rehouse.

However, in some areas the ADHAPs had a predominance of 'landed interest' among their members, who seemed rather more keen to advise for rehousing 'in the interests of efficient agriculture' than might otherwise be the case. The National Union of Agricultural Workers felt there was also growing evidence by 1979 that tied accommodation vacated after such recommendations in some parts of the country was subsequently either being sold as second homes or converted to holiday lets.

In other rural areas the efficient working of the ADHAP system depended upon the local authority accepting the rehousing duty. Andrew Larkin suggests there is evidence that the benefits of the 1976 Act were being diminished by some local authorities who offer only low-standard accommodation to the farmworker.[11] More important, in the longer term, was the question of supply, and of local authorities' willingness to accept their statutory duty. Rural authorities have never been extensive council house builders; the amount of council housing existing in any one village or small town is not great. The 1976 Act put an obligation on local authorities at a difficult time since even had they wished they could not easily expand their building programme to meet it, due to expenditure cutbacks. By late 1979 the proposals to sell council housing began to take effect in rural areas and the ADHAP system came under strain. It seemed possible that ADHAPs might be wound-up as part of the government's package of housing proposals.

Many farmers have argued that tied accommodation is essential in order to attract and keep good workers, because housing is so scarce in rural areas. A Shelter enquiry in 1974 suggested that the majority of farmworkers were content to be in tied cottages until they themselves were faced with eviction.[13] It is still the case that tied accommodation serves to hold down wages, and that if there were an adequate supply of housing in rural areas, at rents within the farmworkers' means (either public or private renting), then the circle of tied cottage–low wage could be broken. However, with most rural new building being for owner-occupation; with the shortage of housing in rural areas exacerbated by the growth of holiday lets and second homes; with the public sector switching to selling and with its building programmes still declining, the problems of the tied cottage and low agricultural wages will continue.

REFERENCES

1. P. HALL, R. THOMAS, H. GRACEY and R. DREWETT, *The Containment of Urban England*, vols 1 and 2, Allen & Unwin, London; Sage Publications, Beverly Hills (1973).
2. R. BLYTHE, *Akenfield: portrait of an English village*, Penguin, Harmondsworth (1972).
3. R. PAHL, *op. cit.* (see ref. 6, Ch. 3).
4. J. M. SHAW, 'The social implications of village development', in *Social Issues in Rural Norfolk*, M. MOSELEY (ed.), Centre for East Anglian Studies, University of East Anglia (1978).
5. R. PAHL, *Patterns of Urban Life*, Longman, London (1970).
6. C. JACOBS, *Second Homes in Denbighshire*, Denbighshire County Planning Office, Research Report No. 3 (1972).
7. C. BELL and H. NEWBY, 'The sources of variation in agricultural workers images of society', in *Working Class Images of Society*, M. BULMER (ed.), Routledge & Kegan Paul, London (1975).
8. C. BOLLOM, 'Attitudes towards second homes in rural Wales', in *Social and Cultural Change in Contemporary Wales*, G. WILLIAMS (ed.), Routledge & Kegan Paul, London (1978).
9. I. EMMET, *A North Wales Village*, Routledge & Kegan Paul,

London (1964).

10. P. DOWNING and M. DOWER, *Second Homes in England and Wales*, Dartington Amenity Trust, Research Publication 7 (1973).

11. A. LARKIN, 'Rural housing: too dear, too far, too few', *Roof*, January (1978).

12. F. THOMPSON, *Lark Rise to Candleford*, Penguin, Harmondsworth (1973); see also ref. 2 above.

13. M. CONSTABLE, *Tied Accommodation*, Shelter (1974).

Chapter nine
URBAN DEPRIVATION
AND THE INNER-CITY QUESTION

The decline in the rural areas of Britain was characterised by the loss of local industry and with it a decline in employment, particularly of skilled jobs. The local population also declined by out-migration, particularly of younger working people and their families. This population decline was compensated by in-migration of predominantly middle-class commuters, and by a growing number of retired people, a changing pattern that continued the long decline of the 'abandonment of the land'.

An examination of urban Britain shows that in the inner-city areas a very similar pattern of decline has taken place, to an extent that perhaps allows us to talk of the 'abandonment of the city'. Here, too, there has been the loss of local industry, and a change and then decline in employment. Here, too, the young skilled workers have moved out, leaving the older and less mobile. More recently the predominantly middle-class have moved in. Both the rural and the urban areas have a housing shortage in the private rented sector. There are important differences between the two areas, however, and the nature and type of the 'abandonment of the city' needs to be examined in more detail, in order that later policies for inner-city regeneration can be evaluated. Much of the dispersal of people out of the central and inner-areas of the major cities of Britain was encouraged by positive policy measures from 1947 onward. In 1976 these thirty years of planned decentralisation were reversed by the government, and the following year the Secretary of State for the Environment, Peter Shore, was introducing new policy measures to combat decay and deprivation in the inner-cities, arguing that although decay and deprivation existed elsewhere in the country, 'there must be particular emphasis on the inner-areas of some of the big cities because of the scale and intensity of their problems and the rapidity of run-down in population and employment.'[1]

PATTERNS OF URBAN CHANGE

The growth of cities that came with Britain's industrial transformation tended to concentrate people and jobs in the central areas. The land around the major cities still remained rural, losing its population and employment to the cities but serving initially as an important source of fresh food.

By the 1880s changes in employment were beginning to take place in the city centres. Factories and industrial premises were being replaced by warehouse and office developments. Such commercial development schemes also contributed to the housing shortage as homes were cleared as well as factories and workshops. 'Shovelling out the poor' was not simply the consequence of slum-clearance. Although much housing, workshops and industry still remained in the city centres, the predominant pattern had changed. 'Business' had replaced 'Manufacture' [doc 20].

From the 1890s people began to move in considerable numbers out of the city centres to the rural periphery. These rural areas now became built-up and 'sub-urban' themselves. Although this process of moving out was not new (the wealthier classes had been causing anxiety among reformers as they removed their 'good example' from the cities from quite early in the nineteenth century) the numbers involved were far greater and the social classes involved were far more varied. This much greater removal came with the development of cheap forms of transport that made the daily journey into work a possibility. From the passing of the Cheap Trains Act 1883 onwards, local trains, special railway fares and, in London, the extension of the underground railway [doc 21], with growing motor-bus and coach services and later the private car, all brought the possibility of a home in the leafy suburbs within the reach of the urban workers. Suburban housing offered a means of upward social mobility for the growing numbers of 'white-collar' workers occupied in 'business' at the city centres.

Not all the suburban dwellings were in the private sector. City councils also began purchasing land on the outskirts and building council estates. Partly this was because of the rising price of land in the city centres, but also because the councils (influenced by the 'Garden City' theories of Ebenezer Howard [doc 22]) believed in the therapeutic benefits of gardens and open space. 'Perhaps also implicit was the hope that a working-class happily cultivating its gardens would be less interested in social change,' commented the Architects of the Greater London Council sixty years later.[2]

By the early 1930s, some concern was being expressed at the unchecked spread of building. 'Ribbon development' of suburban housing along the major roadways out of the city areas led to fears that Britain would become entirely covered with buildings, from Liverpool to London via Manchester and Birmingham [doc 23]. In the city centres, natural increase was keeping the population steady despite the large out-migration that increased as the slum-clearance programmes began to take effect. The process of changing employment patterns continued as factories decentralised. The turmoil of the General Strike and the years of the Great Depression had highlighted the tremendous regional variations in economic growth and employment prospects, in particular the differences between the expanding London and South-eastern areas compared with the declining industrial areas of the North. The Royal Commission on the Distribution of the Industrial Population 1940 (Barlow Commission) in its report saw a national policy for urban dispersal as part of the strategy it proposed for regional regeneration. The imminent possibility of war made its recommendations for national planning, as Hall has pointed out, 'relevant to national survival, for the danger of aerial bombardment of the cities made the dispersion of people and industry seem imperative.'[3]

The aerial bombardment, when it came, certainly hastened the dispersal process, and effected considerable slum clearance along with much else. After the war, however, the Barlow proposals continued to have effect and were echoed in further policy reports, in particular the Report of the Committee of the New Towns (Reith Committee), in 1946 and the Abercrombie Greater London Plan (1947). From Abercrombie came the proposals to contain the spread of London by putting a 'green belt' around it, that is a belt of land upon which no further building would be allowed. Abercrombie also proposed that the London region should be 'zoned' according to its various activities, thus housing development would not be allowed in an area zoned for industrial use, nor industry in a residential zone. The Reith Committee proposed a ring of 'New Towns' to be built initially around London to take the population of the congested inner-areas and allow them room to grow in a new environment with new homes and new jobs [doc 24]. Both these and other contemporary reports put forward an idea that had been growing before the war and was implicit in the Barlow Commission that 'planning has the right and the responsibility to try to shape the life of the community through good physical arrangements.'[3] Their proposals were made law with the Town and Country Planning Act 1947 which established a New Towns Corporation to undertake the development programme. 'Planned dispersal' was the dominant policy; and town planning and 'planners' became an increasingly important part of local government.

The New Towns Corporation was a separate body to the existing local authorities. Funded by sixty-year, fixed interest, Treasury loans its purpose was to buy land and develop complete New Towns with housing, industry and social and recreational facilities. As the housing in these towns was built and let so they would be handed over to the relevant local authority, but the Corporation would keep the commercial property and receive the rental income from it to help fund further projects. The first New Town – Stevenage – was started in 1946 and by 1979 there were twenty-eight New Towns in England, Scotland and Wales. In addition to the New Towns further measures were introduced by the government to encourage migration away from the city centres. 'Overspill Estates' were constructed on the outskirts of city regions, and 'Expanded Towns' designated elsewhere. An Expanded Town was an existing small/medium town – King's Lynn in Norfolk, for example – at which new housing and industry were located with the aid of a series of government grants.

As these policies began to take effect and as the longer trend of migration to the suburbs continued, the city centres suffered a massive drop in population, beginning about 1951 and increasing in velocity after 1961. Between 1961 and 1966, 265,963 people left London, 93,741 left the inner-area of Manchester, and 62,216 the inner-area of Liverpool. Initially, employment still tended to remain fairly concentrated in the central areas – with the consequence of longer and longer journeys to work as people moved further and further out, but from the early 1960s this, too, began rapidly to decentralise.

There was more to this 'abandonment of the cities' than simply policies of 'encouragement' to move to new or expanded towns, or a desire for upwards social mobility and suburban *Lebensraum*. People living in the inner-areas were under considerable pressure to leave. The 'pull' pressures of desire for better living conditions and employment out of town were undeniable, but there were also 'push' pressures as well. These pressures, which can, at the least, be said to have resulted in a marked deterioration in the quality of urban life, are discussed below.

Commercial development

To begin with, there was the pressure from commercial development
and the switch of investment from housing to office development,
serving both to reduce the housing stock and to drive up land values.
Since the Second World War, Britain has experienced two 'property
booms' of speculative office building in city centres. The first
roughly spanned the decade 1954–64 and the second covered the
three years of the 'Barber' boom, 1970–73 (so called after Anthony
Barber, the then Chancellor of the Exchequer).

The first boom of the 1950s and early 1960s began simply enough,
with astute businessmen buying up buildings left empty or bomb-
damaged during and immediately after the war; taking advantage of
the low wartime price of land and waiting for the price to rise when
war ended. Much of this was a consequence of being 'in the right
place at the right time'. But there was more to the property boom
than buying land cheap and selling dear. For a speculator with a plot
of land, the difference in profitability between building a row of
houses and an office block lay in two important factors – value and
expectation: the value of the completed block as a portfolio asset and
the enhancement effect it would have upon neighbouring land
values; plus the expectation of greatly increased rent levels. In many
cases expectation seemed enough of itself to generate profits without
rents actually being obtained. Perhaps the most notorious example
of this was Centrepoint, the thirty-two-storey office block in Central
London built in 1964 and remaining unlet for almost fifteen years to
no apparent disadvantage, indeed with apparent profit, to its
developer. Both in value and in expectation investment in offices was
far more profitable than investment in housing, even at the luxury
end of the housing market.

The spread of new office development, coming as it did at the
same time as the crisis in the private rented sector and the visible
increase of homelessness, contributed to an already sensitive political
situation. Property deals and property dealers, while rarely apparently going outside the law, often appeared to be able to make use of
its loopholes in manners which appeared to the public eye as sharp
practice. It was not surprising, then, that the incoming Labour
government introduced a ban on further office development in
November 1964. Only schemes that were able to obtain a new Office
Development Permit (ODP) would be able to go ahead. Marriott
suggests that, paradoxically, the 'Brown Ban', as it was termed –
after George Brown the Minister who introduced the measure – 'did

most developers a power of good'.[4] It artificially limited supply, thus greatly increasing rental values and enabling previously unlet blocks to be filled up. Also a great many schemes still went forward. This was not least because the Brown ban when introduced to the House of Commons during the afternoon exempted any development for which the contract was signed by midnight of the same day. This move, intended to enable virtually completed contracts to have a final tidying-up, resulted in what Marriott has termed the 'night of the long pens' as property developers rushed to sign contract after contract before midnight.

In many ways the second period of boom was a re-run of the first, but important changes had taken place both within the property companies and in the rôle of financial institutions, changes which had begun during the first boom in the early 1960s. Take-overs, mergers and consolidation had led to what Ambrose and Colenutt term the 'development industry' dominated by giant companies. In 1974 the value of the top three property companies (Land Securities Investment Trust; Metropolitan Estate and Property; and St Martin Property) had a value that exceeded the value of many of the largest industrial firms in the country – Bowaters, for example. These large concerns all had subsidiary companies, so a pattern was established of consolidation at the top and proliferation at the bottom.[5]

No longer was there any possibility of a developer profiting from war-purchased land. Land in the inner-cities was scarce and expensive. From the 1960s the links of the development industry with finance capital became increasingly close and complex. Developments required large loans. These were obtained from the clearing banks, the merchant banks, and (as the Barber boom got under way with a rapid increase in the money supply) a number of secondary banking houses – 'fringe banks'. These attracted money from depositors with high-interest schemes and lent liberally, especially to the development industry – borrowing short and lending long. But when minimum lending rates rose in 1973 from $7\frac{1}{2}$ per cent in June to 13 per cent in November uncertainty crept into the property market; depositors rushed to withdraw their deposits and many fringe banks collapsed, while other financial institutions also found themselves in a precarious position.

The spread of commercial development transformed the face of the inner-cities. New techniques enabled the architects to the property companies to erect office blocks dozens of storeys high where previously there had been a low-rise jumble of old buildings. Vast towers of glass and concrete arose whose style and design provided silent comment on their owners' view of the world. The importance of all this was not simply that it represented a gigantic switch of investment, or that it made the property-developer immensely wealthy – Marriott has commented: 'Since the war Britain is the only country in the world to have had a property boom channelling wealth into the hands of individuals on such a large scale.'[4] – but that it displaced a great deal of housing and the small-scale shops and other facilities that enabled inner-city living to continue. It also provided one of the causes of what may be termed the second 'push' factor – 'planning blight'.

Planning blight

The central areas of cities had already acquired their commercial characteristics before the property boom of the 1960s and 1970s, but the overall building mix was very varied. Large commercial buildings would stand next door to shops and workrooms, often with housing above. The new office developments did away with such untidiness, took up much larger sites, and when they did include shop floor space the much higher rent attracted a more prestigious type of shop. Much of the existing building was old, but this did not necessarily mean it was derelict or in bad repair. Many of the commercial buildings were of historic and architectural merit. Much of the housing – although more likely to need repair – came under the same heading. There were certainly areas that had a 'tough' reputation prior to redevelopment – the Bull Ring in Birmingham for example – and there were certainly pockets of appalling slums, but it is important to remember that many buildings that were pulled down in the late 1950s and early 1960s might well have been 'listed' and 'preserved' had they stayed standing until the late 1970s. One thing was certain, if an area was not in bad repair when potential developers first moved in, by the time they had bought up all the freeholds, obtained planning permission and got ready to build – it often was.

A property company needed patience in 'putting together a site'. That is, gradually buying up the freeholds of separate buildings until a whole area belonged to them. This had to be done with caution and some secrecy to keep the prices down. Often several subsidiary companies were used to make the purchases. Tenants who might be accustomed to fairly frequent changes of landlord would not have any idea that the latest landlord's intention was redevelopment. This could lead to situations of some irony, such as Wates describes in his book *The Battle for Tolmers Square*.[6] In 1963 the then Tolmers Square Tenants Association, all of whom had lived in the square for many years, were protesting about the adjacent Euston Centre redevelopment by D. and J. Levy's Stock Conversion Company, and fighting to get the displaced people rehoused. While they were doing this, Stock Conversion were buying up all the houses in Tolmers Square.

An area where a development site is being put together becomes 'blighted', the whole area gradually being run-down and neglected. Companies purchasing to redevelop do not seek to incur the expense of repairs. 'Putting together a site' often took several years, with further years to pass before planning permission to build was gained, and sometimes more before building started. Buildings that had been low-rent housing might already be needing care and attention, and new neglect simply hastened their decline, when burst pipes were no longer mended, nor tiles replaced on the roofs. Gradually shops would close, and people would be moved out. Sometimes they might be offered housing elsewhere; sometimes they might be rehoused by the local authority (in return for some notional 'gain' to the authority from the proposed redevelopment, such as a road widening, or some land allocated for council housing that was owned by the property company elsewhere in the borough). Most often, the tenants would be offered a sum of money to leave. This process, termed 'winkling out', was sometimes accompanied by implied threats – for example workmen arriving in mid-afternoon and commencing to pull up the floorboards, claiming they 'thought the house was empty'. Even without such harassment a tenant was often disadvantaged, since frequently the sums of money involved were too small to purchase access to owner-occupation, and the shortage of low- and medium-rent accommodation made alternative housing hard to find. Several hundred pounds might seem a large sum to an elderly person or a low-wage earner, but it in no way reflected adequate compensation for their housing loss. Those tenants who refused to move, and survived the tensions of 'winkling out' and of the area being demolished around them, sometimes got higher payments, but ran a much greater risk of harassment unless they had the good fortune to be articulate, aware of their rights, and to have a strong tenancy agreement.

As people moved out an atmosphere of decay and abandonment would settle on an area, as buildings became vacant, shops boarded up and windows broken. Commercial development, however, was not the only cause of planning blight that made the inner-city environment so depressed and put pressure on people to leave. Local authorities during the 1960s also became massive blighters as they designated areas for comprehensive redevelopment themselves. These 'clearance areas' were purchased by compulsory purchase order often some considerable time before the authority was ready or able to begin building.

We saw in the section on squatting how long the Redbridge houses had been empty when the squatters moved in and how two years after that the redevelopment proposals were finally abandoned. Shelter, in its report on slum clearance as late as 1975, when housing policy had markedly changed, was commenting, 'Most local authorities have been over-ambitious and totally unrealistic when drawing up clearance plans; the plans seem to have been drawn up without any reference to the ability of the authority to carry them through within the time period envisaged.'[7] It found that many clearance areas appeared to be 'written off' as far as welfare agencies, educational services and town hall staff generally were concerned and that little attempt was made to collect refuse or keep the areas clean. The report pointed to the great distress experienced by residents of clearance areas due to the uncertainty of their future housing prospects, since no definite rehousing dates and often little information at all was given them; it also drew attention to the concomitant distress people felt seeing their neighbourhood demolished, old people in particular.

These local-authority clearance schemes took place both in the central and the wider inner-city areas. Thus the transformation of the city centres and the demolition of much of the inner periphery, coupled with the existing shift of investment out of private-renting, could lead only to one thing – severe shortage and overcrowding among those people who stayed in the inner-city, and who could not obtain access either to the public sector or to owner-occupation.

Changes in employment

The process discussed above led to considerable changes in both the number and type of jobs available in the inner-cities, and to a growing mismatch between the skills of the people living in the inner-areas and the jobs available for them.

The growth of commercial redevelopment in the city centres led to an increased growth in the number of office jobs available. These were clerical and managerial 'white-collar' posts, with a small number of unskilled jobs in cleaning and maintenance.

The decline and closure of traditional industry and manufacturing meant an overall decline in the number of skilled, semi-skilled and unskilled 'blue-collar' jobs. These jobs were not replaced within the inner-city, so that the likelihood of unemployment served to 'push' blue-collar workers out of the inner-areas. Not all were able to respond to this, though skilled workers were able to find work in the new factories being built on the outer periphery of the city regions, or in the New Towns. These were especially attractive because of the availability of housing there as well.

Unskilled and semi-skilled workers, however, were far less able to respond to the pressure to move. Between 1966 and 1971, for example, only 15 per cent of the people moving out of inner-Birmingham and 16 per cent from inner-Manchester were semi-skilled or unskilled workers. But as a group they were the most vulnerable to the non-replacement of jobs. In Liverpool, where the number of jobs for men fell by 18 per cent between 1966 and 1971, 'the kinds of jobs disappearing were those of warehousemen and storekeepers, packers, caretakers, shop assistants, building labourers and unskilled workmen in the engineering and chemical industries, abattoir workers and food processors, and, most important of all, unskilled dock workers.'[8] In the new factories of the outer-areas new equipment and mechanisation meant that no alternative range of job opportunities were being developed to compensate for this overall decline.

The increase in office jobs did not serve to keep clerical and managerial staff living in the inner-city. White-collar workers were more able to take advantage both of suburban house prices to purchase access to owner-occupation outside the inner-city, and of the 'transport revolution' to commute in to work. Accessibility was an essential prerequisite of the success of the high-rent expectation of central-area commercial redevelopment, and the public-sector road programmes of the 1950s and 1960s guaranteed this for them. A massive programme of road works took place to speed and encourage traffic through from the outer periphery to the central areas. Motorways, clearways, through-ways, dual-carriageways, inter-sections, underpasses, orbital networks, all became facts of urban life. Yet more buildings were demolished to meet the needs of the road programmes. The predominant mode of travel for the commuter was the private car, and from the 1950s there was a massive increase both in the overall ownership of cars and in their use for travelling to work. In 1957, 32 per cent of passenger transport had been bus and coach, 18 per cent had been rail transport and 42 per cent cars. By 1977 cars had increased to 80 per cent of all modes of passenger transport while buses and coaches had fallen to 11 per cent and rail transport to 7 per cent.[9] Along with private cars, commercial traffic also increased by 53 per cent between 1953 and 1963 and continued to increase. The Suez crisis of 1956 and the introduction of petrol rationing briefly slowed the rush to the roads, but the volume of traffic continued to grow thereafter until the fuel crisis of the late 1970s. By 1963 the Steering Group of Traffic in Towns was commenting 'the loss of wealth and amenity that the nation is inflicting upon itself through the congestion of traffic is already very large.'[10]

CONSEQUENCE OF CHANGE FOR THE INNER-CITY AREAS

No urban area is ever quite static. Towns and cities have always been constantly altering and developing. The interaction of the policies and pressures discussed above, however, did effect quite dramatic change on the inner-city areas of Britain in a fairly short space of time. The inner-cities became areas of contrast between old and new buildings and of polarisation and inequality between the people living and working there.

Environmental consequences

The environmental consequences of the process of urban change are plain to see today. High concrete blocks of offices and flats soon began to tower over the older buildings. Some writers have commented that there was more to this contrast than simply the difference in height, and that the new planners and architects were making 'statements in concrete' about how they felt the world should be organised. Both architecture and planning had achieved growth and status during the 1950s and 1960s and become established professions controlling and defining the use and shape of the urban environment. Now, as the new buildings were completed, criticisms began to be made that the built environment had become increasingly alienating and depersonalising; that the new road schemes isolated people and cut them off from parks or shops; that the new blocks of council flats were as much mechanisms of social control as the 'model dwellings' of the nineteenth century; that the new commercial city centres were barren and windswept, deserted by nightfall.

Such criticisms were ironic, in that much of the initial inspiration to post-war urban architecture appeared to have sprung from the architectural movements of the inter-war years, when the aim had been to use the innovations in building materials to create a liberating environment for the motor age. Prominent among these was Le Corbusier, who in his book *The Radiant City*, in 1933, proposed to end the 'tyranny of the street' by building high. The elegant blocks radiating light, standing on columns – pilotis – to enable free circulation of air beneath them, would be surrounded by green space of gardens, parks and sports fields; people and traffic would be totally segregated, yet the Radiant City would be the city of the fast moving car [doc 25]. 'Suburban life is a despicable delusion entertained by a society stricken with blindness,' wrote Corbusier. 'Architecture and city planning are the essential functions required for modern man.'[11] When reading *The Radiant City* it is easy to see how it excited and inspired a generation of architects, and one can also find there the genesis of much that was built in the past twenty years. Yet in practice the new high-rise building schemes seemed to many to fail to measure up to Le Corbusier's ideals. This may have been because the redevelopment of cities did not take place on quite the same total scale that Le Corbusier had recommended (he proposed demolishing the whole of Paris and starting again). A more likely reason could be found in the cost-cutting that characterised the new high buildings both in the commercial and in the public sector. In both sectors Le Corbusier's vision of towers arising from among leafy parkland was replaced only too often by windswept, treeless, open spaces.

There had been other reasons for adopting the high-tower block for public-sector housing as well as those of architectural excitement and inspiration. Policies of containment of urban sprawl had resulted in extreme shortage and greatly increased price of land. Commercial development, massive road schemes and clearance programmes had all done their bit to ensure that there was insufficient housing. The high-rise block, particularly the prefabricated sort, was seen as offering a rapid solution to the problem of slums, waiting lists and land shortage. The use of prefabricated industrial building systems began to be increasingly adopted by local authorities, urged on by central government, who, convinced that industrialised building was cheapest, frequently refused loan sanction to authorities seeking to use other methods. In 1964 industrialised building formed 21 per cent of council housing, by 1967 this had risen to 42 per cent. Most building contractors rapidly came to realise that to cover their massive expenditure on factory plant and make a profit, an annual output of at least one thousand dwelling units needed to be maintained. 'Between these contractors and their less hardy rivals, and between the various suppliers of packaged mechanical services, there ensued some bitter infighting to collar the most wealthy clients: councillors and officials found themselves wined and dined and taken on trips to Paris . . .'[12] The disadvantages of these systems became apparent as soon as they were built. Condensation due to lack of ventilation caused fungus to grow on the walls of many a council tenant's bedroom. Complaints about noise levels, about lack of privacy, of front doors opening straight onto landings, about faulty construction and about isolation came flooding in. 'The Utopian visions of garden estates had now given way to vertical ghettoes',[13] yet as Taylor has pointed out, 'The road to this reinforced-concrete hell was paved with political good intentions.'[12]

The high-rise building boom came to an end in 1968, symbolised by the collapse of Ronan Point, a twenty-three-storey block in East London. A gas explosion in one of the flats caused much of the block to collapse, killing three people. At the subsequent enquiry it emerged that a gust of wind of 60–70 mph could have brought it down just as easily.[14] Although high building virtually ended, the consequences for local authorities continued. Some of the councillors and officers who had been wined and dined in the 1960s ended up in prison on corruption charges in the 1970s, as did John Poulson, one of the major building contractors involved. Although there continued to be debate as to the social implications of high-rise living it became increasingly clear that such blocks were not suitable for families with small children. Maizel's study, *Two to Five in High Flats*,[15] in 1961, had drawn attention early on to the risk of family breakdown such social isolation might cause, and Morton's study for the NSPCC in 1970 confirmed this.[16] In 1972 a DOE report, *The Estate Outside the Dwelling*, found that two-fifths of housewives with children under five were unhappy living off the ground, although this mattered less to the other people surveyed than did the appearance of the estate overall.[17] By 1979 some local authorities were dynamiting their worst blocks.

The consequences of the new building were, on the whole, disastrous for the public sector. As Cooney and others have shown, they did not solve either the problems of land or housing scarcity, nor were they low cost either in social, economic or aesthetic terms. 'So it was that in the middle 1960s many architects stood appalled while high-rise blocks multiplied whose lineage could be traced back to their professions' radical thinking of thirty and forty years previously. They were in the position of the sorcerer's apprentice . . .'[18]

The consequences of the 'transport revolution' were also often less than beneficial for the inhabitants of the inner-cities. Initially, the demolition of houses to build the new roads and to widen existing ones led to the 'decanting' of many people into council housing at a time when pressure was also coming from the rise in homelessness and when waiting lists were already long. Subsequently, people living in the inner-areas suffered from the increase in private cars coming daily into the central areas, both from the increased risks of accidents (by 1963 urban areas were claiming 73 per cent of all road casualties) and from the congestion and delays this caused to public transport. Policies to separate 'environmental areas' such as were suggested by the Buchanan Report[10] led in the short term to concentration of traffic usage to intolerable levels in other areas. Buchanan's longer-term proposals, for Central London at least, echoed Le Corbusier in scope: 'it is clear that any attempt to implement these ideas would result in a gigantic programme of urban reconstruction. We see no reason to be frightened of this . . .'[10]

One increasingly contentious question was whether or not the increased number of cars produced damaging atmospheric pollution from the lead contained in petrol exhaust fumes. Research done in Manchester during 1974 produced disquieting evidence of lead in urban street dust being deposited over wide areas, and that this dust stuck to children's hands and to the food, especially sweets, that they ate. The researchers commented:

We conclude that children in urban surroundings, who may already be ingesting in food and drink an amount of lead approaching a tolerable limit, may considerably increase their daily lead intake by the accidental ingestion of dirt and dust from their surroundings in the course of their everyday activity. This source of lead does not at present seem to be recognised as a potential hazard. . . . We consider that this is an urgent and important problem.[19]

Research in Birmingham on blood lead levels around the Gravelly Hill Intersection (or 'Spaghetti Junction' as it became called) gave similar indications of cause for alarm.[20] But further work done there by a DOE Working Party in 1977 painted a more reassuring picture. The working party found that when the interchange was first opened the blood lead levels of everyone living around increased; they also found that 'a relatively high proportion of very young children living in the inner-city areas had elevated blood lead concentrations', but concluded that this was not due to motorways or street dust, although they conceded that it needed further investigation.[21]

The effects of the Transport Revolution on the environment of the inner-cities provided an example of what Jordan terms the 'continued influence of Benthamite Liberalism' on social policy[22] – an influence that resulted in policies of 'the greatest good for the greatest number'. In this case 'the greatest number' were also increasingly politically forceful. The Buchanan Report had commented on the rise of car ownership: 'Before very long, a majority of electors will be car owners. . . . It does not need the gift of prophecy to foresee that the Governments of the future will be increasingly preoccupied with the wishes of car owners.'[10]

William Plowden has shown in *The Motor Car and British Politics*[23] how well organised and influential pressure groups, particularly of road builders and the British Road Federation, kept the importance of an extensive road programme before government and civil servants. Buchanan's proposals had been to change the cities to accommodate the cars. Not until the development of the anti-motorway pressure groups during the late 1970s were any alternatives to proposals developed. Meanwhile the 'costs' of the benefit of the greatest number were being borne by the lesser numbers of inner-city dwellers. The importance of this becomes clear when we consider who these inner-city dwellers were, and how they became increasingly perceived by policymakers as being a 'problem'.

ECONOMIC AND SOCIAL CONSEQUENCES

It can be seen that the effect of the economic and social changes on the environment of the inner-cities was considerable, and that the interaction of policies for population dispersal with economic and environmental pressures caused many people to leave. From all that has been discussed above, it will be hardly surprising to discover that, at the most general level, the people who left the inner-cities tended to be professional, managerial, clerical and skilled workers, while those who stayed seemed 'trapped' by their lack of economic power and tended to be the less skilled, low-wage earners and those with few job prospects together with many elderly people and people with social handicaps of one sort or another, all vulnerable to the pressures of poverty and bad housing.

But it would be unwise to conclude that the distinction between the inner-areas and the rest of the city region, especially the outer suburbs, was quite so clear-cut between poverty and affluence. For although the picture was true at a general level, poverty, deprivation and bad housing were not purely inner-city phenomena. It was the *concentration of multiple deprivation* that increasingly began to be perceived as the 'problem of the inner-cities' rather than the mere fact that deprivation existed. Thus the fact that 19 per cent of the men living in inner-Liverpool were unskilled (as compared with 10 per cent in the city as a whole) would not have mattered so much had this not been combined with factors such as that 82 per cent of the inner-city's households were lacking an inside toilet, and three-quarters of the city's overcrowded houses were also to be found there.[8] People living in the inner-areas suffered both 'collective' and 'personal' deprivation as their low spending power interacted with the lack of housing, amenities, and unskilled employment opportunities.

For the elderly, the out-migration of the young skilled workers or the dispersal that resulted from clearance programmes often tended to deprive them of a meaningful rôle and status, as neighbourhoods were broken up where previously networks of kinship support had existed. In these neighbourhoods, writers such as Townsend,[24] and also Wilmott and Young in their famous study *Family and Kinship in East London*,[25] have argued that the elderly had a valuable and dignified rôle to play in the life of their extended family. Elderly women, for example, offered valuable support to daughters and grand-daughters by looking after the children while the mothers worked, and in turn received support and care that enabled them to continue living in the community despite the onset of infirmity. Although migration to the outer-areas might work wonders for the migrants, especially the husband 'gradually emerging from the shadows of his previous refuges at pubs and dogs to a more domestic concern with saucepans and nappies', as Taylor[12] remarks, the consequences for the old people left behind were far less pleasant. They were vulnerable both to the pressures arising from the decay of the neighbourhood and from personal isolation.

For children and young people born and growing up in the inner-areas, the consequence of the process of urban change was massively restricted opportunity for education, recreation and employment. In 1954 John Barron Mays had argued that 'Juvenile delinquency is merely one aspect of the behaviour pattern of under-privileged neighbourhoods. Such areas, which seem always located in the older poorer parts of big industrial and commercial cities, may be called delinquency producing.'[26] By 1974 Prosser and Wedge were concluding that children born in the areas of multiple deprivation in the inner-city were 'born to fail'.[27] They, and a host of other commentators, drew attention to the stunting effect, both mental and physical, that bad housing had on child development.

POLICY CONSEQUENCES

By the late 1960s the 'inner-city problem' began to generate a response. As had so often been the case before, it was the combination of fears of rising expenditure with fears of social unrest that acted as the trigger for introducing measures of amelioration. These measures, however, represented important developments in social policy in that their emphasis was territorial rather than individual, and were based on the concept of *positive discrimination*. They drew much of their inspiration from the United States where President Johnson was at the time mounting his 'War on Poverty' in the big cities, and had their beginnings in the fields of education, race and housing.

Education

Expenditure on education has often been justified in terms of 'investment in human capital', together with the argument that an advanced industrial economy, such as Britain's, needs a literate, educated workforce. The Education Act 1944 introduced a system of selection at 11-plus to determine what type of free state education a child would receive. Subsequently, research by Floud and others,[28] which indicated that this system worked mainly to the benefit of children from middle- rather than working-class homes, led to the abandonment of selection and to the policy emphasis being placed on 'equality of access' to education. In 1967 the Report of the Plowden Committee on *Children and their Primary Schools*[29] suggested that equality of access did little good if children did not have the equality of opportunity to benefit from education, due to being socially disadvantaged before they arrived in school. Pointing to the deprivation that many children experienced from bad housing, poor environments and parents with low income and earning prospects, the committee argued that schools situated in areas of multiple deprivation should be given *priority* in resource allocation, that positive discrimination in the form of extra grants, salaries and capital allowances should be made to them. Thus education was to be used to compensate for other inequalities.

Following the Report, the government made funds available to local education authorities to spend on schools in designated Educational Priority Areas (EPAs), the majority of which, inevitably, were in the inner-cities. In addition, Action Research Projects were set up in four widely differing areas to evaluate the effectiveness of educational priority policies. Halsey has defined Action Research as 'small-scale intervention in the real world, usually in administrative systems, and the close examination of the effect of such intervention.'[30] Many of the EPA Action Research Projects involved running nursery school groups, and projects involving parents and children. Quite apart from their findings, the projects were important in that they legitimised action research as a method of approaching the formulation and evaluation of social policy, and were subsequently to be used on a considerable scale by government-funded schemes. The EPA project researchers concluded that educational priority policies did have a part to play in redressing the balance of inequality, but that on their own such policies could not do all that much. Educational priority needed to be a part of a much wider attack on multiple deprivation, especially the deprivation of bad housing and low income.

Race

During the 1950s and 1960s, as the flow of people out of the inner-city areas increased, newcomers began to join the population of the inner-areas from Asia, the West Indies and Africa. They had come to Britain initially as a result of policies to recruit labour to specific industries, such as London Transport or the Bradford Woollen Mills, or as nurses, as Britain at that time was experiencing a shortfall of skilled labour. There were not many of them arriving each year – forty thousand or so people, about the same number as a Saturday afternoon first division football match crowd. From 1960 the numbers of immigrants increased as government curbs on immigration made men hurry to bring their wives and children to join them before it was too late, but even today black British citizens form only about 2 per cent of the population. As newcomers, they sought housing as and where they could find it, inevitably in the private rented sector in the inner-city areas. Here they faced prejudice, high rents and bad accommodation, at the least secure end of private-renting. Many endeavoured to escape from their accommodation problems by purchasing houses, showing, as the Milner Holland Committee remarked, 'a marked capacity for thrift and a strong sense of community which has led to various forms of pooled resources'.[31] Only too often, however, 'the immigrant purchaser finds himself the owner of indifferent, often downright bad, property for which he has paid too high a price, saddled with liabilities . . . it is just these purchasers, simple and inexperienced, who are the natural prey of those who do not scruple to make easy profits out of conditions of shortage.'[31] Such situations frequently led to sub-letting and overcrowding in attempts to meet the liabilities.[32] Black owner-occupiers today equal the national average for owner-occupiers, and pooled resources and shared support continue to be an important characteristic.[33]

Initially, the position of black people in the private rented sector made them particularly likely to be decanted into the public sector as a result of slum clearance and road schemes; but today the number of black council tenants is below the national average. Evidence suggests that council allocation policies worked to the disadvantage of black people and that they were allocated older, inner-city, flats. One study of GLC allocation showed that black tenants were twenty-three times more numerous among pre-war flats than among the outer cottage-type estates.[34] The black population that remained in the private rented sector and were unable to gain access to either council housing or owner-occupation continued to endure severe housing hardship. The Select Committee on Race Relations found in 1971 that black people generally endured the worst housing conditions and had a particularly high level of housing need. It is important to stress that they did not cause the problems of scarcity and bad conditions. These had been present for over a century and were exacerbated by the changes discussed above.[34]

This did not stop them from being blamed, however. Prejudice and panic made it only too easy to blame the newcomers for the 'problems of the inner-city', and the first policy response was to impose restrictions upon immigration in 1961. By the end of the decade it was clear that a more comprehensive policy approach to the problem of the inner-cities was needed. The majority of the black population could no longer be classed as immigrants; they had settled and had families. Evidence showed they were no more likely to be unemployed than their white counterparts, and that they made no greater demand on social-service facilities.[35]

A new generation were growing up who had been born in Britain and shared its indigenous culture. Nonetheless, the 'sheer weight of alien numbers' argument was rehearsed by bigots, and fears of racial conflict in the inner-city areas were stoked by Enoch Powell in his infamous 'rivers of blood' speech in 1968. The government's response was to set up the Urban Programme in May 1968, comprising grants to local authorities and voluntary agencies for special projects in inner-city areas. These were self-confessedly ameliorative, the Urban Programme was 'not intended to do the work of the major social services like education or health; it does not build primary schools, houses or hospitals. It tries rather to encourage projects which have a reasonably quick effect and which go directly to the roots of special social need (i.e. multiple deprivation).'[36] The £3.5 m. funds available were for 'urban areas of special need' and were initially concentrated on expanding and improving nursery schools and similar projects for the under-fives. The scope of projects was widened in 1969 to include community centres, language classes for immigrants, day centres for the elderly, etc. – altogether some 450 projects. From 1968 to 1972, £20–£25 m. was spent on the Urban Programme and a further £35–£40 m. was allocated for 1972–76, by which time the projects had become even more diverse. In 1968 the then Home Secretary – James Callaghan – had echoed a general view of the inner-city problem when he said, 'There remain areas of severe social deprivation in a number of our cities and towns, often scattered in relatively small pockets. They require special help to meet their social needs and to bring their physical services up to an adequate level.'[37] This 'concentration problem' view was later to be questioned.

The year following the introduction of the Urban Programme, the Home Office set up the Community Development Projects. These were to be neighbourhood-based Action Research Projects in twelve selected urban areas, working within a local authority framework and supported by a research team from a university. Very soon the CDP teams were biting the hand that fed them by publishing reports that were fiercely critical of small-scale ameliorative measures such as the Urban Programme, and arguing that the *structural* causes of inner-city decline needed to be understood and changed. As many of the Action Research Projects involved opening and running community advice centres, some CDP workers were soon in conflict with their relevant local authorities over local policy and housing issues as well.[38] As soon as possible the Home Office wound the projects up. But the points raised by the CDP were crucially important ones: they exposed many defects in social policy formulation and administration, and above all they questioned many of the assumptions upon which policy was based.

Housing

I have suggested that the Urban Programme and the CDPs were introduced because of fears of racial conflict; and that the 'problems' of the inner-city were seen as problems of concentration in definable areas of deprivation. A similar approach to the housing problems of the inner-cities was initially adopted in the late 1960s for broadly the same reasons, but with additional financial stimulus. By 1969 the policy of demolish and rebuild was proving to be increasingly costly, and the government squeeze on local-authority spending was reflected in a declining number of new building 'starts'. Councils were faced with increasing building costs, increasing waiting lists, increasing numbers of decants and homeless families to house and decreasing funds. The squatters were drawing attention to the waste of the clearance areas, disillusion was spreading. Housing policy began increasingly to emphasise the need for improvement and rehabilitation of existing homes rather than demolition. That is not to say that slum clearance stopped there and then; about 67,000 dwellings a year continued to be demolished in England and Wales and a further 18,000 in Scotland, and slum clearance was given new impetus under the Housing Finance Act 1972. Nonetheless, there had been a definite change of emphasis.

Following the Report of the Dennington Committee in 1966,[39] the new policy initially concentrated on the general physical improvement of dwellings. As Cullingworth has shown, the take-up of improvement grants by landlords in the private sector had been extremely slow throughout the 1950s, and the (then Conservative) government had introduced powers under the Housing Act 1964 to allow local authorities to *compel* landlords to improve.[40] At that time the government had stressed the need for local authorities to adopt an area approach to improvement as 'something more than a means of providing amenities in individual houses . . . a part of the process of urban renewal.'[41] But the compulsory powers were so hedged about with restrictions as to be unworkable, and the fact that grants were still tied to individual houses made an area approach difficult to adopt. It became increasingly clear, however, that the need for improvement, especially in the private rented sector, was really urgent. The 1966 Census revealed that in Great Britain some 2.5 m. households still lacked exclusive use of a fixed bath, and some 3.9 m. lacked exclusive use of an inside w.c. This information was followed in 1967 by the House Condition Survey, which showed that 8 m. dwellings were 'unfit for human habitation' – more than double the number that had been expected. Clearly current improvement policy was unsuccessful and a new approach was needed. This new approach was laid out on the White Paper *Old Houses into New Homes* [doc 26] and subsequently embodied in the Housing Act 1969. Surprisingly, for a (by then) Labour goverment, the Act removed virtually all restrictions and conditions that had previously applied to the obtaining of improvement grants, and even introduced the possibility of profit making by abandoning the condition that an improved dwelling should not subsequently be quickly sold. Local authorities were given powers to declare General Improvement Areas (GIAs) – 'areas of fundamental sound houses capable of providing good living conditions for many years to come' – and within these areas there were to be additional grants to both landlords and local authorities for environmental improvements, as well as increased improvement grants for dwellings. The emphasis was upon flexibility.

Between 1969 and 1973 the number of improvement grants rose sharply from 124,000 to 454,000 per year. But of these only 16 per cent were in the private rented sector, the rest went to local authorities and owner-occupiers in almost equal proportions. Shelter had offered a cautious welcome to the 1969 Act: 'There is the first hint that a government is prepared to consider a solution to the problems of inner-city slums that encompasses the whole of life.'[42] They established the Shelter Neighbourhood Action Project (SNAP) in Granby, Liverpool, an area where the amount of shared overcrowded private rented property was very high and the provision of basic amenities very low. They succeeded in gaining improvements, establishing a residents' association with street representatives to act as a focus for community development, and they converted an old fire station into a clearly identifiable 'community corner shop', along the lines of the CDP activities taking place elsewhere at the same time. Taylor suggests the GIA policy worked well in 'rooted working-class areas, in a town where few people were any longer on the move or on the make; so there were few ulterior motives at work as people bought their freeholds cheaply and set to work industriously to install bathrooms and loos, while the Ministry planted trees, equipped playgrounds, stopped up cul de sacs and laid out parking bays.'[12]

In other areas a more cautionary tale was told, as criticisms mounted of the way in which the improvement programme was operating. As the whole emphasis of the policy was a physical one, concern to maintain buildings did not extend to maintaining the existing tenants in them. GIA policy was accused of increasing the scarcity of rented housing. In rural areas it became clear that grants were being used to improve 'second homes'. In the inner-cities improvement often brought a substantial change in the class composition of an area as the switch of housing tenures 'winkled out' existing rented tenants and replaced them with a new group of incomers.

Gentrification

The early 1970s was marked by an explosion in the price of owner-occupied housing, and many writers have suggested that the system of improvement grants set up under the Housing Act 1969 was a major contributor to this rise. They argued that the *laissez faire* nature of the improvement programme had introduced a situation whereby housing previously in private renting was 'improved' with the aid of public funds and then put on the market for sale. The process became termed 'gentrification' because the subsequent purchasers of the improved property were 'gentry' or at least were of a higher socio-economic group than the erstwhile tenants.[43]

There were two ways gentrification might take place: Merrett distinguishes between what he terms the 'mediated' and 'unmediated' process, depending on presence or not of entrepreneurial capitalists (landlords, estate agents and developers).[44] I propose to modify Merrett's classifications, and describe the process as taking place either with or without vacant possession:

1. *Without vacant possession.* A dwelling situated in the 'twilight areas' of (by then) decaying Georgian or Victorian inner-city housing, would be purchased from an estate agent by a buyer intending to occupy the property himself. In part of the house there would already be a tenant usually with a controlled tenancy of long standing and low rent. Because of the 'sitting tenant' the price of the house would be relatively cheap. The new owner might try to persuade the tenant to leave or might resign himself to waiting for the tenant's decease. Either way, he would occupy and improve the rest of the property himself, with the help of improvement grants, and possibly a local authority mortgage to help him purchase if he was lucky. Eventually he would be in sole possession of an improved dwelling, which represented an asset rapidly increasing in value.

2. *With vacant possession.* Similar dwellings in similar areas, but in

multi-occupation, would be purchased by entrepreneurial capitalists. They would persuade the tenants to leave – either by winkling or harassment. Merrett quotes Ann Holmes's evidence to the Greater London Development Plan Enquiry, where she stated, 'They will be pushed out. If they are furnished tenants they will get notice to quit. If they are overcrowded the legal enforcement will be applied, if they are timid or ill informed they can be harassed. If they are stubborn the landlord may have to wait or even offer an alternative flat. But in the end the conversion will go through . . .'[44] The vacated dwelling could then be converted with the aid of improvement grants and put on the market for sale at a considerably higher price.

As a result of this process, professional people began to move back into the inner-city areas in some numbers. They were both the cause and the effect of the gentrification process. They were certainly the cause of the rise in price of housing in inner-city residential districts which had previously not faced the scarcity prices arising from competition with commercial usage. As rising fuel costs and increased congestion made commuting both more expensive and unpleasant, and rising demand pushed up the price of suburban housing, the purchase of improved inner-city housing became increasingly attractive to people who might well be defined as 'second generation suburbanites' by birth. These newcomers to the inner-cities benefited not only from improved transport and housing costs; many also appeared to receive 'psychic income' from 'saving the lovely old houses'[45] and from taking part in the possibly more stimulating and cosmopolitan city life. Many inner residential areas in the major cities now became in fashionable demand, and very nice they looked with bright new paint, shining brass and cheerful plants in tubs and window boxes. The only snag to this happy burst of environmental improvement was the question of the previous tenants, who had been moved out of their rented homes so that lawyers, architects, advertising executives, teachers, university and polytechnic lecturers and such like could move in. There was also the matter of public funds being used to increase the profits of entrepreneurial capitalists. In 1972 the *London Property Letter* (circulated privately to estate agents and property interests) had commented, 'Properly done, conversions are the next best thing to counterfeiting for making money,' and recommended the Barnsbury area of London as 'a chicken ripe for plucking, thanks mainly to Islington Borough Council's environmental improvement plans for the area.'[44] All this raised questions as to the purpose of existing legislation. The size of the gentrification profit margin perhaps helped convince government policy-makers that rehabilitation was a possibly cheaper alternative to demolition and rebuilding. The next set of housing proposals for the inner-city could almost have been termed 'gentrification for the lower orders', so much was emphasis placed on rehabilitation, but this time in the context of the 'existing community', as policy began to take regard of social as well as environmental factors.

Participation

The changes effected by slum-clearance programmes and by gentrification took place against a background of protest. Partly stimulated by projects like SNAP and the CDP, sometimes arising from the squatting campaigns, sometimes consequent upon the arrival of middle-class radicals, but very often quite spontaneously and unprompted, a groundswell of complaint arose and grew from the people whose neighbourhoods were being cleared or were being transformed for commercial or gentrified use. Many of the protests centred on road-building schemes, and increased traffic problems; some were purely local, with people blocking busy and dangerous roads; some were on a far larger scale, and 'took on' the road lobby at national planning level.

Protest was in the air on a wider scale during the late 1960s as decisions on social and environmental issues came increasingly to be questioned and citizen participation as the means of preventing or resolving conflict became policy across a wide spectrum of agencies. In education, the Plowden Report[29] had stressed the importance of full parental involvement in children's education, and the subsequent Halsey Report[30] had developed this to include wider neighbourhood involvement in 'community schools'. In personal social services, the Seebohm Committee were urging a 'partnership' between social service departments, voluntary agencies and 'the community' to help 'break down the barriers between givers and takers of services'. The publication of the Skeffington Report, *People and Planning*, in 1968[47] extended this into the field of town planning. The main recommendations were that people should be kept informed of any planning applications relevant to their area (this had previously been secret) and encouraged to participate in the preparation of local-structure plans by helping with surveys and such as well as making comments. Cullingworth commented that 'the mundane nature of many of the recommendations is testimony to the distance which British local government has to go in making citizen participation a reality'[48] and rightly pointed out that what was lacking in the debate on citizen-participation was any consideration of the political implications, which in many cases meant local politics, not party politics. Conflict was almost certain to occur as the participating citizens demanded not only the right to be consulted but the right to help formulate and decide policy. Following Skeffington a wide number of local planning, amenity and neighbourhood groups were formed and many became increasingly vociferous during the 1970s, when citizen-participation gradually became transformed into 'community action' as disillusion with the participation process grew. Many of these groups came from the inner-city areas and while admitting to the physical problems of their areas nonetheless expressed a marked preference for staying there. To what extent the arguments and protests from such groups influenced policy is difficult to say, but they came at a time both of evaluation of the effectiveness of improvement programme and financial constraints on new building. Some of the more widely publicised campaigns may have on occasion posed a threat to social order. Certainly the squatting campaigns were perceived as such. In any event, citizen-participation of a sort entered housing policy with the proposals for Housing Action Areas contained in the Housing Act 1974.

THE 1974 HOUSING ACT AND HOUSING ACTION AREA POLICY

During 1972 and 1973, the government reviewed its policies for older housing. The resulting proposals were published as a White Paper, *Better Homes – the Next Priorities* (June 1973). As the title suggests, the emphasis was upon priorities – the urgent need to treat the worst houses first. There was recognition that the 1969 Improvement Programme had failed to stimulate investment in the private rented sector, and that it had helped the process of gentrification in certain locations. Considerable emphasis was placed on the 'concentration of deprivation' theory and the need for positive discrimination measures to attack these pockets of housing need. The main emphasis of policy was upon 'putting people first'.

Thus the subsequent legislation – the Housing Act 1974 – represented a complete departure from the 'sanitary idea' that had dominated inner-city housing policy for over a century. Slum clearance and redevelopment were no longer seen as the 'solution' to the problems of the inner-city. The 'social function' of housing was seen by the government as having as much importance as physical conditions – even when the physical conditions were bad [doc 27].

The 1974 Act concentrated upon improvement and gradual renewal of inner-city dwellings. It contained measures to strengthen local authorities' mortgage lending, and to encourage housing association activity by the setting up of the Housing Corporation. These, combined with the security of tenure for furnished private tenants provided under the Rent Act 1974, formed the basis of the attempt to offer a new solution to the problems of bad housing concentrations. The measures in the new Housing Act where the social approach to housing was clearest were those for the setting up of Housing Action Areas (HAAs).

Housing Action Area policy was intended for those areas where poor housing stock combined with poor social conditions – an estimated 3 or 4 per cent of the housing stock. The criteria used for determining poor housing were the proportion of houses sharing facilities, the proportion of overcrowding and the amount of private renting. The 'social stress' criteria, in fact, appeared to mean income deprivation in various forms, but it was the *concentration* of deprived groups of people (the elderly, or unemployed or disabled, the single parent or the large family) that was important. Housing Action Areas were to be relatively small areas – three to five hundred or so houses – and the intention was that the 'unsatisfactory living conditions' in those areas should be dealt with within five years.

Active participation in the HAAs by local authorities was seen as crucial to their success. Under the 1974 Housing Act councils were given wider powers to compulsory purchase and for enforcing improvements. Improvement grant levels were raised. Councils were supposed to ensure the 'proper and effective management and use' of housing in the HAA and to have public participation in the management process. They were to play the major rôle in publishing the measures and encouraging landlords and owner-occupiers within the HAA to improve their property voluntarily.

Obviously, if HAA policy were to succeed, extra council funds and officers would need to be deployed, and extra resources would need to be made available by government. Herein lay the first pitfall. Also the determination and vigour required if local authorities were to deal effectively with unsatisfactory living conditions within five years called for a high level of enthusiasm among the local authorities involved – and this was a potential pitfall too.

Many local authorities opposed the HAA idea from the first. Professional opposition came from many Environmental Health Officers (EHOs) who still preferred the 'sanitary' approach to bad housing and overcrowding. Much of the task of assessing conditions in potential HAAs would fall upon the EHOs, and many Public Health Departments were already under strength as public expenditure curbs had led to the freezing of posts. Opposition also came from elected councillors, particularly Labour ones. Many councillors knew the worst housing areas of their boroughs only too well; they had dealt for years with the housing problems these generated; had fought the landlords for years, and they longed to get what they considered to be rotten slums pulled down. The government's proposals for gradual renewal, particularly the suggestion that improvements need not be to full Parker Morris standards, appalled them [doc 28]. Although they might welcome the emphasis upon municipalisation in the proposals, they feared that the purchase of sub-standard properties, subsequently patchily repaired, would create ghettos of 'second-class council housing' (or even third-class, since most councils already had some pretty bad old estates themselves). More importantly, perhaps, they, and many others, argued that diverting resources to HAAs would inevitably mean fewer resources available for the other areas of bad housing and poverty within their boroughs which did not quite qualify for HAA designation. They therefore challenged the concentration theory, while also challenging the government to put up enough money for action.

Many community action groups, however, saw the proposals as offering a weapon in the fight to maintain their neighbourhood, and often seemed to view the 'social function' of housing in more or less the same light as the government. These groups varied widely in type and location, but all shared the same aims of improving the existing buildings in their neighbourhood, and keeping the existing residents in them. Many undertook their own housing condition surveys, thus both pre-empting the 'EHO shortage' plea, and providing material with which to put pressure upon their local authorities. Many had to convince their local councils that a residential use should continue, before going on to argue for improvement. In Workington, for example, the residents of 'the Marsh' argued for HAA designation and improvement of their dwellings despite the area being 'zoned' for industrial use.[49] Similar problems were faced in areas such as Central London, where competition was between housing and commercial use. Residents' groups there saw HAA designation as a means whereby the price of land might be lowered and the existing housing use confirmed.[50] Many hoped that HAA designation might also help maintain the existing infrastructure of shops and small industries, since 'putting together a site' would become that much more difficult, and that designation would also help enforce repairs to historic buildings in residential use. When put to the test, however, the success of such arguments largely depended on factors external to the actual workings of HAA policy.

A few local authorities, Birmingham and Newcastle in particular, did embark upon ambitious HAA programmes, but in general the rate of declaration was slow. By May 1977, three years after the Housing Act had become law, only 194 HAAs had been declared in England, and as Paris commented, 'to apply an admittedly rough measure of the patchiness of the national programme, no fewer than twelve . . . of the government's own list of twenty-eight stress areas had not . . . declared a single housing action area among them.'[51]

Once declared, the task of remedying unsatisfactory living conditions within five years was far from easy – even with local-authority enthusiasm. Councils were expected to 'encourage' voluntary improvement among private owners before resorting to compulsory purchase, and grant levels were increased to help stimulate take-up. The Chairman of Manchester's Housing Committee commented in 1976 that 'the costs associated with the improvement and repair of many of the private houses in these areas (i.e. HAAs) are so high as to prevent their owners, under the present regulations, from proceeding with voluntary renovation schemes.'[51]

But if the problem of repair in the private sector was no more easily solved by the 1974 Act improvement grants than they had been before, attempts to use municipalisation as a solution within HAAs were fraught with difficulty. Although councils were given much wider powers of compulsory purchase under the 1974 Act, the actual process of securing a compulsory purchase order (CPO) was still a long and complicated one. CPOs had to be confirmed by the DOE, who in practice acted with extreme caution and still appeared to view a CPO as a measure of desperate last resort rather than a tool for local-authority initiative. Even when the sale of a property was agreed non-compulsorily between owner and local authority, the expenditure still had to get government sanction. This might be withheld, but even if not it always took time. Those authorities who saw HAAs as being a useful way to attack their worst housing problems still had to carry the DOE with them in getting their schemes through towards anything like completion.

Support for, or opposition to, the HAA proposals, however, were not the crucial determinants. What mattered was money, and when it came to the actual allocation of resources the government failed to pay up. HAAs had been part of a package of housing strategies contained in the 1974 Housing Act. The White Paper on Public Expenditure brought out in January 1975 showed a continued commitment to housing expenditure, but by February the following year the government's allocation to housing had been drastically cut back. Municipalisation, council house building, local-authority mortgage lending, housing association activity, all were severely reduced. Although the government continued to stress the importance it placed on gradual renewal and housing action in the inner-cities, it limited the scope of action available to local authorities both by cutting back on its original allocation to the HAA programme and by restricting the money available to local authorities for their other spheres of housing action. Prior to the cuts many authorities had earmarked the bulk of improvement grant allocation for improving their own properties within the worst areas. Contracts having been signed had to be honoured, but as the allocation was reduced almost at once, this left little or nothing to attack the problems of the private sector. Money and staff, in any case, simply were not adequate to potential requirements. Birmingham's £5 m. for acquisitions in 1975, for example, would have been enough to purchase only 1,000 of an estimated 32,000 tenanted properties in renewal areas.

Yet, had the money and staff been made available on a large scale, the question would have remained as to the efficacy of such area-based strategies as HAAs. So many of the problems these areas suffered were generated by causes outside the areas themselves, particularly the problems of investment in the private rented sector, of building-society activity in restricting loans within 'redline' districts, and particularly the problem of low income. The thinking behind the HAA policy seemed to be that the causes of problems such as bad housing, poor environment and low income all lay with the individuals who lived within the areas, rather than that they might be caused by the workings of the housing, job and investment market. Nor would greater resource allocation have answered the questions raised about bad housing and social conditions *outside* the HAAs. As Paris commented, 'Not only are the HAAs failing to meet the problem, but given present policies they could be yet another wrong answer to the wrong problem.'[51]

THE 1977 WHITE PAPER AND 'TOTAL' REAPPRAISAL

Almost from the beginning criticisms were voiced about the effectiveness of priority-area policies in tackling multiple deprivation in the inner-cities. Analysis of data in the 1971 Census suggested that deprived people were not simply concentrated in small localised areas.[52] Writers such as Donnison and Townsend argued that by concentrating on pockets of deprivation, priority-area policies served to increase inequality among the already unequal, and that national policies of income redistribution aimed at individuals might more effectively help the deprived.[53] The CDP termed the priority-area approach 'gilding the ghetto' and argued that small-scale positive discrimination measures did not attack the underlying structural causes of deprivation.[54]

Although the government rejected the critics' proposals for a national attack on individual poverty, they did concede that priority area policies seemed to be having a limited effect. A review of policy took place and subsequently resulted in the publication of the White Paper *Policy for Inner Cities* in 1977.[1]

Much of the review and the White Paper conclusions were based on evidence from the newly completed *Inner Area Studies*.[55] These studies, begun in 1973, had examined selected areas of inner-Birmingham, Liverpool and London. Undertaken by consultant architects working closely with the relevant local authorities, their remit was to 'look at the needs of the inner-areas from the point of view of the people living in them'. They included several action research projects. They provided detailed accounts of the decline in the quality of inner-city life and of the growing inequalities. Although there were differences between them, the broad recommendations were the same from all three studies:

(*a*) the need for economic regeneration;
(*b*) the need for greater sensitivity and awareness at central and local government level of the needs and wishes of local people;
(*c*) the need for improved housing conditions;
(*d*) the need for an overall approach to the inner-city problems, which included economic as well as social measures.

It is interesting to compare and contrast the inner-area studies with the reports from the CDP, since both were seeking to describe the same processes at much the same time. The inner-area studies were calm, balanced documents, charting inequalities with reasonable compassion and lots of quotes; they were unlikely to offend anybody very much. Much the same could be said about the subsequent White Paper, even though it represented a further reversal of the policies of planned dispersal, industrial relocation and the 'sanitary idea' approach to slum clearance.

The 1977 White Paper could be described, perhaps, as priority-area policy developed and spread wider. It stressed the importance of specific commitment to the ideas of regeneration of the inner-cities and the need for an attack to be made on all fronts – economic, physical and social:

A new balance is required between the inner-cities and the surrounding region. A deliberate effort is needed to reduce, and possibly in some cases end, the loss of people and jobs from the cities as a whole and the inner-cities in particular. This means making the cities more attractive for employers and more attractive for people to live and work in. It means taking steps to match the skills of those in inner-cities with the jobs which are available, and providing the sort of homes people want.[1]

The White Paper specifically rejected the possibility of creating the equivalent of the New Towns corporations for the inner-areas, not least because 'it is important to preserve accountability to the local electorate'.[1] Instead, they proposed to give wider powers to local authorities to encourage industry back into the cities, enhance the Urban Programme, and set out proposals for *partnership schemes* between government and selected local authorities.

The need to attract industry into the inner-cities was to be aided by giving local authorities power to make loans for land purchase of up to 90 per cent of cost; to declare Industrial Improvement Areas, and to provide help with the cost of site preparation. The policy was very similar to the existing system of regional development grants which encouraged industry to move (often out of the inner-areas) to the designated development regions – those areas of the North, Wales and South-west where primary industry had declined and unemployment was high. Indeed the switch of emphasis was most clearly symbolised in the changing function given in the White Paper to the Location of Offices Bureau (LOB). The LOB had for years been helping firms move out of the cities, and had by advertisement exhorted travellers on public transport to 'get out of London, get more out of life'. Now, its task would be to coerce firms back again. (Subsequently, of course, the LOB was 'axed' in 1979 as part of the Conservative government's attack on 'quangos'.)

Strangely enough, the White Paper suggested that 'services and office employment in the centres of cities . . . will help to provide employment'. It did not make clear whether this meant office cleaning and caretaking as the main vehicle for employment of the inner-city unskilled, or whether the proposal was to stimulate more white-collar workers to move house and gentrify. Since office development already characterised the central areas of all the major cities and had in many cases been a contributory factor to the overall decline, the possibility of yet more was perhaps less than helpful.

The enhanced Urban Programme was to become the responsibility of the Department of the Environment, although the Home Office was to remain responsible for race relations. Funds for the Urban Programme were to be increased from around £30 m. per year to £125 m. (£120 m. for England and £5 m. for Wales) in 1978–79. The Scottish increase from £6 m. to over £20 m. reflected the government's concern both with the growing crime and vandalism on the outer-Glasgow estates and the possibility of an electoral swing to the Scottish National Party. The White Paper stated that the government's intention was that the Urban Programme should form part of 'a continuing commitment over the next decade', and that the initial increase would be met by 'modest savings in the new towns programme and by a redirection of resources within other programmes.' The method of funding individual projects under the Urban Programme would continue as before, with a 75 per cent government and 25 per cent local-authority input.

The partnership proposals were a wholly new attempt to achieve a unified approach to policy implementation. They were intended to provide a vehicle for the direct channelling of funds to the most disadvantaged areas on a far wider basis than before. The partnership was to be between central government and selected local authorities [doc 29]. 'The aim will be to see that the powers and finances of central government are used in a unified way to improve economic and social conditions and to deal with physical decay.' Seven partnership schemes were established; these were offered to Liverpool, Birmingham, Glasgow, Manchester/Salford, the London Boroughs of Lambeth and Islington/Hackney and to the London Docklands. (A Statutory Joint Committee of relevant London Boroughs, the GLC and government agencies had already been established and was about to commence an urban renewal programme of the Docklands area.) Each partnership had a small team to analyse each area's needs, draw up a programme for regeneration and help guide it through to fruition, ensuring the while that 'the community are involved in the work'. These programmes were intended to provide the main focus of the unified approach, and to deal with 'the totality of local-authority policies and programmes for the inner-areas and with other public-sector activities, for example industry and employment.'[1] Although the brief was such a large one, the White Paper urged the need to achieve value for money and the need to aim at 'early and demonstrable results'.

I suggested above that the 1977 Inner Cities White Paper represented a change of direction from earlier policies of clearance and dispersal. Such changes might well be based in ideology, but they were not overtly party political in the way many other policy changes so clearly were. When in 1979 the government changed, the notional commitment to inner-city regeneration remained, although there was a marked shift of emphasis within the overall policy framework. The Urban Programme was not immediately wound up, when much else was. What changed was the rôle of local authorities, who had previously been the major deliverers of government resources. In 1979 reduction of local-authority activity was clearly signalled with the government reduction in the Rate Support Grant (which the 1977 White Paper had seen as the principal source of financing local-authority regeneration activities) and greatly curbed HAA activities. The Secretary of State – Heseltine – although initially keeping the partnership schemes, proposed the setting up of three urban development corporations coterminus with three of the partnership areas, where the removal of many planning and development constraints would further curb local-authority powers. The Development Corporation idea had been specifically rejected in the White Paper, and ironically the proposals came at the same time as the government was considering forcing the existing New Town corporations to 'sell off their assets' of housing and possibly of industry.

It is too early to say whether the continued commitment to the inner-city policies simply represented a continuation of the more usual Conservative preference for selectivity, or whether the abolition of planning controls was intended to stimulate a further 'property boom' or even how long-term the commitment was likely to be. Certainly, as the recession in the economy had grown, the distinction between the inner-cities and other areas of high unemployment had become less clear-cut. The 1977 Housing Green Paper had identified five main housing problems in inner-cities – run-down housing and shabby neighbourhoods, bleak local-authority estates, limited choice of tenures, and a disproportionate number of people with special housing needs and limited housing mobility.[56] It became increasingly clear that these characteristics could be found in the outer-city peripheries, on the overspill estates and in a number of urban areas beyond the inner-cities.

CONFLICTING VIEWS OF CITY LIFE

When people talk about the 'housing problem' they usually mean the problems of the private rented sector, of shortage, overcrowding, lack of amenity and homelessness. But these housing problems are only a part of the problems of an urban society, and to concentrate upon the most obvious malfunctions may be to miss the wider implications of the effects of urban change upon town and country. Herbert Gans talked about 'urbanism and suburbanism as a way of life' and described American urban society largely polarised between the rich 'cosmopolites' and the 'deprived' and downwardly mobile 'trapped'. While it is possible to suggest that social polarisation may not be quite so acute in British inner-cities as in American ones, Gans's categories provide valuable insights: 'These . . . types all live in dense and heterogeneous surroundings; yet they have such diverse ways of life that it is hard to see how density and heterogeneity could exert a common influence. . . . Even the well-to-do can choose an expensive apartment in or near a poor neighbourhood, because, if they have children, these are sent to special schools and summer camps which effectively isolate them from neighbours.' He adds, 'The deprived population suffers considerably from overcrowding, but this is a consequence of low income, racial discrimination and other handicaps and cannot be considered an inevitable result of the ecological make-up of the city.'[57]

Gans's statements could be said to be echoed by much of the findings of the inner-area studies, but how closely can we apply his urban/suburban dichotomy to British society? Is it possible to argue that some people are urban dwellers from choice, when they are able to choose? The Lambeth Inner Area study found 48 per cent of their survey sample wished to move out. Subsequently David Jordan, one of the researchers, elaborated on this to suggest that there should be policy measures to facilitate 'rippling out' of population to the outer suburbs and beyond.[58]

The people who wanted to leave Lambeth were mainly young working people with children. They cited the environmental decline, rising crime and other changes that had overtaken their area as the reasons why they wanted to get out of the inner-city altogether. Similar views were expressed by similar people leaving Islington for the New Towns.[59] Further research in South London again confirmed that it was white, working-class, long-established residents who wanted to move out.[60] But would it be right to conclude from this that 'everybody' or 'most people' want to move and that policies should be altered accordingly? Over half the Lambeth sample said they wanted to stay where they were. Many of the people who wanted to stay in Lambeth were comparative newcomers and many were black. They had established a close community locally of kin and friends, and perhaps fitted Gans's 'ethnic villagers' type of urban dwellers. Should we, then, conclude that urban living by choice is something that really characterises only black Londoners? The people of the 'Marsh' in Workington, who were mentioned above – and who were white working-class with children, wanted to stay where they were too.[49] The Covent Garden Community Association, who fought long and hard to stem the redevelopment of their area of London, were also white working-class (albeit with prominent middle-class activists as well).[61] The Tolmers Square tenants association – all long-established working-class residents – also fought to stay where they were until it was no longer possible and they were scattered. It was only then, when the existing community was smashed, that the squatters moved in.[6] It is really hardly surprising that long-standing residents who have suffered the degradation of area decline, slum clearance, planning blight, loss of jobs, change and decay; who have seen their friends and neighbours move out; should perhaps want to go too. In any case the 'push factors' discussed above did not cease to push simply because the government set up the Inner-City Programme. But much of the evidence suggests a resilience to the policy of planned dispersal from people in the inner-cities, and that the expressed desire to move out is at least partly a consequence of thirty years of government action. As one resident of the Small Heath area, quoted in the Birmingham Inner Area study, said, 'Once they've started to plan, everything goes. Now they've made it so you want to get out anyway.'[55] It might be possible to suggest with Gans that 'suburbanism', if not exactly a way of life, might well represent a set of values. Since most local and central government officers do not live in the inner-areas for which they make and administer policy, the effect of suburban values on policies for the inner-cities, could well be important. It might help provide added reasons why the Urban Programme, Housing Action, and the whole Inner-City Policy package were all 'too little too late'. As Holman pointed out in 1972, the total cost of the phases of the urban programme till then 'would not buy the Manchester United football team.'[62]

To help put the inner-city problem into perspective it is worth examining some of the underlying value beliefs that influence policies, in this case particular views of the nature and condition of 'city life'. Broadly speaking there are two main viewpoints: one sees the city as 'the centre of civilised life', the other as 'the infernal wen'. The first viewpoint – taking as its model the ancient Greek city state – sees the development of art, culture and government as an inevitable consequence of city formation. Indeed, Jane Jacobs has argued that without the economy of cities settled patterns of agriculture would not have developed.[63] Perhaps the chief contemporary protagonist for the 'civilised life' viewpoint is Lewis Mumford; in *The City in History* he says, 'The breadth of human experience that the dynamic, still healthy metropolis offers is rivalled by its density and depth, its capacity for making available layer upon layer of human history and biography.'[64]

The phrase 'the infernal wen' was first coined with reference to Tudor London, which commentators at that time saw as spreading out of control, engulfing the surrounding countryside and containing in its dark heart 'abodes of sedition and vice'. In the nineteenth century, many people saw the expanding industrial towns in just the same light. The growth of such cities meant the breaking down of the 'old ways' and bringing together dangerous numbers of people who might all too easily become a mob. I have suggested that much early housing and slum-clearance policy developed from the fear of mob uprising. There were plenty of examples to feed these fears from the eighteenth century and throughout the nineteenth, both at home and overseas. Inevitably the policies that were influenced by the 'infernal wen' viewpoint were policies of social control in housing as in much else. It is important to remember this, even when the outcome of such policies might appear to be quite pleasant. I mentioned above the LCC building 'cottage estates' for workers on the outskirts of London in 1908. On a more sumptuous scale, the wide boulevards of central Paris were deliberately created by Hausmann when he rebuilt the city after the uprising of the 1870 Commune, to provide clear lines of fire for troops in the event of a repetition. Social unrest and conflict continued to influence policy in the twentieth century, and although I have suggested that it was, in the main, the fear of racial conflict that generated the Urban Programme, the view that the inner-cities still contained 'abodes of sedition and vice' continued to be expressed, particularly by those who saw poverty as a form of vice.

Views and opinions about city life tend to generate a complementary set of views about rural life. Those who hold the view of the civilising city tend to stress the 'dullness, lack of society, low wages, lack of amusements and general decay' of country life.[65] Those who see the city as the 'infernal wen' see rural life as representing 'the old ways, human ways, natural ways'.[66] Much of the debate about these views tends to concentrate on definitions and examples of 'community' and 'association'. I do not propose to go into the detail of these theories; very full explanations can be found in Ray Pahl's *Patterns of Urban Life*[67] and Gwyn Jones's *Rural Life*.[68] Briefly, the terms were first defined in 1887 by Tönnies[69] who suggested that 'Community' (*Gemeinschaft*) was generated by close patterns of relationships mainly within extended kinship groups, with no distinction between work and home activity, whereas 'Association' (*Gesellschaft*) occurred where patterns of relationship were formal and distant, outside the extended-kinship network and where work and home activities were separate and distinct. Thus 'Community' was more likely to be found in close rural settlements where everyone was related and where all shared, to varying degrees, in the work of the land, while Association was the typical pattern of relationships in urban settlement, where the individual was isolated from kin and where workplace and homeplace were distinct. Thus the phrase 'the urban community' represented a contradiction in terms. Since this was precisely what later commentators on the state of the inner-cities argued ought to be maintained and developed, it would be a mistake to see 'Community' and 'Association' as purely a rural/urban dichotomy. Yet the images of city and country retain great force, and influence. Williams suggests that

. . . in their main bearing they are forms of response to a social system as a whole. Most obviously since the Industrial Revolution, but in my view also since the beginnings of the capitalist's agrarian mode of production, our powerful images of country and city have been ways of responding to a whole social development. . . . It is significant, for example, that the common image of the country is now an image of the past, and the common image of the city an image of the future. That leaves, if we isolate them, an undefined present. The pull of the idea of the country is towards old ways, human ways, natural ways. The pull of the idea of the city is towards progress, modernisation, development. In what is, then, a tension, a present experienced as tension, we use the contrast of country and city to ratify an unresolved division and conflict of impulses which might be better to face in its own terms.[66]

If we look at the policies for the inner-cities as being 'forms of response to a social system as a whole', as Williams suggests, then the problems of urban change, bad housing and unemployment clearly become part of the wider problem of structural poverty within a particular type of economy.

REFERENCES

1. DOE, *Policy for Inner Cities*, Cmnd 6845 (1977), HMSO.
2. GREATER LONDON COUNCIL, *Home Sweet Home: housing design by the LCC and GLC architects 1888–1975* (1976).
3. P. HALL *et al.*, *op. cit.* (see ref. 1, Ch. 8).
4. O. MARRIOTT, *The Property Boom*, Pan, London (1967).
5. P. AMBROSE and B. COLENUTT, *The Property Game*, Pelican, Harmondsworth (1975).
6. N. WATES, *op. cit.* (see ref. 5, Ch. 7).
7. SHELTER, *Slum Clearance Report* (1975).
8. DEPT OF ENVIRONMENT, *Change and Decay: Final Report of the Liverpool Inner Area Study*, HMSO (1977).
9. DEPT OF TRANSPORT, *Great Britain: transport statistics 1967–77*. Table 11. Passenger transport, by mode, HMSO (1978).
10. MINISTRY OF TRANSPORT, *Traffic in Towns: a study of the long-term problems of traffic in urban areas* (Buchanan Report), HMSO (1963).
11. LE CORBUSIER, *The Radiant City* (first published 1933. Reprinted Faber & Faber, London, 1964).
12. N. TAYLOR, *The Village in the City*, Temple Smith, London (1973).
13. COMMUNITY DEVELOPMENT PROJECT, *Whatever Happened to Council Housing?*, London (1976).
14. MINISTRY OF HOUSING AND LOCAL GOVERNMENT, *Collapse of Flats at Ronan Point, Canning Town: Report of the Enquiry*, HMSO (1968).
15. M. MAIZEL, *Two to Five in High Flats*, Housing Centre Trust, London (1961).
16. A. MORTON, *Children in Flats: a family study*, NSPCC (1970).
17. DEPT OF ENVIRONMENT, *Design Bulletin No. 25* (1972).
18. E. W. COONEY, 'High flats in local authority housing in England and Wales since 1945', in *Multi-Storey Living: the British working class experience*, A. SUTCLIFFE (ed.), Croom Helm, London (1973).
19. J. P. DAY, M. HART and M. S. ROBINSON, 'Lead in urban street dust', *Nature*, vol. 253, 31 January (1975).
20. H. WALDRON, *Lead Levels in Blood in Residents near the M6–*

A38M Interchange, ibid.

21. DEPT OF ENVIRONMENT, CENTRAL UNIT ON ENVIRONMENTAL POLLUTION, Pollution Paper No. 14. *Lead Pollution in Birmingham: Report of the Joint Working Party on Lead Pollution around Gravelly Hill*, HMSO (1978).

22. B. JORDAN, *Freedom and the Welfare State*, Routledge & Kegan Paul, London (1977).

23. W. PLOWDEN, *The Motor Car and British Politics*, Pelican, Harmondsworth (1976).

24. P. TOWNSEND, *The Family Life of Old People*, Pelican, Harmondsworth (1965).

25. P. WILMOTT and M. YOUNG, *Family and Kinship in East London*, Pelican, Harmondsworth (1967).

26. J. B. MAYS, *Growing Up in the City: a study of juvenile delinquency in an urban neighbourhood*, Liverpool University Press, Liverpool; John Wiley, New York (1954).

27. P. PROSSER and H. WEDGE, *Born to Fail*, Arrow Books, London (1973).

28. J. FLOUD, A. HALSEY and F. MARTIN, *Social Class and Educational Opportunity* (first published 1957; Bath/Cedric Chivers, London, 1972).

29. CENTRAL ADVISORY COUNCIL FOR EDUCATION, *Children and their Primary Schools* (Plowden Report), HMSO (1967).

30. DEPT OF EDUCATION AND SCIENCE, *Educational Priority. Vol. 1. EPA Problems and Policies*, A. HALSEY (ed.), HMSO (1972).

31. MINISTRY OF HOUSING AND LOCAL GOVERNMENT, *op. cit.* (see ref. 2, Ch. 4).

32. J. REX and P. MOORE, with A. SHUTTLEWORTH and J. WILLIAMS, *Race, Community and Conflict*, Oxford University Press, London (1967).

33. M. FENTON, *Asian Households in Owner Occupation*, University of Bristol/Social Science Research Council, Working Paper on Ethnic Relations No. 2 (1977); see also B. INEICHEN in *New Society*, 22 August (1979).

34. RUNNYMEDE TRUST, *Race and Council Housing in London: census returns examined by the Runnymede Trust Research Staff* (1975); see also HOME OFFICE, *Race Relations and Housing: observations on the report on housing of the Select Committee on Race Relations and Immigration*, Cmnd 6232. HMSO (1975).

35. F. FIELD and P. HAIKIN (eds), *Black Britons*, Oxford University Press, Oxford (1971).

36. HOME OFFICE, *Notes on the Urban Programme* (1972).

37. HANSARD, 22 July, col. 4, HMSO (1968).
38. R. LEES and G. SMITH, *Action Research in Community Development*, Routledge & Kegan Paul, London (1975).
39. CENTRAL HOUSING ADVISORY COMMITTEE, *Our Older Houses: a Call for Action* (Dennington Report), HMSO (1966).
40. J. B. CULLINGWORTH, *op. cit.* (see ref. 7, Ch. 2).
41. MINISTRY OF HOUSING AND LOCAL GOVERNMENT, *Circular 53/64*, HMSO (1964).
42. SHELTER, *Reprieve for Slums* (1972).
43. RUTH GLASS, *London Aspects of Change*, Centre for Urban Studies, London (1969).
44. S. MERRETT, 'Gentrification', *Housing and Class in Britain*, papers presented at the Political Economy of Housing Workshop of the Conference of Socialist Economists, University of Sussex, Brighton (1976).
45. DEPT OF ENVIRONMENT, *Inner London: policies of dispersal and balance. Final Report of the Lambeth Inner Area Study*, HMSO (1977).
46. Seebohm Report, *op. cit.* (see ref. 15, Ch. 2).
47. MINISTRY OF HOUSING AND LOCAL GOVERNMENT, *Report of the Committee on Public Participation in Planning* (Skeffington Report), HMSO (1968).
48. J. B. CULLINGWORTH, *op. cit.* (see ref. 1, Ch. 2).
49. MARSH AREA ACTION GROUP, *The Future of the Marsh*, 35 South Marsh St, Workington, Cumbria (1977).
50. FITZROVIA NEIGHBOURHOOD ASSOCIATION, *The Fitzrovia Housing Survey*, 39 Tottenham St, London W1 (1977).
51. C. PARIS, 'Housing action areas: will they really work?', *Roof*, January (1977).
52. S. HOLTERMAN, 'Areas of urban deprivation', in *Social Trends 1975*, E. THOMPSON (ed.), HMSO (1976).
53. D. DONNISON, 'Policies for priority areas', *Journal of Social Policy*, vol. 3 (1974); see also P. TOWNSEND, 'Urban deprivation policies', *New Statesman*, 6 August (1976).
54. COMMUNITY DEVELOPMENT PROJECT, *Gilding the Ghetto*, London (1976).
55. DEPT OF ENVIRONMENT, *Unequal City: final report of the Birmingham Inner Area Study*, HMSO (1977); see also above, refs. 8 and 45.
56. DEPT OF ENVIRONMENT, *op. cit.* (see ref. 8, Ch. 2).
57. H. G. GANS, *People and Plans: essays in urban problems and solutions*, Pelican, Harmondsworth (1969).

58. D. JORDAN, 'How we can free the housing market', *Roof*, January (1977).

59. N. DEAKIN and C. UNGERSON, *Leaving London: planned mobility and the inner-city*, Heinemann Educational Books, London (1977).

60. A. FASEY and G. LLEWELLYN, *Social and Economic Consequences of Housing Association Activity: an inner-London case study*, Polytechnic of Central London Occasional Paper. Unpublished (1979).

61. T. CHRISTENSEN, *Neighbourhood Survival*, Prism Press, London (1979).

62. R. HOLMAN and L. HAMILTON, 'The British urban programme', *Policy and Politics*, vol. 2 (1972).

63. J. JACOBS, *The Economy of Cities* (first published New York, 1969; paperback edn, Pelican, Harmondsworth, 1970).

64. L. MUMFORD, *The City in History* (first published 1961; paperback edn, Pelican, Harmondsworth, 1966).

65. F. J. OSBORN, 'Ebenezer Howard and the Garden City Idea', in *Cities in Modern Britain*, C. LAMBERT and D. WEIR (eds), Fontana, London (1975).

66. R. WILLIAMS, *The City and the Country*, Chatto & Windus, London (1964).

67. R. PAHL, *Patterns of Urban Life*, Longman, London (1970).

68. G. JONES, *Rural Life*, Longman, London (1973).

69. F. TÖNNIES, *Community and Association* (first published 1887); reprinted Routledge & Kegan Paul, London, 1974.

Part four
HOUSING AND SOCIAL JUSTICE

Chapter ten
EVALUATION

It will have been seen from the foregoing chapters that the housing situation we have today has been historically determined through change arising from economic processes. Housing policy has tended to be reactive and incremental, responding to particular situations and building on policies that had gone before. Policy was often the result of fears and conflicts, and was usually firmly based in values and ideological beliefs that mostly, but not always, were aligned with a particular political perspective.

Certainly it would seem that housing policies to date have rarely if ever 'solved' the various problems that have arisen. Often, as we have seen, policies to solve one problem in one area created new and further problems in others, not least because housing policy has tended to be particularistic – 'single-problem orientated' – rather than holistic. The only attempt to evaluate housing policy as a whole – the 1977 Green Paper[1] – proved to be a rather tired statement of the existing situation rather than the herald of a new approach.

No society is static, and British society like any other is constantly changing. Changes in housing policy and the housing system reflect this. If we take the years since the Second World War it is clear that major changes have taken place within the British housing market. There have been changes caused by population increase and the growth of the overall number of households, with earlier marriage and healthier old age. There have been changes in the size and relationship of the various housing sectors. Owner-occupation, a relatively small sector after the war, dominated by 1979 with 53 per cent of all housing tenures; council housing had also grown to take 32 per cent of all tenures by then. The private rented sector, which had been most people's form of tenure after the war, now had shrunk almost away to a mere 14 per cent of all tenures. The real beginnings of these changes were established much earlier, and received major impetus in 1919 and 1923, but it was not until the 1950s that the impact of change began to make itself felt. These changes have caused and been caused by policies and were an integral part of the social processes of the time, no policy – housing or any other – is ever made in a vacuum.

Housing is a *commodity*. In some locations and at some price levels it is a very scarce commodity. Although at the moment there is a crude surplus of dwellings to population in the country overall, there is a mismatch between dwellings and people in terms of location, household type and available income and employment. Like other commodities, housing can be bought in the market place. Choice there depends upon economic power. There is considerable state intervention in the workings of the housing market. Growth and decline have been fostered by subsidy, dwellings have been provided that are not dependent upon economic power for allocation. We have seen that the highest subsidies go to those who are already advantaged in both housing and income terms. Housing is still most scarce for those who lack economic power and who are unable to gain access to the public sector. For them competition for housing – often for the worst housing – is fiercest.

Housing is a *physical undertaking*. There are always time-lags between a policy decision and its realisation in bricks and mortar or concrete. Attempts to speed up the process by cutting corners, lowering standards or introducing new building systems have often proved to be short-term expedients with disastrous long-term financial and social consequences. The physical nature of housing means that the rôle of finance, planning and of the construction industry are of particular importance, since they – as pressure-groups, suppliers and contractors – determine the social as well as the physical landscape. People have to live with the consequences of these groups' actions for years to come.

Housing is a *social reality*. The design and location of buildings can be said to have 'visual symbolism'. Lowenthal and Price noted that each age fashions its environment to suit and reflect existing social norms.[2] The built environment is thus no accident, but a series of statements about the architect's view of the world, about the people who commissioned the building, and about the people who live there. Harvey has commented, 'The design of a medieval church has much to say about the nature of social hierarchy simply through the spatial relationship which an individual has to the central focal point. It is no accident that those in the choir somehow seemed closer to God (and hence more privileged) than those in the nave.'[3]

If we take Harvey's analogy and look around at the built environment it becomes clear that some people are 'closer to God' than others. This raises questions. Is it simply a matter of costs and budgetry constraints that make a council estate so instantly recognisable? What can the neglected houses of the inner-city tell us about their owners and their occupants? Should we conclude that 'good' people live in 'nice' houses? Or ought we to perhaps consider that the important dimensions of the social reality of housing are the dimensions of class, status and power?

As well as being all the things mentioned above, housing is also a *social good*. Above all, it is a fundamental human need. Without adequate shelter the business of human life cannot really be adequately conducted. Clearly, there are massive inequalities in the way housing is socially distributed in Britain. Inequalities of class, race, sex and income are all manifested in housing. Are these inequalities desirable, or ought they to be redressed? There are writers who argue that most inequality is inevitable and ought not to be redressed. Such commentators, particularly Friedman[4] and Hayek,[5] suggest that inequality is a necessary spur to competition and achievement and they see failure to achieve as essentially an individual's personal problem (much as the Poor Law commissioners did in the early nineteenth century). These writers might argue that if some people are badly housed, then this is largely their own fault, and that were they more thrifty, or had they worked harder, they too could enjoy the better housing experienced by others. Other writers see inequality as reflecting the social and economic structure of our society, of industrial capitalist society as a whole and the power relationships within it. Many argue, as Tawney did in 1931, that inequality is costly and wasteful of both financial and human resources.[6] To illustrate Tawney's point, consider how the stress of bad housing and of homelessness so often leads to sickness and to family break-up, with costly consequences both for the people involved and for the wider society.

If we agree with Tawney that inequality is wasteful, it follows that inequality ought to be redressed, if only on the grounds of saving waste. But is inequality redressed by the establishment of greater equality? It is possible to suggest that what should be considered are questions of greater *equity* of distribution rather than equality as such. Equality means 'equal shares' – if three people have a cake a policy of equality would ensure that each got one-third. Equity means 'fair' shares. Thus if two of the cake-owners have had tea but the third has arrived late and also missed lunch then it is equitable that this person should receive a larger piece of the cake than the other two. Inevitably, discussions of equity within a society go very much further than arguments about the wastefulness of inequality. To talk about equity and fairness is also to talk about justice.

SOCIAL JUSTICE

It was Kant who, in the eighteenth century, first developed the concept of 'justice as fairness' which was to develop in turn into theories of *social* justice, which are today increasingly being used in the evaluation of social policy. The major contemporary theorist is John Rawles, whose massive work took over twelve years to complete.[7] Rawles built a theoretical model of justice as fairness based upon the social contract theories of Locke[8] and Rousseau.[9] These attempted to determine how a group of rational human beings in a state of nature (i.e. with no political knowledge or experience) would agree as to the best way to conduct the affairs of society. Runciman, applying Rawles's theories to the study of relative deprivation, elaborated this to suggest that a socially just society would not necessarily be an equal one, but that 'Three specific principles would be agreed in advance to be capable of justifying such inequalities as might occur – need, merit and the contribution to the common good.'[10] These remaining inequalities, Runciman suggested, would be inequalities of status 'in the sense that Picasso has higher status as a painter than does an ungifted amateur, not the sense in which a duke has higher status than a labourer.'[10] David Harvey, however, referred back to Rawles's essentially utilitarian position by commenting that 'The concept of social justice is not an all-inclusive one in which we encapsulate our vision of the good society. It is rather more limited. Justice is essentially to be thought of as a principle (or set of principles) resolving conflicting claims.'[3] David Miller went further than this by suggesting that there were three fundamental interpretations of social justice, in which no one interpretation could be assimilated into either of the others, but which were, in fact, in conflict with one another. He argued that there was a relationship between different conceptions of social justice and different conceptual models of society. That conceptions of social justice had an ideological background.[11]

Miller defined his three concepts of social justice as:

(a) *Justice as the protection of rights*, which he referred to as 'conservative justice' since its purpose was to preserve the established order from disruption by preserving the established distribution of rights and goods. This concept he matched with the conceptual model of society as a 'hierarchical order', where emphasis was laid upon people keeping to the station in life to which they were born.

(b) *Justice as distribution according to desert* conflicted with the previous concept since rights depend upon convention, and deserts upon an individual's actions and qualities. Miller pointed out that desert could be interpreted a number of ways, but in each case a personal feature which is generally held in high regard forms the basis – features such as effort, moral virtue, achievement and so on. This interpretation of justice was supported by a model of society as a competitive market, where individuals through their efforts acquire unequal amounts of wealth 'and thereby win esteem'. 'Such social organisations as there are come into existence through the voluntary act of association between free individuals, and they are consciously designed to serve individual ends.'[11]

(c) *Justice as distribution according to need* Miller saw as conflicting with both the previous concepts. 'A person may have an acknowledged right to something which he does not need; while a hungry man who steals a loaf needs what he has no right to. Again, we should not expect the most deserving man (for instance the man who contributes most to some common project) also to be the man with the greatest needs. At best it would be a happy accident if desert and deed coincided.'[11] 'Need' implies a deficiency of some kind, the lack of which is harmful, thus it cannot be said to be the same thing as 'want'. Distribution according to need implies a degree of collective and altruistic behaviour within a society, and thus Miller suggested that the concept corresponded most closely to a model of society as 'solidaristic community'.

This linking of concepts of social justice with conceptual models of society serves both to widen our understanding and to pose further questions. If the concept of social justice itself has an ideological background, as Miller suggests, then there is the distinct possibility of injustices arising if resources are distributed on the basis of any one of the three interpretations he gives. Can these injustices, these inequalities, be justified? Runciman claimed that in particular cases inequalities of status were justifiable, but would this claim adequately justify inequalities in, for example, housing distribution?

HOUSING AND SOCIAL JUSTICE

It is possible to suggest that housing resources in Britain today are distributed mainly on the basis of one of the interpretations above, or rather that housing policy in the main is underpinned by a particular set of ideologies. At first glance it may appear that all three conceptions of social justice can be applied in turn to discrete sectors of the housing market – in the private rented sector the property *rights* of landlords and the tenure *rights* of tenants are safeguarded (more or less); owner-occupation being income linked is distributed on the basis of *desert*, with those having highest income or wealth being most deserving and advantaged; council housing, on the other hand, has been allocated for the last thirty years on the basis of *need* (although there may appear to be very little 'solidaristic community' operative within the allocation process). In fact, as we have seen, such discrete categorisations cannot be applied due to the overlap and interaction of policies for the housing sectors. In the light of Miller's intepretations of the theory of social justice, however, let us examine one particular recent set of policy proposals – the sale of council housing – which many claimed to be a socially just measure.

Councils had had the powers to sell their council housing for owner-occupation if they so wished under a 'general consent' given them by the Conservative government during the 1950s. Sales, however, had never been on any significant scale. Even at the time of the Housing Finance Act 1972, when political debate on housing was reaching heights of controversy and the number of council houses being sold off reached its highest point, sales amounted only to 1 per cent of the total stock of council housing. By 1978, over the twenty-five years since the consent had been given, the number of houses sold per year rarely reached ten thousand dwellings, and exceeded that number on only six occasions.

In 1979 the Conservative government proposed to make the power to sell council housing for owner-occupation a statutory duty of local authorities. All council tenants were to be given the right to buy their homes at substantial discount prices, up to 50 per cent depending on length of residence. There was talk of allowing elderly tenants to 'buy' their homes for nothing. Local authorities were to arrange mortgages for tenants wishing to buy, and put their remaining property on the market as it became vacant. Empty council dwellings were to be offered at full market rates.

The proposals had formed part of the Conservative election manifesto, and the size of the Conservative majority in the House of

Commons suggested a degree of support for the sales policy among the electorate. The intended consequence was to be a massive transfer of dwellings across the housing sector, to allow a far greater number of people to benefit from what was clearly the most financially advantageous and morally desirable form of housing tenure. Thus it appeared that the proposals were clearly 'socially just' since they would involve redistribution of wealth on an unprecedented scale. The Secretary of State – Michael Heseltine – argued that the proposals offered 'a chance for council tenants to take their place in the sun'. What council housing remained was to have a strictly 'welfare' function for the disadvantaged few unable to join the property-owning democracy. The proposals to sell formed part of a package of housing proposals that appeared to aim for measures of social justice across the housing sectors. Those council tenants that remained were to have enhanced freedom of choice and opportunity. A 'Tenants' Charter' detailed a list of rights for council tenants – for example the right to undertake their own repairs and redecoration, to take in lodgers and to have a say in estate management. In the private sector the new 'shortholding' proposal was presented as offering a just adjudication between the conflicting claims of landlord and tenant.

Much of the Tenants' Charter proposals had, in fact, formed part of the Housing Bill that the previous, Labour government had been intending to introduce. Apart from those the package of housing proposals in party political terms was red hot. For all the tacit commitment of recent Labour governments to owner-occupation, council housing still formed a major part of Labour policy, and municipalisation had remained a very important part of the housing strategies of Labour local authorities. Indeed, many such had stepped up their activity as part of their response to the Inner Cities White Paper. Since one of the first actions upon taking office of the new administration had been to stop all further acquisitions by local authorities (whereby private-sector housing with tenants was acquired by agreement) and to introduce further cuts in public spending with the threat of withdrawal of rate-support grant, these authorities tended to view the proposals as a direct attack upon their autonomy, as well as upon their politics.

There were commentators outside the Conservative party who favoured the idea of council house sales in some form. Frank Field, while Director of Child Poverty Action Group (he was later Labour MP for Birkenhead), had argued that selling would give power, in terms of capital assets, to a wide range of people who were currently powerless, as well as encouraging a more flexible approach to administration among local authorities. David Donnison also advocated greater flexibility and responsiveness to demand by housing authorities. He commented:

The sale of council houses should be considered on its merits without prior commitments for or against the idea. There will always be some areas of scarcity where the council will always need publicly-owned subsidised housing. There, council housing should not be sold. But elsewhere sales may help to keep the whole stock of council property in houseproud use and retain people – particularly the children of present tenants – in neighbourhoods which they otherwise might desert altogether.[12]

On the other hand there were commentators within the Conservative party who if not exactly opposed to the idea of council house sales at least had some reservations. Local authorities in areas with ageing local populations and a high proportion of holiday lets and second homes expressed anxieties that in the longer term what had been council housing would become lost to the local-housing stock.

To evaluate whether or not the council house sales policy could be called 'socially just', as its protagonists claimed, it is necessary to consider both the benefits and the costs. Inevitably one person's welfare is another's diswelfare, and 'justice as fairness' should perhaps aim to achieve equity between the two. It is not enough to claim that 'a great many' or 'a majority' will benefit, since it is the nature and extent of benefit and disbenefit that is important. A policy that brings immense benefit to a few, while bringing little or no disbenefit to the many, may perhaps be a fairer policy than one which immensely benefits the many while massively disbenefiting a few. More important, perhaps, is the question 'who benefits' and at what social and economic cost to whom?

WHO WOULD BUY?

Initially it seemed that the majority of dwellings sold were those already empty and being offered by councils on the open market. Council tenants themselves appeared to move more slowly.

Just how many were unwilling to take on the financial commitment of a mortgage at a time when unemployment was rising and financial uncertainty increasing is hard to calculate. But, as in the days of the philanthropic housing associations, continued secure earnings did seem to be a prerequisite for taking on such a debt. Should a council tenant become unemployed and be forced to apply for social security, the amount received would include the rent.

Social security did not allow for mortgage payments, however, although interest could be met as a temporary measure. Just how many were waiting to see the outcome of the political confrontation is also impossible to guess.

In city areas, where scarcity had pushed up land prices and thus the cost of all types of housing, the price of house purchase, even at 50 per cent discount, was beyond the reach of even many quite high-income workers. This was particularly true of new property. The rents of council housing are 'pooled' – the high costs of new building are added to the historic costs of earlier, therefore cheaper, buildings and the rent averaged out between them. Mortgages, on the other hand, were calculated at current market value, and any discount would be based on this. Council rents varied widely, some were low, some relatively high, all were inclusive of rates, and were subject to rebate – which, of course, mortgages were not. Already in 1979 as the recession deepened many existing owner-occupants were unable to keep up with their rising mortgages. The government's exhortation to sell below construction cost did not also mean that local authorities could sell too far below the market price.

It appeared that in any case at least half of all council tenants were in no position to buy. Twenty-five per cent of all council tenants, about 1.5 m. people, were on supplementary benefit, and a further 12 per cent of all council tenants were already receiving rent rebates. In addition 15 per cent could be found among the unemployed, low-income families and single-parent families not on supplementary benefit. Suggestions by government ministers that disadvantaged tenants be encouraged to buy their dwellings on a 'room by room' basis was met with reserve, even by local authorities in favour of selling, because of the administrative cost implications.

Critics of the policy to sell council houses focused on the financial and social costs to others. Some estate agents began to sound warning notes about the long-term implications for property prices of increased supply. Some building societies warned that interest rates and mortgage costs would be bound to rise. At the other end of the spectrum Shelter argued that the inequalities created and exacerbated by the policy were unjustifiable. If this were so then the policy could not be termed a socially just measure. 'Somebody will have to pay', argued Shelter, and they seemed in no doubt as to who. 'The prospect for the next five years is that the adequately housed will be made better off at the direct expense of the badly housed and homeless.'[13] There were three major areas where the 'costs' of the policy were most likely to be incurred. These were the social-cost areas of housing stress and of divisiveness, and the financial costs of loss of housing stock to the public sector. They need to be examined before any consideration is given as to whether or not they are justifiable.

THE 'COSTS' OF COUNCIL HOUSE SALES

The cost of housing stress

People generally applied for council housing because they were badly housed. Usually they could not find a 'decent' home within their means to rent in the private sector, and their income was too low to allow access to owner-occupation. The strain of bad housing, coping with lack of amenities such as no hot water; sharing a lavatory; the problems of dirt, damp and decay that come with lack of repair; overcrowding; all contribute to place a household 'at risk' of breaking up. The cost of family breakdown is spread between different agencies, but is borne in the end by all of us as tax-payers. It is very expensive to keep a child in care in an ordinary community home let alone a more specialised establishment, and what price do we put on distress and despair? Because of scarcity council housing is rationed through the points system. Already due to rising costs and successive cuts in finance, council building had slowed down, rehabilitation programmes had been curtailed and scarcity had increased. Allowing for variations in policy and geography many councils were only able to rehouse 'decants' from slum-clearance schemes or families whose situation was so desperately bad that they made it to the very top of the points list or got into the social services quota. The amount of time a family in bad housing waited to be rehoused must be included in the cost of housing stress, for the longer they wait the greater the risk of breakdown became. Should a council sell all or most of its housing stock, movement *into* the public sector would virtually cease. Already in 1979 some councils were holding back empty property, waiting to sell rather than reletting.

The costs of replacement and loss

There is still a high level of demand for council housing. Many urban local authorities have waiting lists of ten thousand and over. As this does not include those who have been unable to gain access to the list there is also a high level of 'hidden demand'. It can be argued that if people on the waiting list could afford the market value of an owner-occupied house they would already have bought one. In 1979 the government set an annual target for council house sales of 250,000 dwellings a year, which if achieved would diminish in one operation housing stock which local authorities had built up over the century. This could not be replaced anything like as quickly. Even were finance available, the actual process of building takes time. Local authorities in the 1960s had become the construction companies' biggest clients. By 1978 these companies were already concerned by the collapse of public-sector house-building starts. The sales proposals clearly meant that public-sector building would be further curtailed. The employment repercussions of this were considerable since the private-sector house-building part of the industry was in no position to take up any slack. Major contractors were expressing anxiety in 1979 that scarce mortgage funds would be diverted from private-house building to council mortgages 'to prop up the scheme'.[14]

As well as the overall cost of replacement there was the question of just which properties would most likely be sold and need replacing. Many local authority housing estates had themselves become slums by now. In some cases this was due to the passage of time, but others had major faults of design and construction arising from recent attempts to cut building costs. This was particularly true of much council housing built during the Macmillan drive of the 1950s. In 1979, for example, the repair bill of sixty local authorities for housing built by them during that period came to £200 m. each.[15] The widely differing standards of design and construction had been causing concern long before the 'selling off' of properties had been launched. The Parker Morris Committee[16] had attempted to rectify this by laying down standards for space and equipment in new council building. The cost yardstick, mounting inflation and government cuts in public expenditure, led inevitably to the erosion of these standards by the 1970s. In addition, many councils owned estates of old tenements and dwellings. Some of these were inherited from the philanthropic trusts, others the councils had built themselves earlier in the century when different concepts of 'minimum standards' were operative. All these were now in urgent need of repair, improvement, of money being spent on them. These properties were unlikely to be in much demand by possible purchasers.

Critics of the proposals argued that it was inevitable that the 'better' properties, both old and new, would be the ones that would sell. In rural areas many small pre-war cottage-type estates offered considerable charm at the government's suggested price of about

£5,000. In the urban areas many new council flats were of excellent design and the municipalisation programme had rehabilitated many fine older buildings to a high standard. The consequence of this would be that local authorities would be left with the repair burden of the poorly built estates and the declining old ones: council tenants in these, and in the tower blocks of the 1960s, would be unable to transfer to better or more suitable dwellings as they became vacant. Wilson, calculating the financial implications of council house sales policy in 1977 for the Institute of Cost and Management Accountants, concluded that there would also be considerable long-term cost to the tax-payer due to the effect of inflation and rising costs.[17] Shelter calculations in 1979 came to the same conclusion [doc 30].

The cost of social divisiveness

The physical problems of the older estates had often been worsened by the reluctance of council officers to put those they perceived as 'problem' families into 'good' housing. Thus many estates became dumping grounds for such families and a vicious cycle of deprivation developed. Already, as I have suggested, there was a 'class within a class' division in the development of council housing. By the late twentieth century this division could be said to have manifested itself within the public sector as a polarisation between the 'decent tenants/steady workers' who tended to be allocated the better housing and the 'problem families/rent dodgers' who were put in the 'sink' estates. We have seen in the section on homelessness how attitudes to the homeless played an important part in turning them from 'ordinary decent Londoners' into 'problem families'. Many similar attitudes existed to tenants with rent-arrear cases and it is worth pausing to examine this since attitudes, labels and perception are important parts of the cause and effect of social divisiveness. Of course there were tenants who spurned attempts to intervene by housing managers and social workers and who maintained a feckless and cavalier approach to rent-paying. Recent studies,[18] however, suggest that such tenants are the exceptions and that 'Rent arrears are concerned with poverty, and not seldom maladministration. They are sometimes an unusual form of protest against insufferable living conditions. . . . Arrears are also about emergencies and what happens when there is nothing in the bank to tide the tenants over.'[19] Maladministration, of course, brings us back to the points raised earlier about the rôle and power of the local state and its officers and politicians. The strike in 1974 of the National Association of Local Government Officers, for example, led to the building up of massive arrears when no rents were collected and no benefits paid, also the decision by some councils to end door-to-door rent collecting almost invariably brought an increase in arrears.

The potential polarisation between 'good' and 'bad' council tenants was bound to be increased when the 'good' tenants became owner-occupiers, taking their 'place in the sun'. Some commentators, pointing to the American experience, where welfare housing in the inner-cities often represented the worst slums and ghetto areas, argued that the effect of such social divisiveness might well be a threat to social order, with at the very least an increase in cases of vandalism and crime. Other writers drew attention to the implicit clash of interest between 'housing classes' and thus the intensification of the 'housing class struggle'. The concept of housing class had been developed by Rex and Moore who attempted to define a series of housing class categories competing with each other for scarce resources: 'We follow Max Weber who saw that class struggle was apt to emerge wherever people in a market situation enjoyed differential access to property, and that such class struggles may therefore arise not merely around the use of industrial production but around the control of domestic property.'[20] Later writers, particularly Saunders, pointed out that, in fact, there could only really be two housing class distinctions – owners and renters – since it was only between these two groups that a real clash of interest lay.[21] Others rejected the whole notion of housing class interests, and located the debate about inequality back with the system of economic relations. After all, as Engels had pointed out in 1872, to make the working-class owner-occupiers did not make them capitalists:

Capital is the command over the unpaid labour of others. The little house of the worker can therefore become capital only if he rents it to a third person and appropriates a part of the labour product of this third person in the form of rent. But the house is prevented from becoming capital precisely by the fact that the worker lives in it himself, just as a coat ceases to be capital the moment I buy it from the tailor and put it on.[22]

Nevertheless, there were those who argued that the policy to sell council houses was, in fact, a form of social control, of 'dividing the working-class against itself'. Owner-occupation was thus seen as a form of 'embourgeoisement' whereby those workers able to take advantage of the sales policy would be encouraged to distance themselves from those remaining in council renting. For, as Engels had also said, 'The worker who owns a little house to the value of a thousand talers is, true enough, no longer a proletarian. . . .'[22] A full implementation of the sales policy would have ensured that what council housing remained would serve a purely residual 'welfare' function, thus further underlining the distinction between the deserving and the undeserving.

If, in fact, the overall consequences of the change in policy did not result in as great a switch of tenures as the government had envisaged, it would, nonetheless, widen the already considerable housing inequalities. Those people who were in bad housing in the private rented sector became even less able to find a better alternative. People in bad housing in the public sector could no longer hope for transfer to something better. In both town and country the main effect was to exacerbate the existing housing shortage. Many previous council tenants did benefit from the policy and buy their own homes. But the cost of these benefits appeared to be mainly borne by people who were already disadvantaged. People who through age or low-earning capacity; through having a large family or being a single parent; through illness, disability or unemployment were unable to 'take their place in the sun'.

These clashes over the policy of council house sales illustrate the conflict between two of the interpretations of social justice – justice as distribution by desert, and justice as distribution by need. Once desert is accepted as the criteria for distribution of housing benefits, then a policy that increases the disbenefits for those perceived as undeserving is socially just and consequent inequalities justifiable. That this interpretation is ideologically based seems obvious – as do the bases of the other interpretations developed by Miller. Those people who interpret social justice as distribution by desert do also appear to construct and operate on the basis of a conceptual model of a competitive market society, where the emphasis is upon individualism. There are very many people who justify housing inequalities in terms of individual failings – as has been shown in the sections above, particularly that on homelessness – and who see the broader issues of poverty and inequality in the same terms. It should not automatically be assumed, however, that this perception of poverty and this interpretation of social justice simply correlates with one broad set of economic relationships. A study of the perception of poverty in Europe, undertaken in 1977 for the European Economic Commission, suggests that there may be other dimensions such as national characteristics to take into account. From the sample studied there, the three most common causes of poverty were felt to be 'deprived childhood', 'lack of education' and 'sickness or ill health'. Alone out of the nine countries, Britain gave 'laziness' as the primary cause. The EEC researchers also attempted a typological analysis, grouping the perceptions of poverty into types ranging from 'cynics' to those they termed the 'militants for justice'. The militants for justice, who 'blamed society for these situations in which they consider the poor are inescapably trapped', were largely represented in France and Italy. The cynics on the other hand 'are the hard core of social egoism and conservatism of the most reactionary type. . . . This type is particularly common in the United Kingdom, which seems to suggest that it is tied up with a set of beliefs whereby the poor are primarily responsible for their social disgrace.'[23]

Sadly, it seems that the set of beliefs that so characterised the Poor Law, beliefs which time and time again have proved wasteful, inefficient, uneconomic and just plain wrong, still appear to characterise the perception of poverty in Britain today. We would seem to have a long way to go before social justice is determined upon Runciman's criteria of 'need, merit and contribution to the common good'.

At the end of their Report in 1965, the Milner Holland Committee concluded, 'Housing has for too long been the sport of political prejudice. The need now is for a common approach to the problem and for an understanding of the whole housing situation, purged of irrelevant prejudices against landlords, tenants, or any other group of the population. . . .'[24] That their plea mainly fell on deaf ears is hardly surprising. To try to separate housing, or any other field of social policy, from the beliefs and values that underly its formation and implementation is to forget that policy is the means to achieve specific ideological ends.

Any study of the rôle of policy in the housing market must inevitably raise more questions than it answers, including important questions about the nature of our society. Today, after more than a century of state intervention in the housing market, a great many of our fellow citizens live in unsatisfactory housing conditions, or have no home at all. Is this 'just'? Berry has called housing policy 'the great British failure' in that it has so often increased rather than diminished housing inequalities. However, this becomes understandable when we consider how policy has been constructed over the years. Richard Titmuss suggested that the way in which a society constructed its welfare systems had an important impact on its overall 'moral climate'. Thus welfare systems that were constructed upon the basis of individualism helped develop a moral climate where egoism and intolerance dominated; whereas where welfare systems were constructed upon a universalist basis (with free access to all citizens outside the working of the market mechanism) a moral climate of tolerance, compassion and altruism could grow. Titmuss argued that social policy should be more than simply ameliorative, it should be a powerful instrument for achieving social justice with need as the only criterion.[25] Yet 'need' itself is open to subjective interpretation, and perhaps we should look beyond the need itself to its causes. 'Hunger is hunger. But the hunger that is satisfied with cooked meat and fork is another hunger than that which swallows raw meat with the aid of hands, nails and teeth. The mode of production produces both objectively and subjectively, not only the object consumed, but also the manner of consumption.'[26] Thus it can be said that while there will always be unequal distribution of mental and physical attributes among people, other forms of scarcity and inequality are not inevitable facts of life, but the products of particular social and economic structures.

In 1647, Colonel Rainsborough asserted, 'For truely I believe, that the poorest he that is in England hath a life to live as the greatest he.'[27] Many would assert the same today. Perhaps there needs to be a new interpretation of social justice as a right, based not upon tradition and hierarchy, but upon what Bill Jordan terms a 'true Welfare State',[28] where citizenship, personal liberty and state intervention are held in balance by collective activity. A society that asserted, and believed, that each of its members had a fundamental *right* to a proper home according to *need*, might perhaps so structure itself as to make the achieving of that right a possibility.

REFERENCES

1. DEPT OF ENVIRONMENT, *op. cit.* (see ref. 8, Ch. 2).
2. D. LOWENTHAL and H. PRICE, 'The English landscape', *Geographical Review*, vol. 54 (1964).
3. D. HARVEY, *op. cit.* (see ref. 15, Ch. 3), Edward Arnold, London (1976).
4. M. FRIEDMAN, *Capitalism and Freedom*, University of Chicago Press, Chicago (1962).
5. F. A. HAYEK, *The Constitution of Liberty*, Routledge & Kegan Paul, London (1960).
6. R. TAWNEY, *Equality*, Allen & Unwin, London (1931).
7. J. RAWLES, *A Theory of Justice*, Clarendon Press, Oxford (1972).

8. J. LOCKE, 'Of civil government', in *Two Treatises of Government: a critical edition*, P. LASLETT (ed.), Cambridge University Press, London (1960).

9. J.-J. ROUSSEAU, *The Social Contract and Discourses* (first published 1762; Everyman edn, J. Dent & Sons, London, 1955).

10. W. G. RUNCIMAN, *Relative Deprivation and Social Justice* (first published 1966; paperback edn, Pelican, Harmondsworth, 1976).

11. D. MILLER, 'The ideological backgrounds to conceptions of social justice', *Political Studies*, vol. 22 (1974).

12. D. DONNISON, *op. cit.* (see ref. 18, Ch. 2).

13. SHELTER, 'King Midas out of touch', *Roof*, May (1979).

14. SHELTER, *The Facts on Council House Sales* (1979).

15. J. DARWIN, 'Build cheap now – pay more later', *Roof*, May (1979).

16. CENTRAL HOUSING ADVISORY COMMITTEE, *op. cit.* (see ref. 9, Ch. 2).

17. J. P. WILSON, *Accounting for the Sale of Council Houses*, Institute of Cost and Management Accountants (1977).

18. L. ALPREN, *The Causes of Serious Rent Arrears*, Housing Centre Trust, London (1977).

19. A. HARVEY, *Remedies for Rent Arrears: a study of the London Borough of Camden*, Shelter (1979).

20. J. REX and P. MOORE *et al.*, *op. cit.* (see ref. 32, Ch. 9).

21. P. SAUNDERS, *Sociology and Urban Politics*, Hutchinson, London (1979).

22. F. ENGELS, *The Housing Question* (first published 1872–73; reprinted in paperback, Progress Publishers, Moscow, 1975).

23. COMMISSION OF THE EUROPEAN COMMUNITIES, *The Perception of Poverty in Europe: a report on a public opinion survey carried out in the member countries of the European Community as part of the programme of pilot projects to combat poverty* (1977).

24. MINISTRY OF HOUSING AND LOCAL GOVERNMENT, *op. cit.* (see ref. 2, Ch. 4).

25. R. TITMUSS, *The Gift Relationship* (first published 1970; paperback edn, Pelican, Harmondsworth, 1970); see also R. PINKER, 'Social Policy and Social Justice', *Journal of Social Policy*, vol. 3 (1974).

26. K. MARX, quoted in A. SCHMIDT, *The Concept of Nature in Marx*, New Left Books, London (1971).

27. D. M. WOLFE (ed.), *Leveller Manifestos of the Puritan Revolution*, Nelson, London (1944).

28. B JORDAN, *op. cit.* (see ref. 22, Ch. 9).

Part five
DOCUMENTS

Document one
THE AWFUL GROWTH OF TOWNS

Engels came to live in England in 1842, when he was twenty-two years old. He lived and worked as a businessman in Manchester and was well situated to observe and consider the phenomenon of industrialisation. Many other contemporary writers shared his horror and concern, even when they did not necessarily share his analysis of the causes, and there are many similar descriptions, both fact and fiction, to suggest that Engels did not overstate or exaggerate what he saw. One joke of the time was the question, 'What is the quickest way out of Manchester?' The answer was 'Drink'. The American, Henry Coleman, remarked, 'Every day that I live, I thank Heaven that I am not a poor man with a family in England.'

Every great city has one or more slums, where the working-class is crowded together. True, poverty often dwells in hidden alleys close to the palaces of the rich; but, in general, a separate territory has been assigned to it, where, removed from the sight of the happier classes, it may struggle along as it can. These slums are pretty equally arranged in all the great towns of England, the worst houses in the worst quarters of the towns; usually one or two-storied cottages in long rows, perhaps with cellars used as dwellings, almost always irregularly built. These houses of three or four rooms and a kitchen form, throughout England, some parts of London excepted, the general dwellings of the working-class. The streets are generally unpaved, rough, dirty, filled with vegetable and animal refuse, without sewers or gutters, but supplied with foul, stagnant pools instead. Moreover, ventilation is impeded by the bad, confused method of building of the whole quarter, and since many human beings here live crowded into a small space, the atmosphere that prevails in these working-men's quarters may readily be imagined. Further, the streets serve as drying grounds in fine weather; lines are stretched across from house to house, and hung with wet clothing.

From: *The Condition of the Working Class in England*. F. Engels (first published 1845), 1969 edn, p. 60.

Document two
TRAINING THE POOR

Someone once said of Octavia Hill that she was 'as firmly encased in her middle-class values as she was in her corset', and indeed her answers to questions about her housing system do have the ring of utter certainty. She was not unusual in this, of course; self-doubt, or what Beatrice Webb called the 'class consciousness of sin', was still far from general among the superior classes of late Victorian Britain. What the tenants felt about the firm but kindly interest of Miss Hill and her lady visitors has not been recorded.

3258.   Take Edward's-place, the population is of such a kind that you would not care to re-house them? – I should care very much indeed to re-house them.

3259.   You think they are improvable? – I always believe in people being improvable; they will not be improvable without a good deal of moral force, as well as improved dwellings. If you move the people they carry the seeds of evil away with them; they must be somewhere, and they want improved dwellings that they can inhabit, and care taken of them.

3260.   Do you think they would go into any new dwellings if they were offered to them? – I think they would if the dwellings were properly arranged. First of all there must be more of these single rooms than are built, and I think that a good deal should be done by volunteer work in the buildings before you touch the very poor; they have not the courage to face the large cleaner places, unless somebody knows them and introduces them. I do not believe that this difficulty will ever be met, except by a good deal of volunteer work; whether the large societies will enlist volunteers, or whether it will be done by private enterprise, I do not know; but I am certain you can hunt the poor about from place to place, rout them out of one place and drive them to another; but you will never reach the poor except through people who care about them and watch over them.

From: *Report of the Select Committee on Artisans' and Labourers' Dwellings Improvement*, 1882. Minutes of evidence, paras 3258, 3259 and 3260.

Document three
EARLY COUNCIL TENANTS

Occupations of those persons who in March 1912 were tenants of the Council's dwellings

Nature of Occupation	Number	Nature of Occupation	Number
Agent and commercial traveller	202	Carried forward	1,765
Artist and draughtsman	25	Clerk	495
Barman	30	Coachbuilder	30
Basket and brush maker	10	Collector	15
Boilermaker	15	Commissionaire	52
Bookbinder	54	Compositor	124
Bootmaker	101	Cook	80
Boxmaker	34	Costermonger	24
Brass finisher	27	Cutter	25
Bricklayer, mason and plasterer	65	Distemperer and paperhanger	20
Butcher	65	Domestic servant	26
Butler and servant	21	Dressmaker	93
Cabdriver and chauffeur	17	Electrician	76
Cabinet maker	208	Engine and crane driver	43
Carman, carrier and coachman	235	Engineer	115
Carpenter and joiner	151	Engraver	13
Carpet planner	18	Farrier	37
Cellarman	18	Fireman	42
Charwoman and cleaner	272	Fitter and plumber	131
Checker	29	Florist	14
Chemist and analyst	11	Flusher and sewerman	10
Cigar and cigarette maker	128	Foreman	75
Clergyman and churchworker	29	Furrier	11
		Gardener and park keeper	24
		General dealer and hawker	48
		Glazier and glassworker	22
Carried forward	1,765	Carried forward	3,410

Nature of Occupation	Number	Nature of Occupation	Number
Carried forward ..	3,410	Carried forward ..	6,602
Hairdresser	37	Post office and telegraphist	48
Hat and cap maker ..	32	Postman	127
Horsekeeper	38	Railway worker, guard	
Housekeeper	48	and signalman	31
Inspector	47	Salesman	286
Instrument maker ..	52	Sawyer	17
Jeweller	11	Seaman and coastguard ..	145
Journalist	16	Shipwright	19
Labourer	549	Silversmith and goldsmith	31
Lamplighter	17	Soldier	15
Laundry worker	13	Sorter	56
Leather worker	46	Stevedore	38
Lighterman	42	Steward	20
Machinist	71	Stoker	58
Manager and manageress	31	Storekeeper	43
Mechanic	26	Superintendent and	
Messenger	69	caretaker	63
Metal worker	39	Tailor and tailoress ..	205
Milkman and dairyman ..	18	Teacher	43
Miscellaneous	511	Theatre worker	21
Musician and artiste ..	30	Timekeeper	22
Newsagent	18	Tinsmith	22
Nurse	34	Turner	28
Omnibus and motor		Umbrella and stickmaker	12
driver	204	Upholsterer	29
Omnibus and motor		Waiter and valet	125
conductor	111	Waitress	11
Packer	115	Warehouseman	194
Painter and decorator ..	139	Watchmaker	15
Pensioner	73	Watchman	25
Platelayer	20	Waterman and boatman ..	12
Police constable, sergeant,		Wheelwright	16
and detective	349	Wireman and linesman ..	19
Polisher	47	Woodcarver	19
Porter	339		
Carried forward ..	6,602	Total	8,417

From: *Housing of the Working Classes in London: Notes on the action taken between the years 1895 and 1912 for the better housing of the working classes in London with special reference to the action taken by the London County Council between the years 1889 and 1912.* LCC, 1913, Appendix X, p. 158.

Document four
TOWARDS A DEFINITION OF COUNCIL TENANT

Until 1936 the term 'working-classes' had never been defined for housing purposes nor subject to any general judicial interpretation. Now, judicial opinion held that chauffeurs could be members of the working-class but police superintendents could not. This was to be disregarded after the war, when the government sought to allow for local authorities to provide for all social classes. Later still, the concept of 'housing need' in effect broadened the definition yet again.

The expression 'working-class' includes mechanics, artisans, labourers, and others working for wages, hawkers, costermongers, persons not working for wages, but working at some trade or handicraft without employing others, except members of their own family, and persons other than domestic servants whose income in any case does not exceed an average of three pounds a week, and the families of any of such persons who may be residing with them.

From: The Housing Act 1936. 26 Geo 5 and 1 Edw. 8. Schedule 11 – Rehousing by Undertakers of Persons of the Working Classes, section (e).

Document five
DIFFICULTIES OF EARLY BUILDING SOCIETIES

The Royal Commission on the Housing of the Working Classes, instigated by Lord Shaftesbury, numbered the Prince of Wales and Cardinal Manning among its members. Much of the evidence they received testified to the failure of existing legislation to solve the problems of overcrowding, rack renting, and the social dangers inherent in this. Yet their final Report urged more efficient administration rather than any more radical reforms. Mr Eli Sowerbutts, who gave evidence concerning 'his' Building Society, told the Commission that it numbered the Mayor of Manchester, the Medical Officer of Health and many leading citizens among its members. It also housed a 'respectable' class of purchaser.

13,848.   (*Chairman.*) You are an accountant and public auditor for the purposes of the Industrial and Provident Societies' Acts; you live at Manchester, and you are secretary to the Oddfellows Co-operative Building and Investment Company, Limited? – That is so.

13,849.   That company was formed, I believe, in the year 1869 for the purpose of providing healthy and comfortable dwellings either for sale or to let on rent? – That is so.

13,850.   The company has a considerable amount of property in and about Manchester, has it not? – Yes.

13,851.   The reason for promoting the company was, I believe, that the ordinary building societies did not meet the case of the provident working man who desired, and could afford to become, the owner of one house only? – That is so, and that is one reason why the building societies have failed.

13,852.   You think that allowing persons to become middle-men has been a cause of failure? – Not merely that, but they have been playing into the hands of the jerry builders. I suppose you know what a jerry builder is?

13,853.   Yes, perfectly – We call them 'brick-on-edge' men in Lancashire. I heard a Lancashire miner say that when he went to live in one of these houses, and he went to knock a nail up to hang his clock up, he knocked down all the clocks in the row. . . .

13,859. The first blocks of dwellings built by the company comprised 59 houses, did they not? – That is so.

13,860. And those are inhabited by the following purchasing tenants, are they not, namely, about 31 artizans, four widows of artizans, about 20 shopmen, clerks, agents, or travellers, three policemen, and one surgeon? – That is so.

From: Royal Commission on the Housing of the Working Classes. Cd 4402–1, 1884. Vol. II, Minutes of Evidence, paras 13,848–13,853, and 13,859–13,860.

Document six
LABOUR: THE PARTY OF THE HOME OWNER

The Wilson administration re-elected in 1965 had ambitious plans for housing. A target of half a million new houses to be built every year to 1970 – half of which were to be in the public sector, with the other half built for owner-occupation by the private market. A massive building programme was initiated which achieved 400,000 housing completions in 1967–68. But at the same time there was a retreat from the earlier Labour policy of a target of council housing for all.

But once the country has overcome its huge social problem of slumdom and obsolescence, and met the need of the great cities for more houses let at moderate rents, the programme of subsidised council housing should decrease. The expansion of the public programme now proposed is to meet exceptional needs; it is born partly of a short-term necessity, partly of the conditions inherent in modern urban life. The expansion of building for owner-occupation on the other hand is normal; it reflects a long-term social advance which should gradually pervade every region.

From: *The Housing Programme 1965–1970*. Cmnd 2838, 1965, p. 8.

Document seven
CENTRAL GOVERNMENT CONTROL OF HOUSING

The process of allocation and control is described here by Dame Evelyn Sharp, who was Permanent Secretary to the Ministry of Housing and Local Government from 1955–66. A formidable and competent civil servant before whom Ministers quailed, she has been described by Richard Crossman in his *Diaries of a Cabinet Minister*.

The Ministry has always controlled the amount of house-building which local authorities may do – if only because it generally attracts subsidy. Nowadays all capital expenditure by public authorities is programmed by the country's economic managers; and this applies to housing as to other forms of investment. The awkward thing for house-building, which accounts for two-fifths of the value of all new building in Great Britain, is that the 'programme' applies to all housing, whether private or municipal. Public housing can be controlled through the loan sanction machinery; but there is no power to control the number of houses built privately. . . . In 1965 the Government embarked on an attempt, in co-operation with the building societies and builders, to programme private house-building – or at least to achieve reasonably accurate forecasting. But how successful this can be remains to be seen.

It having been settled, usually in the late summer, how many houses public authorities may start in the following year, the Ministry must then break this total down to the individual authorities. This is done in the regional offices, each of which receives an allocation – together with instructions about the priorities to be observed. For example, authorities with a great many slums still to clear, or serious overcrowding to eliminate, must be allowed to build all that they can, any necessary cuts falling on those with only a general need for more houses. After getting from their authorities their idea of the number which they could – and need to – build (usually a much too optimistic or deliberately inflated estimate) the regional officers settle how much they can afford to each authority in the light of their instructions, and notify them of the 'starts' for which they can in principle expect to get loan sanction.

The annual exercise in distributing the local authority share of the new housing programme has never been easy. As already remarked, there are about 1,200 housing authorities in England alone; there have been even more in the not very distant past. It is no use pretending that the Ministry knows all these authorities, and their housing situation, well enough to be able to judge their comparative needs with any sort of precision, whatever the standards by which needs have currently to be judged. The establishment of six regional offices has made things a good deal easier, but it is still a difficult job. Much of it falls on the principal regional officer (in the south-east, where there is no regional office, the appropriate Assistant Secretary at headquarters). Provisional allocations are always followed by a certain amount of complaint, correspondence and discussion, and sometimes by deputations from dissatisfied local authorities to the Minister or a Parliamentary Secretary. On the whole, however, decisions have been accepted philosophically, even at times when the Government have felt it necessary to reduce the level of local authority building.

From: *The Ministry of Housing and Local Government.* E. Sharp, 1969, pp. 78–80.

The Seebohm Committee is perhaps best known for its proposals to integrate the social service function of local authorities into one 'generic' department. However, the Report also contained wide-ranging discussion and evaluation of housing policy in the public sector.

396.   In addition to a broader interpretation of their housing responsibilities we consider housing departments should pay more attention to families in greatest need. Some families are at greater risk than others of becoming homeless or grossly ill-housed; for instance, the very young family, the large family with a low income or the fatherless family. They are not numerous; for example, only 8 per cent of all households in England and Wales contain three or more children and only 2 per cent five or more. About 2 per cent of households comprise fatherless families and many of them, and many large families as well, are already adequately housed. Although the proportion of families who are particularly vulnerable is small the problem is urgent. If it is set aside by local authorities, not only may families be endangered but considerable social costs incurred to the community.

397.   At present there are particular difficulties facing such families in obtaining a council house. Two are especially important. First, they tend to be mobile (or, as with immigrants, they have been mobile) and to gravitate to areas of greatest housing need which are also generally areas with a high demand for labour. As a result they may find it difficult to get on to a housing list, or be given a low priority, because they lack residential qualifications. Second, because they are often poor, they may not be able to afford the rents of the council houses offered them.

398.   We recognise that the Housing Act 1957 requires local authorities to give reasonable preference to large families, among other groups, when allocating houses. Successive Ministers of Housing and Local Government, endorsing recommendations of the Central Housing Advisory Committee, have also urged local authorities to look critically at allocation schemes involving residential qualifications, to introduce rent rebate schemes to assist poorer tenants, and to provide for special groups such as unmarried

mothers. Nevertheless, the problem remains of vulnerable families who have little hope of getting (or, in some cases, keeping) a council house for a long time. The problem is not solved by leaving certain families to fend for themselves, or shuttle between accommodation for homeless families, 'half-way housing', unlicensed caravan sites, unsatisfactory lodgings and the streets.

399. The problem of the family which cannot really afford council housing, or which is not thought fit or qualified to have it must be faced. The present methods of subsidising housing do not necessarily help families to obtain accommodation appropriate to their needs. The distribution of subsidies is inequitable and in large measure accidental, being based on categories of housing rather than need. Within local authorities the adoption of rent rebate arrangements can help if they are framed to give maximum benefit to the poorer tenants; we hope such schemes become more widespread.

From: *Report of the Committee on Local Authority and Allied Personal Social Services*, Cmnd 3703, 1968, paras 396–99.

Document nine
THE GRADING OF HOUSING APPLICANTS

90.   We have found considerable variation not only in the extent to which local authorities 'grade' their tenants, but also in the reasons why grading is thought to be necessary. On a very limited scale the justification for grading is that some tenants will not take care of a new house: at the extreme they may wreck it. It would not be sound policy to allocate a high-standard house to such an 'unsatisfactory tenant'. But such families are very few in number, though they pose problems for the local authority out of all proportion to their numbers. It is a far cry from allocating specially selected houses to unsatisfactory tenants to grading all according to their 'fitness' for particular types of houses. We were struck by the simple fact that the approach of a number of local authorities to this seemed to vary according to the range of house types they had available. A local authority with a small range (e.g. all post-war houses) see no need for careful grading. On the other hand, a local authority with a great range tend to see a necessity for fine grading. . . .

96.   Part of our concern here stems from the feeling that there is a danger that applicants are graded according to an interpretation of their desert. This even extends, on occasion, to a rejection of some from the council house sector. We were surprised to find some housing authorities who took up a moralistic attitude towards applicants: the underlying philosophy seemed to be that council tenancies were to be given only to those who 'deserved' them and that the 'most deserving' should get the best houses. Thus unmarried mothers, cohabitees, 'dirty' families, and 'transients' tended to be grouped together as 'undesirable'. Moral rectitude, social conformity, clean living and a 'clear' rent book on occasion seemed to be essential qualifications for eligibility – at least for new houses. Some attitudes may reflect public opinion – in the same way that they induce policies unfavourable to newcomers (white and non-white), but this is a case where local authorities must lead public opinion.

97.   Whatever justification such attitudes may have had when council housing was on a small scale (which is by no means self-evident), they cannot be upheld in a situation where council housing forms a large and ever-increasing proportion of the available rented accommodation. The simple fact is that it is becoming increasingly difficult for those excluded

from publicly-provided housing (on whatever grounds) to find satisfactory alternatives. Indeed, one feature of current housing policy (which it is not for us to question) is the concentration of effort on clearance and redevelopment. This has the effect of reducing the alternatives for those ineligible for council housing. There is thus a severely practical reason why local housing authorities should be paying particular attention to the needs of those who face acute social problems.

From: *Council Housing: Purposes, Procedures and Priorities*. Ninth Report of the Housing Management Sub-Committee of the Central Housing Advisory Committee (Cullingworth), 1969, Ch. 3, paras 90, 96 and 97.

Document ten
BANKS v. BUILDING SOCIETIES

THE NEED FOR FAIR COMPETITION

The clearing banks welcome the increased competition in financial markets because it fosters efficiency and benefits customers. In order for competition to be effective, however, it is of paramount importance that all institutions compete on fair terms. This principle underlays the reform of the credit control arrangements in 1971, as a result of which all commercial banks were placed on more or less the same footing. But it remains the case that many of the mutual and public sector institutions with which the banks are in competition are endowed with artificial competitive advantages. Examples include the fiscal advantages enjoyed by the building societies, savings banks and national savings in the payment of interest on savings, the totally inadequate capital base on which the Giro is being allowed to expand its range of banking services and the unequal application of monetary and credit controls. The clearing banks strongly believe that these competitive advantages should be terminated. They lead to a misallocation of resources in financial markets and distort the market shares of different types of institution. Any subsidies which the government wishes to provide should relate to particular financial functions, not to particular financial institutions.

The building societies have a less direct but important fiscal advantage in the arrangements whereby the societies are allowed to pay income tax on behalf of their depositors at the agreed 'composite rate'. This acts as an inducement to those paying income tax to place their funds with building societies rather than with banks; the societies benefit from the fact that tax-paying investors are evidently more sensitive to interest differentials than non-taxpayers. Building societies also have the advantage of a special low rate of corporation tax (40 per cent); moreover neither building societies nor savings banks are liable to corporation tax on gains arising on the sale of government securities, provided they have held them for more than twelve months.

From: Evidence by the Committee of the London Clearing Banks to the

Committee to Review the Functioning of Financial Institutions (The Wilson Committee), 1977. Subsequently published as *The London Clearing Banks*, 1978, paras 18.11 and 18.13.

The building societies have come in for criticism over their policy of 'red-lining' certain districts and refusing to lend within them. There are signs of change, but significant inroads are unlikely to be made by the societies into lending in the inner-cities, not least because of the high opportunity costs which may tempt landlords to sell for redevelopment rather than owner-occupation.

'RED-LINING' MOTION WITHDRAWN AT HALIFAX MEETING

Criticisms of societies' lending policies in inner-city areas were made at the Halifax Building Society annual general meeting on 23rd May when supporters of Shelter attempted to move a motion deploring 'red-lining' and expressing concern about the lack of information available on the geographical distribution of mortgages. In the event, the motion was not voted upon. Instead, members voted in favour of an amended resolution proposed by A. J. Thayre, Halifax chief general manager, which stated that the meeting disapproves of unreasonable discrimination in lending on mortgage in inner-city areas but notes with approval the society's lending policy in this respect.

The original motion was moved by Mr Ross Midgley, a Shelter supporter, who told members of the Halifax at the meeting: 'You are being asked to deplore the practice of "red-lining" – refusing a mortgage solely because of the location of a house. This motion does not suggest that the Halifax lend on houses which are due for demolition or are about to collapse. But there are many other houses in perfectly good condition, not threatened by road schemes, or planning blight, which are shunned by building societies for no reason other than location.

PROTECTING INVESTORS' MONEY

'This should be deplored for three reasons – it deprives many families of the chance to own their own homes, it makes a mockery of the Government's plans to revitalise the inner-cities, and it contributes actively to the decline of inner-cities. If this motion is successful it will not force the Halifax to make risky investments. What it will do is show that you, the members, recognise that the society has a responsibility to the community.' The motion was seconded by Mr Jim Wintour, Shelter's housing policy officer.

The society's chairman, Mr Raymond Potter, said the society had a duty to protect investors' money and also to protect borrowers from buying something which they ought not to buy. He said that whether or not Mr Midgley's motion was successful it could not detract from the Board's responsibility to conduct the society's lending policy in a manner which safeguarded the interests of investors and helped to deal with the country's housing problems.

Mr Thayre said he did not think that anyone at the meeting had disapproved of the society's lending policy and he then suggested his amendment, which was carried overwhelmingly by a show of hands.

From: *The Building Societies Gazette*, July 1977, p. 686.

Document twelve
THE RACHMAN AFFAIR: NOT A NEW STORY

Sir, – There is one aspect of the Rachman affair which should be brought out – the fact that the story is not new at all.

I am not shocked by the current 'revelations' of the 'Rachman racket'. I find it shocking that such well-known matters have become hot news and have at long last caused some general concern, only within the context of an exceptional series of hot sensations. Many people who lived in, or who were acquainted with, the North Kensington and Paddington districts knew of such rackets long ago – not only the tenants themselves but the Housing Ministry, local authorities, members of Parliament, the police, journalists, social workers and investigators. Several local councillors, together with local associations, encouraged harassed tenants to bring their cases before rent tribunals. And as the recent revelations have confirmed, the 'racketeers' themselves tend to have an extensive range of acquaintances, from the lower to the upper ranks of the social ladder. For some time there has been outspoken criticism of their practices; there has also been complacency.

Moreover, the general public could not plead ignorance of the situation in these districts. For several months after the Notting Hill riots in September, 1958, and again after the (still unexplained) murder of Kelso Cochrane, a West Indian, in May, 1959, there were extensive reports on the area in the press, on radio, and television. The housing conditions of Notting Hill were under observation; and so the manipulations which Rachman's name now symbolizes were soon discovered – and brought into the open. Readers of *The Times* were certainly informed of the essentials of these matters, especially through two articles by your Special Correspondent in your issues of May 21 and May 29, 1959. Although Rachman's name was then rarely mentioned in print, it was already notorious; and it was known to be only one of several more impersonal, more pervasive elements of a versatile system of profiteering.

There was no lack of condemnation of that system four years ago. It was obvious then that a double method of extortion was used – the exploitation of housing needs in central London, aided by the exploitation, and indeed by the manufacture, of racial tensions. And yet nothing happened. If anyone was censured, it was those who were exploited, not the exploiters. Since then the Commonwealth Immigrants Act has been passed – hardly an obstacle against real estate profiteering. But no significant measures have been taken to stop the spiral of urban land values and rents. Are memories so short? Apparently they are: and it is that which points to the moral of the Rachman story. It is one of many recent examples of delayed reaction, of inertia and apathy, in matters of social policy.

Of course, it may be said better late than never. But I am not quite sure. It is all to the good that Rachman's methods are now scrutinized, provided that attention does not remain focused on one individual, or on the lurid features of rack-renting. Many of these operations are a rather humdrum routine – and no less ugly. They exist, and can exist, irrespective of the presence of coloured or other immigrants; many solid citizens are exposed to them. Nor is the physical brutality – the intimidation of tenants – which occurs in such cases the most deplorable feature. The financial brutality to which all kinds of people in need of housing are subjected is far more widespread in the inner areas of our cities. It is with its eradication that we should be primarily concerned. Yours faithfully,

Ruth Glass, Director of Research, Centre for Urban Studies, University College London.

From: *The Times*, 20 July 1963, p. 9.

Document thirteen
HOW THE FAIR RENT POLICY WAS ARRIVED AT

Wednesday evening was the big evening for our rents policy meeting. I was pretty anxious when I went over to my room in the Ministry after dinner and found some fourteen people there. We were late as usual because we had had to do a division on the Finance Bill. I got them all round a table and we sat down to work, discussing the Rent Bill on the basis of the paper provided by Arnold Goodman and Dennis Lloyd as a result of our meeting on the previous Monday. It was a paper in which the idea of the fair rent was sketched out for the first time. It really was an astonishing meeting because we managed to get something like agreement between these fourteen people, many of them lawyers, all of them knowing a great deal about the subject and with experience ranging from that of Arnold Goodman, a commercial lawyer in Fleet Street, on the one hand and his friend Professor Dennis Lloyd, a pure academic, on the other. Then we had, at the other end of the scale, young Labour lawyers, and one property speculator. And finally our own officials, Waddell and Rogerson, and we had Jim MacColl and Dame Evelyn and myself. We started at 8.15 and at 11.45 we sat back because our job had been done. Of course, it says a great deal for Arnold Goodman's powers of persuasion, but basically it was the idea of the fair rent that he had worked out which made it acceptable to this mixed gathering. I was also relieved to find that on other secondary issues, like the problem of service cottages, furnished lodgings and so on, we were very near the kind of detailed policy agreement that I desired.

I couldn't help feeling proud as I saw us there working together, our ideas men from outside the Ministry and the officials from inside, moulded into a team. And I must confess I couldn't help smugly reflecting on the contrast between what we were doing in the Ministry of Housing and the miserable performance going on at the Ministry of Land and Natural Resources.

From: *The Diaries of a Cabinet Minister*. Richard Crossman, Vol. 1, 1976 edn, pp. 77–78.

Deserted by her husband, and in the middle of divorce proceedings, after various attempts to find accommodation, Mary Cecil and her three children were admitted to homeless family accommodation in Newington Lodge, London.

It is not only the workhouse buildings and stark interiors that draw one back into Dickens, but the faces of both warders and inmates. Behind the great iron gate is a little office where on entering one is interrogated. I delivered my set of facts mechanically, having related them so many times to officials and friends and accommodation agencies. Harrowing though it was to me and my children, I now knew it meant nothing to anyone else. Between appointments we had tramped the streets, two in the pram and one dragging behind, but where furnished rooms are concerned, the No Coloured bar is equalled by the No Children one. We had been occupying an exquisite drawing-room for ten days, and its owners could stand the sacrilege no longer. . . .

My story having been taken down laboriously, we were directed to what are called the family quarters, though no husbands are allowed there. A nurse issued us with a knife, fork, spoon and teaspoon apiece, and the warning: 'If you lose 'em you don't get no more.'

By the end of our week we were managing with one fork and two teaspoons between us, though how and when the rest were nicked I have no idea.

Then we were taken to a cubicle – you couldn't call it a room – connected by an opening to a similar space occupied by another family. Apart from two narrow beds and my own cot, the only article of furniture was a battered chest-of-drawers. The inch-deep mattresses and the pillows might have been filled with sand. Boarding school and hospital beds are Dunlopillo by comparison. My seven-year-old girl lay sobbing, the four-year-old boy lay sucking his thumb. His eyes seldom left my face these days. A nurse looked in to tell the girl off for making a noise, so I read them a Beatrix Potter and heard their prayers. In the morning I would hear their nightmares.

There is no ruder awakening than one's first morning here. A bell clangs, nurses bang on doors and shout, and from a low rumbling and whining there mounts a steady crescendo of sub-human sounds reaching deafening proportions in the dining hall. The mingled smells of food and bodies is loud, too. The children again wept and recoiled from the sheer impact of it all. They would not sit at a table but queued with me, the boy removing his thumb to say quietly 'I am going everywhere you go,' which had been almost his sole utterance for weeks.

We took grey porridge and greasy kippers to a table, but were not hungry. I hesitate to condemn the food, since it may well have been the conditions under which it was eaten that made it so revolting. There was certainly plenty of it, and plenty left on plates which we carried to the sinks in which we washed ourselves, the debris first being slung into great bins in the same room. After two or more meals they were brimming with an indescribable glutinous mess. We rinsed dishes and our precious cutlery in running hot water without soap powder. A lot of food was slopped on the way down the stone passage, on either side of which were the sleeping quarters. Volunteers swept up, but even cleaning operations here induced nausea, whether caused by the dirty brooms, the type of filth they were sweeping, the straggle-haired women behind them or simply the bare, battered, bleak background.

After breakfast we cowered in our cubicle until a nurse put her head in and said sharply: 'Get this room cleaned. Clear all that stuff off of the dressing-table and window-sill.'

The children were making brave attempts at home-making by arranging their empty packets and cotton reels along ledges.

'What's that cup doing in here?'

I explained I must drink water, for the baby's feeds.

'I'll have to ask Matron about that. Now look lively. Once your room's tidy you have to stay out of it during the day. Everything must be in the drawers or in cases under the beds.'

There was neither playroom nor playground for the swarms of children, and it was not safe to put a baby outside in its pram in case its eyes were attacked by an older child. The small common room at the end of the corridor was therefore crammed with seedy prams and push-chairs, as well as women and children. This room was as desolate as everywhere else; some broken and bashed-about chairs, a rickety table, no radio, telly or tinny piano, not even a proper window. It was like a communal cell, a painting by Hogarth . . .

From: *New Statesman*, 12 January 1962, pp. 38–39.

Document fifteen
LIFE IN BED-AND-BREAKFAST

Life in such places was awful. Often a whole family would live in one room, with nowhere to cook – meals had to be bought in a local café. Facilities for washing clothes would often be non-existent. In many places families were required to leave the guest house after breakfast and walk the streets all day, until they were allowed back in the evening. Families with babies would often have to smuggle in electric kettles or small stoves in order to be able to heat up bottles. As one family told me: 'We do our ironing on a tiny coffee table or on the floor. The only meal you get here is breakfast and you can't cook so we either live on sandwiches or fish and chips. The kids have to sit on the beds and eat their chips: we haven't had a Sunday dinner for nearly a year.' In short, life in bed-and-breakfast is no 'holiday on the rates' – rather it makes normal family life impossible.

From: *The Homeless and the Empty Houses*. R. Bailey, 1977, p. 23.

Document sixteen
SINGLE PEOPLE NEED HOMES TOO

In 1972 the Office of Population Census and Surveys undertook an examination of Hostels and Lodgings for Single People (Peter Wingfield Digby, 1976, HMSO). Here the findings are being evaluated by CHAR, who comment: 'It is a clear indictment of housing policy that so many thousands of people have to rely on sub-standard overnight accommodation as a substitute for a permanent home which most people take for granted.'

RESIDENTS' PREFERENCES
One of the ways in which the 1972 survey improved on the 1965 National Assistance Board survey was that it investigated the attitudes of the residents to the accommodation surveyed. They were asked if they liked living in the hostel or whether they would like an alternative:

Owner	*% of residents wanting an alternative*
Local Authority	61%
Salvation Army	50%
Church Army	40%
Voluntary bodies	35%
Private commercial	44%
Commercial organisations	60%

In other words, half the residents interviewed would have preferred to live somewhere else and of these, 50 per cent stated a preference for a flat, a room or a bedsitter. Voluntary organisations appear to be the least disliked – while Local Authority and Salvation Army and commercial hostels would seem to run the most unpopular establishments. This unpopularity of hostels and a wish for greater privacy and independence has been borne out by other enquiries. The DOE's own study of the housing needs of single people in 1971 reported that the overriding need was for privacy and independence in a place of their own – 'A self-contained one- or two-roomed flat with a kitchen and bathroom would have satisfied the great majority of them.' In 1974, After Six Accommodation Advisory Service for single people asked their clients whether a hostel would be acceptable. In a period of a month 60 callers said a hostel would be acceptable while 125 said it would not. Half the callers who said a hostel would be acceptable were homeless at the time. It is extremely doubtful if lodging houses were ever built with the preferences of residents in mind, but certainly the great majority of those who are resident now are not living in the place of their choice. One man summed it up:

Just think of living in your own room with your own key, hot water and even your own cooker. With no bully boy of a porter to tell you when you may go up to bed in a domitory which you share with 80 other men. Just think of being able to leave your gear safe, knowing it will be there when you return. Of being able to go away for a night or two without fearing that your bed will have been sold to someone else in your absence.

The way in which institutional living in demeaning surroundings affects a man's view of himself and his ability to determine his own life is reflected in the following recollection by a former hostel resident:

When I first managed to afford a night in Rowton House after a month in the Sally, the thing I really enjoyed was having my own room and being able to get up out of bed and switch the light off myself.

Lodging houses like those described above are often more than a temporary refuge. The 1972 survey showed a third of residents had been living in the same establishment for at least two years. This increases to as many as 60 per cent of residents over the age of 65. In 1974 a resident at Carrington House, a lodging house in Lewisham, died at the age of 90. He had lived there continuously since 1904. Three hundred of the 734 men at Carrington House are pensioners. The DHSS 1972 survey shows that one in five hostel users is an old-age pensioner.

From: *Standards of Accommodation for Single People*. D. Ormany and A. Davies (CHAR & PHAS), 1977, p. 3.

PRIORITY NEED

The *Code of Guidance* issued to local authorities to help them interpret the Housing (Homeless Persons) Act 1977 outlined four main categories of people who should have priority for accommodation:

(*a*)   A person has priority need if he has one or more dependent children living with him or who might reasonably be expected to live with him. The Act contains no definition of dependent children. The Secretaries of State consider that authorities should treat as such all those under the age of 16, and others under the age of 19 who are either receiving full-time education or training or are otherwise unable to support themselves. Dependants need not necessarily be the children of the applicant, but they may be related to the applicant in some other way (e.g. his grandchildren) or they may be adopted or foster-children. Child custody orders should not be required. One-parent families, including battered women with their children, are included. Children need not actually be living with the applicant at the time. They may, for example, be staying temporarily with other relatives. Where, however, children are in care (but see paragraph 4.2 below) the Secretaries of State consider they should be included only where it is reasonable that they live with the applicant. The advice of social services authorities will be important in any cases of this kind.

(*b*)   A person has priority need if he became homeless or threatened with homelessness as a result of an emergency such as fire, flood, or other disaster. In some cases, such as larger scale emergencies, the obligations of housing authorities under the Act may be discharged by action under section 138 of the Local Government Act 1972 such as the provision of special forms of temporary accommodation (church halls, schools, etc).

(*c*)   A person has priority need if he is, or if his household includes one or more members who are, vulnerable for one of the following reasons:

  i.   Old age. Authorities should treat as vulnerable those above normal retirement age (65 for a man, 60 for a woman) and any others approaching normal retirement age who are particularly frail or in poor health or vulnerable for any other reason.

ii. Mental illness or handicap or physical disability. This includes those who are blind, deaf, dumb or otherwise substantially disabled mentally or physically. Authorities are asked to take a wide and flexible view of what constitutes substantial disability, recognising that this will depend on individual circumstances. The help of the area health authority and the social services authority will be appropriate in assessing a number of these cases.

iii. Any other special reason. Authorities should have particular regard to those who are vulnerable but do not come within either of the above categories. In particular, the Secretaries of State consider that it would be appropriate under this heading for authorities to secure whenever possible that accommodation is available for battered women without children who are at risk of violent pursuit or, if they return home, at risk of further violence; and for homeless young people who are at risk of sexual and financial exploitation (the problems to which such people may be exposed were indicated in the report, published in July 1976, of the Working Group on Homeless Young People, which is available on request from the Department of Health and Social Security).

(d) Pregnant women, together with anyone who lives, or might reasonably be expected to live, with them; this includes all pregnant women irrespective of the length of time they have been pregnant.

From: Housing (Homeless Persons) Act 1977: *Code of Guidance (England & Wales)*. DOE/DHSS/Welsh Office, 1978 edn.

RURAL DECAY

The crude population increases in rural areas over the past decade are no guide for prediction. The loss of facilities have a vital bearing on the quality and type of village life.

Growing villages	Facilities or services lost	Facilities or services gained	Pop. Growth (1961–71)		Pop. Size (1971)
			%	No.	
Trunch	1 of 2 foodshops 1 of 2 pubs	None	71.2	242	582
Stalham	1 of 2 doctors	2 foodshops, child health clinic	40.6	483	1,673
Trimingham	None	Surgery	34.6	80	311
Ludham	None	Child health clinic	28.9	256	1,142
Horning	1 of 4 pubs	1 foodshop	28.0	213	975
Catfield	3 of 6 foodshops both doctors' surgeries	None	25.9	169	822
Sutton	Both pubs	Child health clinic	25.1	113	564
Felmingham	The only pub	None	23.4	94	496
Antingham	None	None	18.0	43	282
Sloley	None	None	16.9	33	228
Lessingham	2 of 4 foodshops	None	14.2	34	254
Suffield	None	None	12.7	18	160
Tunstead	1 of 2 foodshops	None	12.1	65	601
Neatishead	2 of 5 foodshops	None	11.3	53	523
Ashmanhaugh	None	None	11.3	17	168

'Changes in Facilities in Growing Villages (1961–71), North Walsham Area.' From: 'The Social Implications of Village Development'. J. M. Shaw in N. Moseley (ed), *Social Issues in Rural Norfolk*, 1978, pp. 77–102.

THE NATIVES ARE RESTLESS

At their October meeting the way in which old Cornish fishing villages are being bought up by non-Cornish and used as holiday cottages, thus meaning that they remain empty through the winter, was deplored. At one nearby village it was stated that during the winter months the place is practically empty, the Cornish having to live in council houses at the top of the hill. If something were not done it seems likely that the coastal areas will become non-Cornish areas with the Cornish people limited to interior, engaged in menial tasks in industry, the towns, the tourist trade – a situation like that in Ireland arising where Bernadette Devlin said the Irish are becoming the 'chambermaids' of the English. At their November meeting the way in which big landlords, the National Trust, the landed gentry, paid little heed to the needs of rural communities, amalgamated holdings, allowed farmhouses to fall into ruin, allowed rapacious farming to be practised was condemned. On account of this policy numerous young Cornish farmers were unable to get started in their careers and the life of rural communities being irreparably harmed.

From: *Cornish Nation* (newspaper of the Cornish National Party), December, 1970, p. 10.

Document twenty
INDUSTRIAL DECLINE IN THE INNER-CITY

By 1971 the industrial and commercial scene had changed radically compared with fifty years earlier. The city centre was still thriving. Much of it had been rebuilt since the war. Lord Street, the main shopping centre, had been rebuilt after the blitz. A new covered shopping centre, the St John's Precinct, had replaced earlier shops and the market. New offices were being built to the north, at Old Hall Street. A scattering of new hotels had opened. Only Dale Street and Castle Street with the municipal buildings and town hall remained substantially unchanged. And east of the city centre, even more new construction was to be found in the growing complex of university and hospitals.

In contrast, the docks, railways and industries were in decline, much of their employment lost. Now, for several miles north and south of the city centre, the docks lie idle. What is left of the trade has been rationalised into the Seaforth complex, north of Bootle. The collapse of the docks has hit nearby industry hard. The north end is crumbling and polluted but tobacco warehousing, sugar refining, brewing and food processing struggle on. But it is a precarious survival. Tate and Lyle, whose vast bulk overshadows all and in which several thousand workers are employed, has been threatening to pull out for years.

The industrial scene in the south end is, if anything, still more depressing. Acres of docks lie unused, save for a little storage and packaging. The impact of abandoned docks, empty warehouses, crumbling factories and mills and acres of derelict land add up to a form of environmental anarchy. The firms that survive and the new ones that spring up, often only for months, use the buildings and their surroundings virtually as they please. But for those who live in the nearby tenements, such dereliction can only remind them that their jobs have been taken away.

The most obvious impact of industrial decline in the study area itself is in the railways. Edge Hill station was the terminus for the first railway passenger line in the world. Opened in 1830, on the inauguration of the Liverpool to Manchester railway, all trains into Liverpool finished their journey here until the tunnel to Lime Street station was built.

From: *Change and Decay: Final Report of the Liverpool Inner Area Study*, DOE, 1977, p. 42.

SUBURBIA – TWO CONTRASTING VIEWS

The Association of Municipal Corporations are quite right in condemning the haphazard manner in which new districts around London are being developed. New suburbs are being created without method or plan, and, for the most part, without the redeeming touch of the architect's hand. Country lanes, open fields, private parks, pleasure grounds, and gardens are giving place to dreary and fearsome streets. Hedges, trees, and shrubs are ruthlessly destroyed simply with the object of crowding the maximum number of houses on the minimum area of land. To the average speculative builder, trees that have taken centuries to reach perfection are of no account, and are cut down whether they are in the way or not of his barrack-like houses. All around London, and even in semi-rural districts where land is cheap, the builder insists on running up long rows of structures, consisting simply of two rectilinear walls covered with a roof and divided at regular intervals into compartments, which are supposed to be, or at any rate are termed, houses. In some places, it is true, we find semi-detached and detached villas bearing evident traces of architectural design, but these are mere oases in the rapidly-growing desert.

From: *The Builder*, 4 May 1907, p. 528.

. . . Smoothly from HARROW, passing PRESTON ROAD,
   They saw the last green fields and misty sky,
At NEASDEN watched a workmen's train unload,
   And, with the morning villas sliding by,
They felt so sure on their electric trip
That Youth and Progress were in partnership.

And all that day in murky London Wall
   The thought of RUISLIP kept him warm inside;
At FARRINGDON that lunch hour at a stall
   He bought a dozen plants of London Pride;
While she, in arc-lit Oxford Street adrift,
Soared through the sales by safe hydraulic lift.

Early Electric! Maybe even here
   They met that evening at six-fifteen
Beneath the hearts of this electrolier
   And caught the first non-stop to WILLESDEN GREEN,
Then out and on, through rural RAYNER'S LANE
To autumn-scented Middlesex again.

From: *The Metropolitan Railway*, John Betjeman, *Collected Poems*, 1977 edn, pp. 212–13.

THE GARDEN CITY IDEA

Ebenezer Howard argued that it was the decaying environment of cities that caused social problems, and that the solution was to build new cities on carefully planned lines. When published in 1902, his *Garden Cities of Tomorrow* was initially rather poorly received. *The Builder* commented, 'This is a very utopian publication, which is based upon the theory that an attempt should be made to unite, for the purposes of habitation, town and country. It is so fanciful, and the projects suggested so impossible of realisation, that it does not appear desirable to comment upon it at length' (9 Aug. 1902, p. 129). The idea gained ground, however, and two Garden Cities – Letchworth and Welwyn – were built, although they departed from Howard's brief in many ways. His more direct heirs were to be found in the New Towns movement, whose views still influence policy.

'Thorough sanitary and remedial action in the houses that we have; and then the building of more, strongly, beautifully, and in groups of limited extent, kept in proportion to their streams and walled round, so that there may be no festering and wretched suburb anywhere, but clean and busy street within and the open country without, with a belt of beautiful garden and orchard round the walls, so that from any part of the city perfectly fresh air and grass and sight of far horizon might be reachable in a few minutes' walk. This the final aim.' John Ruskin, *Sesame and Lilies*.

The reader is asked to imagine an estate embracing an area of 6,000 acres, which is at present purely agricultural, and has been obtained by purchase in the open market at a cost of £40 an acre, or £240,000. . . .

. . . The objects of this land purchase may be stated in various ways, but it is sufficient here to say that some of the chief objects are these: to find for our industrial population work at wages of *higher purchasing power*, and to secure healthier surroundings and more regular employment. To enterprising manufacturers, co-operative societies, architects, engineers, builders, and mechanicians of all kinds, as well as to many engaged in various professions, it is intended to offer a means of securing new and better employment for their capital and talents, while to the agriculturists at present on the estate as well as to those who may migrate thither, it is designed to open a new market for their produce close to their doors. Its object is, in short, to raise the standard of health and comfort of all true workers of whatever grade – the means by which these objects are to be achieved being a healthy, natural, and economic combination of town and country life, and this on land owned by the municipality.

Garden City, which is to be built near the centre of the 6,000 acres, covers an area of 1,000 acres, or a sixth part of the 6,000 acres, and might be of circular form, 1,240 yards (or nearly three-quarters of a mile) from centre to circumference. . . .

Six magnificent boulevards – each 120 feet wide – traverse the city from centre to circumference, dividing it into six equal parts or wards. In the centre is a circular space containing about five and a half acres, laid out as a beautiful and well-watered garden; and, surrounding this garden, each standing in its own ample grounds, are the larger public buildings – town hall, principal concert and lecture hall, theatre, library, museum, picture-gallery, and hospital . . . on our way to the outer ring of the town, we cross Fifth Avenue – lined, as are all the roads of the town, with trees – fronting which, and looking on to the Crystal Palace, we find a ring of very excellently built houses, each standing in its own ample grounds. . . .

Noticing the very varied architecture and design which the houses and groups of houses display – some having common gardens and co-operative kitchens – we learn that general observance of street line or harmonious departure from it are the chief points as to house building, over which the municipal authorities exercise control, for, though proper sanitary arrangements are strictly enforced, the fullest measure of individual taste and preference is encouraged. . . .

On the outer ring of the town are factories, warehouses, dairies, markets, coal yards, timber yards, etc., all fronting on the circle railway, which encompases the whole town. . . .

From: *Garden Cities of Tomorrow*, E. Howard (first published 1902), 1974 edn, pp. 50–55.

Document twenty-three
SUBURBAN SPRAWL AND RIBBON DEVELOPMENT

By the 1930s a reaction to the outward spread of towns had begun to develop, although it was not to materialise as policy until after the Second World War. The following extract illustrates one writer's lack of enthusiasm for the way the Garden City idea was being carried out.

During the past forty years there are towns of from sixty to seventy thousand inhabitants that have sprung from hamlets within the memory of this generation. Villas alternate with cottages, each on its little plot of land, and they extend for miles. They do not combine; they merely continue. There is no attempt to express a communal or civic spirit; 'it is the worship of petty individualities on a gigantic scale.' The country cottages – often excellent in themselves – are not in the country; they are in a borough, and there are three or four miles of them along the tram route. To complete the anachronism, the new palatial town hall, the civic centre of this drowned suburb, will be the latest thing in neo-grec, and much too grand for any provincial company. The whole thing is a misfit; it is the expression of confused thinking, or rather, perhaps, of the absence of thinking. Idealism in housing matters is undefined; its scope is confined within narrow limits, and the end is muddle. The problem is far bigger than our social reformers have realised, and something more is required than warm-heartedness and cheap land. Expressed in the genuine garden city is an ideal which is good, architecturally and socially, but the popular interpretation of the garden city is a twentieth-century freak, neither garden nor city.

From: *The Builder*, 18 July 1903, p. 99.

Document twenty-four
THE NEW TOWN IDEA

At the end of the Second World War the Reith Committee was set up to determine how to establish a series of New Towns, and to ensure that these should be 'self-contained and balanced communities'. While their Recommendations show a clear debt to Ebenezer Howard, and reflected the enthusiasm for social change current at the time, in practice the New Towns tended to be neither 'self-contained' nor 'balanced'.

There may, however, be some doubt as to the full significance of a 'balanced' community, and still more as to how that is to be achieved. So far as the issue is an economic one, balance can be attained by giving opportunity for many sorts of employment which will attract men and women up to a high income level. Beyond that point the problem is not economic at all nor even a vaguely social one; it is, to be frank, one of class distinction. So far as these distinctions are based on income, taxation and high costs of living are reducing them. We realise also that there are some who would have us ignore their existence. But the problem remains and must be faced; if the community is to be truly balanced, so long as social classes exist, all must be represented in it. A contribution is needed from every type and class of person; the community will be the poorer if all are not there, able and willing to make it.

Where possible, therefore, businesses and industries established should include not only factories, shops, and the businesses and services meeting local needs, but head-offices and administrative and research establishments, including sections of government departments and other public offices. It is most desirable that proprietors, directors, executives and other leading workers in the local industries and businesses should live in the town and take part in its life. Many professional men and women, writers, artists, and other specialists not tied to a particular location should find a new town a good place in which to live and work. So also should retired people from home and overseas, from every kind of occupation, as well as people of independent means. All these should find interest and scope in playing their part in the development of the social, political, artistic, and recreational activities of the town.

In order to attract and retain all these groups, the character of the town as one of diverse and balanced social composition must be established at the beginning. If all the dwellings built in the first years are of the minimum standard, however good that may be, the town will be stamped as a 'one-class town', and it will be difficult to redress the balance later. In the first section built there should be some groups of larger houses of varying sizes, provided by the agency, by housing associations or by private builders for sale and letting, as well as sites for houses to be built to suit owner-occupiers. Owing to the housing shortage, the availability of houses on short lease and of facilities for having them built will for some years be a powerful attraction. Once the balanced character of the population is established, it will be relatively easy to maintain it. In this connection, and indeed in general, the importance of a close and cordial relationship between the agency and the dispersing authorities will be obvious. The advantages of living in a new town will be real and apparent and each social or interest group will attract its like.

From: *The New Towns Committee: Final Report.* Cmnd 6876, 1946, paras. 22–24.

Document twenty-five
THE RADIANT CITY

For the task before us is to satisfy men's hearts.

Every day the anxiety and depression of modern life spring up afresh: the city is swelling, the city is filling up. The city simply builds itself anew on top of itself: the old houses towered in a cliff at the edge of the streets; the new houses still tower in new cliffs along the same streets. All the houses are on streets, the street is the basic organ of the city, and the house is the individual, infinitely repeated mould. The street becomes appalling, noisy, dusty, dangerous; automobiles can scarcely do more than crawl along it; the pedestrians, herded together on the sidewalks, get in each other's way, bump into each other, zigzag from side to side; the whole scene is like a glimpse of purgatory. Some of the buildings are office buildings; but how is it possible to work well with so little light and so much noise? Elsewhere, the buildings are residential; but how is it possible to breathe properly in those torrid canyons of summer heat; how can anyone risk bringing up children in that air tainted with dust and soot, in those streets so full of mortal peril? How can anyone achieve the serenity indispensable to life, how can anyone relax, or ever give a cry of joy, or laugh, or breathe, or feel drunk with sunlight? How can anyone *live!* . . . The problem is to create the Radiant City. . . .

I shall explain the plan for this city, and the explanation will be neither literary nor an approximation. It will be technical and rigorously precise.

The general characteristics of the plan are as follows: the city (a large city, a capital) is much less spread out than the present one; the distances within it are therefore shorter, which means more rest and more energy available for work every day. There are no suburbs or dormitory towns; this means an immediate solution to the transportation crisis that has been forced upon us by the paradox of the city + garden cities.

The garden city is a pre-machine-age utopia.

The population density of the new city will be from three to six times greater than the idealistic, ruinous and inoperative figures recommended by urban authorities still imbued with romantic ideology. This new intensification of population density thus becomes the financial justification for our enterprise: *it increases the value of the ground.*

204

The pedestrian never meets a vehicle inside the city. The mechanical transportation network is an entirely new organ, a separate entity. The ground level (the *earth*) belongs entirely to the pedestrian.

The 'street' as we know it now has disappeared. All the various sporting activities take place directly outside people's homes, in the midst of parks – trees, lawns, lakes. The city is entirely green; *it is a Green City*. Not one inhabitant occupies a room without sunlight; everyone looks out on trees and sky.

The keystone of the theory behind this city is the *liberty of the individual*. Its aim is to create respect for that liberty, to bring it to an authentic fruition, to destroy our present slavery. The restitution of every individual's personal liberty. Waste will also have its throat cut. The cost of living will come down. The new city will break the shackles of poverty in which the old city has been keeping us chained.

Its growth is assured. It is the Radiant City. A gift to all of us from modern technology. Those are the outlines of this new city. And I intend to fill in those outlines later, down to the smallest detail.

From: *The Radiant City*. Le Corbusier (first published 1933). Reprinted 1964, pp. 36, 94.

A NEW APPROACH TO IMPROVEMENT

By 1968 much of the worst housing had been replaced, although it was obvious that new house-building programmes would have to continue for many years if all unfit housing were to be eradicated. The government's intention was to slow the decay of what old housing remained by encouraging improvement, and in addition try to cut costs. Despite the admission that individual initiative had produced only a 'patchy' response, there was no swing to compulsion.

Local authorities should have power to declare General Improvement Areas. The aim in these areas would be to help and persuade owners to improve their houses, and to help them also by improving the environment. Authorities would be able to buy land and buildings and carry out work for this purpose. They would also have power to buy houses for improvement and conversion and to buy any houses which were unfit and which stood in the way of the improvement of the whole area.

The success of area improvement will depend on local authorities securing the co-operation of householders in improving their houses with grants. In the Government's view the voluntary principle must be the guiding one, although powers of compulsory purchase would be available. It is essential that the wishes and needs of people in the area should be fully considered, and that the authority's plans for the area should be fully explained. For this reason, and to avoid delay, it is not proposed that the declaration of the area and the plans for it should be formally submitted to the Minister or Secretary of State for inquiry and approval. What is needed at this stage is informality of approach and good public relations . . .

From: *Old Houses into New Homes*. Cmnd 3602, 1968, p. 3.

Document twenty-seven
REDEVELOPMENT, NO! REHABILITATION, YES!

The Government believes that, in the majority of cases, it is no longer preferable to attempt to solve the problems arising from bad housing by schemes of widespread, comprehensive redevelopment. Such an approach often involves massive and unacceptable disruption of communities and leaves vast areas of our cities standing derelict and devastated for far too long. Regardless of the financial compensation they receive, many people suffer distress when their homes are compulsorily acquired. Increasing local opposition to redevelopment proposals is largely attributable to people's understandable preference for the familiar and, in many ways, more convenient environment in which they have lived for years. Large-scale redevelopment frequently diminishes rather than widens the choice available to people in terms of the style of houses, their form of tenure, and their price.

Some local authorities, recognising the heavy financial and social costs involved in major redevelopment schemes, have begun to draw up programmes in which new building and rehabilitation are carefully integrated, house improvement being used to phase urban renewal in ways which allow continuous, flexible and gradual redevelopment on a relatively small scale. The Government wishes to encourage this concept of gradual renewal which allows groups of the worst houses to be cleared and redeveloped quickly; some to be given minor improvement and repair pending clearance in the medium term; others comprising predominantly sounder houses to be substantially rehabilitated and possibly included in general improvement areas. This approach also means that fewer homes, at any point in time during the process of renewal, are lost from the stock of available dwellings – a very important consideration in areas of housing scarcity.

From: *Better Homes: The Next Priorities*. Cmnd 5339, 1973, p. 4.

Document twenty-eight
RENEWAL BECOMES EVEN MORE GRADUAL

The DOE circular outlining how the government saw the Renewal Strategies of the 1974 Housing Act being implemented, marked the furthest point in the retreat from the 'sanitary idea' approach to bad housing.

Gradual renewal is a continuous process of minor rebuilding and renovation which sustains and reinforces the vitality of a neighbourhood in ways responsive to social and physical needs as they develop and change. Rehabilitation should take place to varying standards to match the effective demand of individual occupiers. Successful management of rehabilitation, in particular, will call for a more flexible attitude by local authorities towards the rate at which desirable standards of renovation are adopted. It must be accepted – and willingly – that some houses of low quality meet a real need for cheap accommodation, a need which might not otherwise be satisfied. It would not always be sensible to press for the immediate rehabilitation of all dwellings in an area to the full ('ten-point') standard or more, or to clear them, until they cease to fulfil their present social function. For example, sub-standard dwellings occupied by elderly persons could, *if this were the residents' wish*, remain largely undisturbed for the time being, except for the carrying out of basic repairs and elementary improvements (e.g. hot-water supply, better heating) with the help of the new grants where appropriate. Authorities should also consider the possibility of selective acquisition of dwellings, or rehousing of certain residents, to prevent the undue deterioration of a neighbourhood or enable better use to be made of the housing stock.

From: DOE circular 13/75, January 1975. *Housing Act 1974: Renewal Strategies*, para. 23.

70.   The Government consider that if real progress is to be made in tackling some of the major concentrations of problems, special efforts must be focused on a few cities in the next few years. Inner-area problems are interdependent and complex. There is much fuller understanding of their character now, but they remain to be tackled successfully. The powers and finances of central and local government will need to be used in a unified and coherent way. New forms of organisation and new methods of working may need to be tried. In the Government's view, success is more likely to be achieved by concentrating special attention and the major part of urban aid on a few major areas initially. Spread too thinly, any special efforts will achieve much less.

71.   The Government intend, therefore, to offer special partnerships to a strictly limited number of authorities – districts and counties – to assist in the regeneration of inner-city areas. The participation of central government is intended to underline the Government's commitment to the inner areas and to instil confidence in their future; it will help to bring national experience to bear; it will enable ways of unifying the actions of central and local government to be worked out. The initial task of the partnerships will be to draw up an inner-area programme for early implementation, based on an analysis of local conditions. These inner-area programmes will be supported by Urban Programme grants. They will also help to indicate the priorities within the main policies and programmes of central and local government. For example, inner-area programmes will be taken into account in settling block housing allocations to local authorities; and the work of central government agencies will take account of programmes in whose preparation they will have had a hand. The results of the programmes will be monitored.

78.   *Joint machinery.*   The Government envisage joint machinery for each partnership to secure the preparation and implementation of inner-area programmes. Different arrangements may be needed for different areas, especially for the London Docklands where a Statutory Joint Committee is already in being. The Government will wish to discuss them in each case with the authorities concerned. In general, however, the intention is to

bring together the local authorities – at district and county level (London Boroughs and the Greater London Council) – and central government, through departments and agencies, e.g. Manpower Services Commission, Health Authorities. Local communities will need to be involved in the planning and execution of the programmes.

79.   It is envisaged that there will need to be a small team to analyse inner-area needs, to draw up the programme and to oversee its implementation; together with some steering machinery comprising representatives of central and local government (including Ministers and local-authority elected members) to guide the preparation and implementation of the programme, co-ordinate central and local government activities relating to it, help to remove constraints in the way of action, ensure that the community are involved in the work, and monitor the effectiveness of the programme. The Government will take the necessary steps to concert their contributions and responses to each inner-area programme. These arrangements must take account of the separate responsibilities of the Secretary of State under his statutory functions relating to any matter which comes before him for determination under statutory provisions, including planning appeals, applications for confirmation of compulsory purchase orders and the like.

From: *Policy for the Inner Cities*. Cmnd 6845, 1977, paras 70, 71, 78 and 79.

THE FINANCIAL EFFECT OF COUNCIL HOUSE SALES

Shelter was fiercely critical of the sales policy and calculated that in the long run there would be considerable cost falling on the tax-payer, as well as the social cost falling on the poor and badly housed.

Assumptions:

In this note we are accepting the following assumptions made by the Environment Secretary, Michael Heseltine, in his Conservative Party Press Release GE590/79, 19 April 1979.

* average council house sold for £5,000
* interest rate 11 per cent
* length of mortgage 20 years
* rents minus repairs (i.e. net receipts) £260 a year

We are also assuming that:

* the inflation rate is 8 per cent throughout the period and that rents, house prices, and repair costs rise in line with inflation and therefore that the discount rate is 3 per cent
* mortgage tax relief at 30 per cent is given on 90 per cent of houses when first sold (90 per cent of houses in Leeds, and 94 per cent of GLC houses sold were given council mortgages); tax relief is given on 50 per cent of resold houses And (as estimated by Forrest and Murie) the average date of sale is after 20 years
* the first sale is at a 40 per cent discount (i.e. the market value of the house is £8,333)
* the house has a forty-year life

Some of Mr Heseltine's assumptions on rents and average house prices are questionable but these mainly affect the cross-over point where sales first begin to make a loss. The assumptions on inflation and the discount rate crucially affect the result. Yet we have some confidence in our results as they are similar to those found by the Institute of Cost and Management

Accountants in their more sophisticated study, *Accounting for the Sale of Council Houses.*

IN THE FIRST YEAR THERE IS A GAIN TO THE PUBLIC PURSE

Mortgage receipts (11 per cent of £5,000)	£550
less cost of mortgage tax relief (30 per cent of 90 per cent of £550)	−£149
less loss of net receipts from rent	−£260
Net Gain	£141

BY THE SIXTH YEAR THESE GAINS HAVE TURNED TO A LOSS AS INFLATION REDUCES THE REAL VALUE OF MORTGAGE REPAYMENTS AND RENTS RISE IN STEP WITH INFLATION

Mortgage receipts (11 per cent of £550)	£550
less cost of mortgage tax relief (30 per cent of 90 per cent of £550)	−£149
less loss of net receipts from rent (£260 at 8 per cent inflation for six years)	−£412
Net Loss on Sale	−£ 11

OVER A PERIOD OF FORTY YEARS THE COMMUNITY SUFFERS A SUBSTANTIAL LOSS

Net present value of mortgage payments less tax relief on first mortgage (i.e. £400 a year, for 20 years, 8 per cent inflation and 3 per cent real discount rate)	£3,185
Net present value of capital sum received on resale (£5,000 at year 20)*	£ 509
Net present value of tax relief on mortgage when house is sold after 20 years (i.e. mortgage tax relief on £38,840 house, for half of all purchasers, at 11 per cent interest rate, tax rate assumed to be 30 per cent)	−£ 611
Net present value of loss of net receipts from rent (£260 for 40 years assuming that rent increases and inflation are equal and there is a real discount rate of 3 per cent)	−£6,010
Net overall loss from sale of council house	£2,957
say	£3,000

* We have taken the slight liberty of assuming that the money is repaid all at year 20 by a sinking fund rather than gradually by an annuity mortgage. The difference this would make would be approximately balanced by a corresponding reduction in the level of mortgage interest payments.

From: *The Facts about Council House Sales.* Shelter, 1979, Appendix.

TABLE OF STATUTES

1381 Forcible Entry Act
1848 Public Health Act
1855 Metropolitan Building Act
1855 Labourers' Dwelling Act
1868 Citizens' and Labourers' Dwelling Act
1874 Building Societies' Act
1875 Artisans' Dwellings Act (Cross Act)
1882 Artisans' Dwellings Act (Cross Act)
1883 Cheap Trains Act
1890 Housing of the Working Classes Act
1894 Housing of the Working Classes Act
1893–94 Provident Societies Act
1900 Housing of the Working Classes Act
1909 Housing and Town Planning Act
1915 Rent and Mortgages Restriction Act
1919 Housing and Town Planning Act (Addison's Act)
1923 Housing Act
1930 Housing Act
1936 Housing Act
1944 Education Act
1947 Town and Country Planning Act
1948 National Assistance Act
1948 Children's Act
1957 Rent Act
1957 Housing Act
1959 House Purchase and Housing Act
1964 Housing Act
1964 Protection from Eviction Act
1965 Rent Act
1967 Housing Subsidies Act

1969 Housing Act
1971 Fire Precaution Act
1972 Housing Finance Act
1972 Local Government Act
1974 Housing Act
1974 Rent Act
1975 Land Act
1976 Rent (Agriculture) Act
1977 Housing (Homeless Persons) Act
1977 The Empty Houses (Prevention of Squatting) Bill
1977 Criminal Law Act
1979 Housing Bill

TABLE OF REPORTS

The Reports of Government Committees almost always deserve reading. They frequently give much background detail to the subject under discussion, and often provide a review of other relevant material. Discovering the membership of a Committee can sometimes be almost as instructive as reading their Report. The verbatim Minutes of Evidence of the earlier Reports provide invaluable source material as to how people thought and acted, and what sort of world they lived in.

1881–82   Select Committee on Artisans and Labourers' Dwellings Improvement, 1881 (358) vii 395; 1882 (235) vii 249.
1884   Royal Commission on the Housing of the Working Classes. First Report, Minutes of evidence, Appendices and Index 1884–85 (C 4402) xxxl; Second Report (Scotland) 1884–85 (C 4409) xxx I; Third Report (Ireland) 1884–85 (C 4547) xxx I.
1890   Report of the Standing Committee on the Housing Acts (29) xiii I.
1902   Report of the Joint Select Committee on the Housing of the Industrial Population of Scotland, Rural and Urban, 1917–18 Cd 8731 xiv 345.
1961   Central Housing Advisory Committee, *Homes for Today and Tomorrow* (Parker Morris Report), HMSO.
1963   Ministry of Transport, *Traffic in Towns: a study of the long term problems of traffic in urban areas* (Buchanan Report), HMSO.
1965   Ministry of Housing and Local Government, *Report of the Committee on Housing in Greater London*, Cmnd 2605 (Milner Holland Report), HMSO.

1965   Ministry of Housing and Local Government, *Rents and Security of Tenure: the Rent Bill*, Cmnd 2622, HMSO.

1966   Central Housing Advisory Committee, *Our Older Houses: a call for action* (Dennington Report), HMSO.

1967   Central Advisory Council for Education, *Children and their Primary Schools* (Plowden Report), HMSO.

1968   *Report of the Committee on Local Authority and Allied Personal Social Services*, Cmnd 3703 (Seebohm Report), HMSO.

1968   Ministry of Housing and Local Government, *Collapse of Flats at Ronan Point, Canning Town: Report of the Enquiry*, HMSO.

1968   Ministry of Housing and Local Government, *Report of the Committee on Public Participation in Planning* (Skeffington Report), HMSO.

1969   *Royal Commission on Local Government in England*, Cmnd 4040 (Redcliffe Maud Report), HMSO.

1969   Housing Management Sub-Committee of the Central Housing Advisory Committee, Ninth Report, *Council Housing: purposes, procedures and priorities* (Cullingworth Report), HMSO.

1971   Department of the Environment, *Widening the Choice: the next steps in housing*, Cmnd 5280, HMSO.

1972   Department of Education and Science, *Educational Priority. Vol 1. EPA Problems and Policies*, edited by A. Halsey, HMSO.

1972   Study Group on Local Authority Management Structure, *The New Local Authorities: management and structure* (Baines Report), HMSO.

1977   Department of the Environment, *Change and Decay: Final Report of the Liverpool Inner Area study*, HMSO.

1977   Department of the Environment, *Inner London: policies of dispersal and balance. Final Report of the Lambeth Inner Area study*, HMSO.

1977   Department of the Environment, *Policy for Inner Cities*, Cmnd 6845, HMSO.

1977   Department of the Environment, *Review of the Rent Acts: a consultative document*, HMSO.

1977   Department of the Environment, *Unequal City: Final Report of the Birmingham Inner Area study*, HMSO.

1977   Department of the Environment, *Housing Policy: a consultative document*, Cmnd 6851, and the *Technical Volume*, parts 1, 2 and 3, HMSO.

1977   Supplementary Benefits Commission, *Annual Report for 1976*, HMSO.

1978   Department of the Environment Central Unit on Environmental Pollution, Pollution Paper No. 14, *Lead Pollution in Birmingham: Report of the joint working party on lead pollution around Gravelly Hill*, HMSO.

SELECT BIBLIOGRAPHY

ALPREN, L., *The Causes of Serious Rent Arrears*, Housing Centre Trust, London, 1977.

AMBROSE, P. and COLENUTT, B., *The Property Game*, Pelican, Harmondsworth, 1975.

ARDEN, A., *Housing: security and rent control*, Sweet and Maxwell, London, 1978.

BAILEY, R., *The Homeless and the Empty Houses*, Pelican, Harmondsworth, 1971.

BAILEY, R., *The Squatters*, Penguin, Harmondsworth, 1973.

BARCLAY, I., *People Need Roots*, National Council for Social Services, London, 1976.

BERRY, F., *Housing: the great British failure*, Charles Knight, London, 1974.

BLYTHE, R., *Akenfield: portrait of an English village*, Penguin, Harmondsworth, 1972.

BULMER, M. (ed), *Working Class Images of Society*, Routledge and Kegan Paul, London, 1975.

CASTELLS, M., *City, Class and Power*, Macmillan, London, 1979.

CHARLES, S., *Housing Economics*, Macmillan, London, 1977.

CHRISTENSEN, T., *Neighbourhood Survival*, Prism Press, London, 1979.

COATES, K. and SILBURN, R., *Poverty: the forgotten Englishmen*, Pelican, Harmondsworth, 1970.

COCKBURN, C., *The Local State*, Pluto Press, London, 1977.

COHEN, S., *Folk Devils and Moral Panics*, first edn 1972; second edn, Martin Robertson, Oxford, 1980.

COMMISSION OF THE EUROPEAN COMMUNITIES, *The Perception of Poverty in Europe: a report on a public opinion survey carried out in the member countries of the European Community as part of the programme of pilot projects to combat poverty*, 1977.

COMMUNITY DEVELOPMENT PROJECT, *Gilding the Ghetto*, London, 1976.

COMMUNITY DEVELOPMENT PROJECT, *Whatever Happened to Council Housing?*, London, 1976.

CULLINGWORTH, J. B., *Essays on Housing Policy*, Allen and Unwin, London, 1979.

CUTTING, M., *A Housing Rights Handbook*, Prism Press and Penguin Books, London, 1979.

DEAKIN, N. and UNGERSON, C., *Leaving London: planned mobility and the inner-city*, Heinemann Educational Books, London, 1977.

DONNISON, D., *The Government of Housing*, Pelican, Harmondsworth, 1967.

ENGELS, F., *The Housing Question*, first published 1872–73, reprinted in paperback, Progress Publishers, Moscow, 1975.

FIELD, F. and HAIKIN, P. (eds), *Black Britons*, Oxford University Press, Oxford, 1971.

FRIEDMAN, M., *Capitalism and Freedom*, University of Chicago Press, Chicago, 1962.

GANS, H. G., *People and Plans: essays in urban problems and solutions*, Pelican, Harmondsworth, 1969.

GAULDIE, E., *Cruel Habitations: a history of working-class housing 1780–1918*, Allen and Unwin, London, 1974.

GINSBERG, N., *Class, Capital and Social Policy*, Macmillan, London, 1979.

GREVE, J., GREVE, S. and PAGE, D., *Homelessness in London*, Scottish Academic Press, Edinburgh, 1971.

HADDEN, T., *Housing: repairs and improvements*, Sweet and Maxwell, London, 1979.

HALL, P., THOMAS, R., GRACEY, H. and DREWETT, R., *The Containment of Urban England*, Vols 1 and 2, Allen and Unwin and Sage Publications, London and Beverly Hills, 1973.

HARVEY, D., *Social Justice and the City*, Edward Arnold, London, 1976.

HAYEK, F. A., *The Constitution of Liberty*, Routledge and Kegan Paul, London, 1960.

HEYWOOD, J., *Children in Care*, Routledge and Kegan Paul, London, 1965.

JACOBS, J., *The Economy of Cities*, first published New York, 1969, paperback edn, Pelican, Harmondsworth, 1970.

JOEL-BARNETT, M., *The Politics of Legislation*, Weidenfeld and Nicolson, London, 1969.

JONES, G., *Rural Life*, Longman, London, 1973.

JORDAN, B., *Freedom and the Welfare State*, Routledge and Kegan Paul, London, 1977.

LAMBERT, C. and WEIR, D. (eds), *Cities in Modern Britain*, Fontana, London, 1975.

LANSLEY, S., *Housing and Public Policy*, Croom Helm, London, 1979.

LE CORBUSIER, *The Radiant City*, first published 1933, reprinted Faber and Faber, London, 1964.

LEES, R. and SMITH, G., *Action Research in Community Development*, Routledge and Kegan Paul, London, 1975.

MARRIOTT, O., *The Property Boom*, Pan, London, 1967.

MERRETT, S., *State Housing in Britain*, Routledge and Kegan Paul, London, 1979.

MILLER, D., *Social Justice*, Oxford University Press, Oxford, 1979.

MUMFORD, L., *The City in History*, first published 1961, paperback edn, Pelican, Harmondsworth, 1966.

MURIE, A., NINER, P. and WATSON, C., *Housing Policy and the Housing System*, Allen and Unwin, London, 1976.

ORMANDY, D. and DAVIES, A., *Standards of Accommodation for Single People*, CHAR, 1977.

PAHL, R., *Patterns of Urban Life*, Longman, London, 1970.

PAHL, R., *Whose City?*, first published 1970, paperback edn, Penguin, Harmondsworth, 1975.

PARIS, C. and POPPLETON, C., *Squatting: a bibliography*, Centre for Environmental Studies Occasional Paper 3, 1978.

PEARSON, G., *The Deviant Imagination*, Macmillan, London, 1974.

PLOWDEN, W., *The Motor Car and British Politics*, Pelican, Harmondsworth, 1976.

PROSSER, P. and WEDGE, H., *Born to Fail*, Arrow Books, London, 1973.

RAWLES, J., *A Theory of Justice*, Clarendon Press, Oxford, 1972.

REX, J. and MOORE, P. with SHUTTLEWORTH, A. and WILLIAMS, J., *Race, Community and Conflict*, Oxford University Press, London, 1967.

RUNCIMAN, W. G., *Relative Deprivation and Social Justice*, first published 1966, paperback edn, Pelican, Harmondsworth, 1976.

SAUNDERS, P., *Sociology and Urban Politics*, Hutchinson, London, 1979.

SHELTER, *Roof*, fortnightly, London, 1977 onwards.

STEADMAN JONES, G., *Outcast London: a study in the relationship between classes in Victorian Society*, Penguin, Harmondsworth, 1976.

SUTCLIFFE, A. (ed), *Multi-Storey Living: the British working class experience*, Croom Helm, London, 1973.

TAWNEY, R., *Equality*, Allen and Unwin, London, 1931.

TAYLOR, N., *The Village in the City*, Temple Smith, London, 1973.

THOMPSON, F., *Lark Rise to Candleford*, Penguin, Harmondsworth, 1973.

TITMUSS, R., *The Gift Relationship*, first published 1970, paperback edn, Pelican, Harmondsworth, 1970.

TOWNSEND, P., *The Family Life of Old People*, Pelican, Harmondsworth, 1965.

TOWNSEND, P., *Poverty in the United Kingdom*, Penguin and Allen Lane, London, 1979.

WARD, C., *Housing: an anarchist approach*, Freedom Press, London, 1976.

WATES, N., *The Battle for Tolmers Square*, Routledge and Kegan Paul, London, 1976.

WILLIAMS, R., *The City and the Country*, Chatto and Windus, London, 1974.

WILMOTT, P. and YOUNG, M., *Family and Kinship in East London*, Pelican, Harmondsworth, 1967.

WINSTANLEY, G., *Winstanley: The Laws of Freedom and other writings*, Pelican, Harmondsworth, 1973.

INDEX

Abbey National Building Society, 11, 36, 40
Abercrombie Greater London Plan, 106
access
    to caravan sites, 99
    to council housing, 27–32, 99
    to inner cities, 113–14
    to owner-occupation, 35, 39–43
    to tied housing, 100
Action Research Projects, 121, 123
'Addison's' Act 1919, 8
Afan, 78
Agricultural Dwelling Housing
    Advisory Panel (ADHAP), 101–2
agricultural workers, 92, 100–2
Artisans' Dwellings Acts 1875 and
    1882, 5

Bailey, Ron, 85, 86
Balfe, Richard, 90
banks, 36, 41, 109, doc 10
battered wives, 77
bed-and-breakfast hotels, 68–9, doc 15
Birmingham
    blood lead levels, 117–18
    employment changes, 113
    housing policy, 27, 29–30
    inner city development, 110, 132,
        136, 139
    rents (1972), 20
Bradford, 40
Buchanan Report, 117, 118
building regulations, 10
building societies
    competition with banks, 36, doc 10
    early clubs, 10, doc 5
    lending policies, 39–41, 98
    permanent, 11–13, 35–7
    red-lining policy, 40, 133, doc 11
Building Societies Act 1874, 11

Callaghan, James, 123
Campaign for the Homeless and
    Rootless (CHAR), 74–5, 76, 80
capital expenditure programme, 25,
    doc 7
Catholic Housing Aid Society, 76
Cathy Come Home, 66, 85
Centrepoint, 108
Chadwick, Edwin, 3, 5
Chamberlain, Neville, 12
Cheap Trains Act 1883, 105
Child Poverty Action Group, 76, 154
children, 71–2, 119–20, 120–1
Children's Act 1948, 64
choice in housing, 29
cities, see inner cities
Citizens' and Labourers' Dwelling Act
    1868, 3
Clacton, 79
Clay Cross, 22
commercial development of inner cities,
    108–12, 131–2
Community Development Projects
    (CDPs), 123, 125, 128
commuter villages, 93–6
compulsory purchase, 9, 112, 130, 132
Conservative Party policies, 18–19, 26,
    38, 53, 56
    Rent Act 1957, 47–9
    sale of council houses, 153–5
Cornwall, 98, doc 19

corporate management, 26
cost yardstick, 24, 25–6, 158
cottage estates, 105, 140, 158–9
council houses, 5–6
    allocation of, 29–32
    building of, 18, 68, 105, 133, 140,
        157–8
    government policies on, 13, 17–24
    increases in, 8, 17, 18, 148
    prefabricated, 115–16
    sale of, 42, 102, 153–9
    see also tenants
Covent Garden, 139
Criminal Law Act 1977, 88
Crosland, Anthony, 23
'Cross' Acts 1875 and 1882, 5
Crossman, Richard, 49, doc 13
Cullingworth Committee, 27, 28, 29,
    31, 76, doc 9

Denning, Lord, 87
Department of the Environment
    (DOE), 25, 132, 136
desert and social justice, 152, 153, 161
discrimination in council house
    allocation, 30–1
disrepair procedures, 47, 48–9
District Auditor, rôle of, 22

Education Act 1944, 120
Educational Priority Areas (EPAs), 121
elderly people, 47, 95, 119
employment changes, 92–3, 112–14,
    135–6
Empty Houses (Prevention of
    Squatting) Bill 1977, The, 87
Engels, F., 2, 160–1, doc 1
Environmental Health Officers, 131
eviction, 48–9, 50, 65–6, 86, 88

'fair rents', 20–2, 49–50, 50–1, 57,
    doc 13
finance
    and building societies, 10, 11–12,
        35–7
    and local authorities, 19, 24–6, 133,
        doc 7
    of owner-occupation, 35–7, 37–8
    of private rented sector, 46
Fire Precautions Act 1971, 74
five per cent philanthropy, 4

'folk devil' squatters, 87, 88
Forcible Entry Act 1381, 83–4
Francis Committee, 51, 54

Gans, Herbert, 138
Garden City theories, 105, doc 22
General Improvement Areas (GIAs),
    125–6
gentrification, 126–8, 136
Glasgow, 8, 136
Green Papers
    on housing policy, 23, 40, 42–3, 63,
        137, 148
    on Rent Acts, 52–3

Halifax Building Society, 11, 36
Halsey Report, 128
harassment, 48–50, 65–6, 86, 111, 127
Hertfordshire, rural, 93
Heseltine, Michael, 137, 154
high-rise building, 114–17
Hill, Octavia, 3, doc 2
holiday lets, 83, 96, 97, 98–9, 101
homeless families
    in bed-and-breakfast hotels, 68–9,
        doc 15
    consequences of, 70–2
    one-offer system for, 28, 67
    in Part III accommodation, 64–5,
        67–8
    reasons for, 69–70, 75
    as squatters, 88, 89–90
homelessness, 64–81
    intentional, 78–80
    as result of Rent Acts, 49, 50, 65
    and squatting, 83–4
'Homes for Heroes', 8, 12, 83
homesteading scheme, 41–2
hostels for the homeless, 69, 73–6, 84
House Purchase and Housing Act 1959,
    98
Housing Act 1923, 12
Housing Act 1930, 9
Housing Act 1957, 17
Housing Act 1964, 124
Housing Act 1969, 125, 126
Housing Act 1974, 56, 57, 129–33,
    doc 28
Housing Action Areas (HAAs), 130–3,
    137

Housing and Town Planning Act 1909, 7

Housing and Town Planning Act 1919, 8

Housing Association Grant (HAG), 56

housing associations
government-funded, 54–8, 133
philanthropic, 4–6, 54
and squatters, 86

Housing Bills 1979, 30, 38

Housing Commission, 22, 81

Housing Corporation, 55–8, 130

Housing Finance Act 1972, 20–2, 52, 81, 124, 153
repeal of, 22–3

Housing (Homeless Persons) Act 1977, 76–81, doc 17

Housing of the Working Classes Acts 1890, 1894 and 1900, 5

housing shortages, 7–8, 12–13, 27, 99
in inner cities, 112, 115, 116

Housing Subsidies Act 1967, 25

Howard, Ebenezer, 105, doc 22

'husbands' revolt' at King Hill Hostel, 84

immigrant families, 70, 89, 121–3

improvement grants, 54, 124–5, 126–7, 130, 133

industrial decline, 105, doc 20

Industrial Improvement Areas, 135

industry, relocation of, 135

'infernal wen', 140, 141

inner cities, 54, 57, 58, 62–3, 74, 104–42
industrial decline in, 105, doc 20

investment in private rented sector, 46, 53, 133

Islington, 127–8, 136, 138

Kensington, 83–4, 87

King Hill Hostel protest, 84, 85

Labour Party policies, 18, 22–4, 154, doc 6
'Brown ban', 108–9
in private rented sector, 18, 22, 49, 56

Labourers' Dwellings Act 1855, 10

Lambeth, 28, 136, 138, 139

Land Act 1975, 58

land scarcity, 58, 109, 115–16

Le Corbusier, 115, doc 25

Leeds Permanent Building Society, 11, 36

Liberal Government reforms, 7

Liverpool, 68, 107, 113, 119, 125, 136

loans
for commercial development, 109
for house purchase, 35–7, 39–41, 42–3
to housing associations, 55
to Housing Corporation, 56–7

loan sanction, 24–5, 115

local authorities
clearance and improvement of inner cities, 112, 124–6
and council house sales, 153–8
early rôle of, 5, 9
loans, 55, 135
mortgages, 41, 130, 133, 153, 155–6
obligations to the homeless, 64, 67–9, 74–5, 76–81, 101
participation in HAAs, 130–3
partnership schemes, 135–7, doc 29
planning in commuter villages, 96
reactions to squatters, 84, 85, 86
restructuring of, 26–7
and tied accommodation, 101

Location of Offices Bureau (LOB), 135

lodging houses, 72–4, 75

London
Abercrombie Plan, 106
effects of Rent Acts, 49, 51
homelessness in, 66–7, 68
housing shortage, 8
LCC house building, 17, 140
migration from, 107, 138–9
redevelopment of inner city, 5, 41–2, 127–8, 131–2, 136, 138–9
Ronan Point collapse, 116
slum clearance, 5, 140
squatting in, 83–4, 84–6, 87, 88
see also Covent Garden, Islington, Kensington, Lambeth, St Pancras, Redbridge, Tolmers Square

London Squatters' Campaign, 85–6

Manchester, 68, 107, 113, 117, 132, 136

Metropolitan Building Act 1855, 10

migration, 92–5, 99, 104–7, 118

Miller, David, 151–2, 153

Milner Holland Report, 49, 66, 121–2, 162

minimum standards of housing, 4, 9, 45–6, 158

Ministry of Housing and Local Government, 25

model dwellings, 4–6

mortgages, 12, 37–8, 39–41, 98, 130
  for council houses, 153, 155–6, 158

multiple occupation of houses, 72, 75, 89, 127

National Assistance Act 1948, 64
  Part III accommodation, 64–7

National Council for One Parent Families, 76

National Women's Aid Federation, 76

need, housing, 16–17, 27–9, 30, 77–80, doc 8, doc 17
  defined, 152
  and social justice, 153, 161, 163

Newcastle upon Tyne, 132

New Lanark, 2

New Towns, 106–7, 113, 136, 137, doc 24, doc 25

New Towns Corporation, 107

Norfolk, 68, 93–4, doc 18

one-offer system, 28, 67

Owen, Robert, 2

owner-occupation, 148–9, 153
  access to, 35, 39–43
  advantages of, 37–9
  in commuter villages, 95–6
  by immigrants, 121–2
  policy on, 18–19, 23–4, 35, 40, 42–3, doc 6
  through building societies, 10, 11, 12, 35–7, 39–41

Paris, 6, 140

Parker-Morris standards, 25, 131, 158

partnership schemes, 135–7, doc 29

Part III accommodation, 64–7

Peabody Trust, 4–5, 54

planning, 106–7
  blight, 110–12
  in commuter villages, 96

Plowden Report, 120, 128

points system for council housing, 28, 30

policy, housing, 62, 148–51
  on commuter villages, 96
  on council housing, 18–24
  Green Papers, 23, 40, 42–3, 63, 137, 148
  and homelessness, 77
  on inner cities, 137, 140–1, 148
  on owner-occupation, 18–19, 23–4, 35, 40, 42–3
  on private rented sector, 21, 46–7, 53–4, 56
  see also Conservative Party policies, Labour Party policies, White Papers

poor, the, 16, 58, 99, 159–60, 161–3
  training of, 3, doc 2

Poor Law, 64, 65, 81, 162

poverty traps, 11, 52

Powell, Enoch, 122–3

prefabricated buildings, 115–16

priority areas, 129–34, 135

priority groups for accommodation, 27–9, 77–80, doc 17
  see also need

prisons, model, 5

private housing market, see owner-occupation, private rented sector housing

private rented sector housing, 45–58, 153
  before World War I, 12
  classification of tenants in, 42
  encouragement for, 47–8, 53–4, 58
  in inner cities, 124–6, 126–7
  minimum standards in, 45–6
  post-World War II decline of, 13, 38–9, 45, 48, 50, 148
  rent policies, 8, 38–9, 47–54
  scarcity of, 17, 70, 74, 98–9

Profumo, John, 49, 66

property booms, 85, 108–10

Protection from Eviction Act, 1964, 49, 68

Provident Societies Act 1893–4, 54

Provincial Building Society, 40

public health, 3–4, 131

Public Health Act 1848, 10

public sector housing, see council houses

Public Works Loan Board (PWLB),
    19, 25

Rachman, Perec, 48, 49, 65, doc 12
racial discrimination, 31
racial prejudice, 122–3
rateable value, 47–8
Rate Support Grant, 24, 137, 154
Rawles, John, 151
reception centres, 74–5
Redbridge, 85–6, 112
redevelopment of city centres, 74,
    84–5, 108–12
'red-lining', 40, 133, doc 11
Rees Davies, William, 77
Reith Committee, 106, doc 24
Rent Act 1957, 38–9, 47–9, 52, 65–6
Rent Act 1965, 21, 38, 39, 49–51, 52,
    68
Rent Act 1974, 52, 130
Rent (Agriculture) Act 1976, 100,
    101–2
Rent and Mortgage Interest
    (Restrictions) Act 1915, 8
rent arrears, 50, 69–70, 78, 80,
    159–60
Rent Assessment Panels, 51
rent control, 8, 39
    see also the Rent Acts above
rent decontrol, 47–9, 50
rent levels, 4, 19, 20–3
Rent Officers, rôle of, 49–50, 51
rent rebates, 20–3, 52
ribbon development, 106, doc 23
Rossi, Hugh, 87
Rowton House Group, 74
Royal Commissions, 6, 7–8, 26, 106
rural areas, 68, 92–102, 104–5, 141

St Pancras, 22, 54–5
sale of council houses, 42, 102, 153–9
sanitary idea, 3–4, 9, 129–30, 131, 135,
    doc 28
Scotland, 7–8, 136
second-home ownership, 96–8, 101,
    doc 19
security of tenure
    in owner-occupation, 37
    in private rented sector, 39, 49, 51,
        52, 130
    in tied housing, 100, 101
Seebohm Committee, 27, 76, 128,

    doc 8
Shaftesbury, Lord, 4, 5, 6
Shelter, 66
    enquiry into tied housing, 102
    as pressure group, 22, 40, 76
    quoted on council house sales,
        156–7, 159, doc 30
    quoted on homelessness, 65, 69, 76,
        78–9, 80
    quoted on landlords, 58
    quoted on slum clearance, 112
    SNAP in Liverpool, 125, 128
Shore, Peter, 23, 104
shortages, see housing shortages
shortholds, 53, 154
single homeless, 65, 72–6, 77, 80,
    doc 16
    as squatters, 88–90
Single Homeless Action Campaign
    (SHAC), 28, 30, 76
single-parent families, 28, 30
Skeffington Report, 128
Slough, 79
slums, 6–7, 131, 158–9
    clearance of, 5, 8–9, 65, 105, 112,
        124
social justice, 151–2, 153–5, 161–3
Southside Investment Co., 69
squatters, 83–90
    classification of, 72, 88–90
stabilisation of interest rates, 37
state control of housing, 24–6, doc 7
state intervention in housing, 3–9, 17,
    45, 62
subsidies, 24, 38, 43
    for house building, 8, 12, 24
    for housing associations, 55
    for rents, 8, 19, 22, 52
suburbia, 105, 138–9, doc 21, doc 23

tax relief, 38, 43
temporary housing, 64–9, 77, 86
tenants, council
    classification of, 6–7, 32, 42, 159–60,
        doc 3
    and council house sales, 155–7
    definition and selection of, 9, 16–17,
        27–9, doc 4
    grading of, 29–30, doc 9
    licensed, 86, 90
    in rural areas, 94

tenants, tied-housing, 100–2
Tenants' Charter, 154
tied housing, 99–102
Tolmers Square, 110–11, 139
'Torrens' Act 1868, 3
Town and Country Planning Act 1947, 106–7
towns, growth of, 2, doc 1
transport revolution, 92, 98, 117–18
   and increased commuting, 93, 105, 113–14, doc 21

urban deprivation, 62–3, 104, 110–35
urban development corporations, 137
Urban Programme, 123–4, 135–7, 139

vacant possession, 47, 48–9

waiting lists, 27–9
Wales, 78, 97–8, 136
White Papers, 133
   Better Homes – the Next Priorities, 129, 130, doc 27
   Fair Deal for Housing, 21
   Housing the Next Step, 18
   Old Housing into New Homes, 125, doc 26
   Policy for the Inner Cities, 134–8, 154, doc 29
winkling out, 111, 126, 127
winter lets, 98–9
Woolwich Equitable Building Society, 36
workhouses, 5, 65, doc 14
Workington, 131, 139
World War I, 8

Also from Longman

RESOURCES FOR THE WELFARE STATE
John F. Sleeman
First published 1979

This text sets out the economic implications of the welfare state and pays particular attention to the means of raising the resources needed to provide social services and the effects that the use of these resources have on the working of the economy. The author discusses the implications of the rapid expansion of government spending in the early 1970s coupled with Britain's relatively slow economic growth, inflation and balance of payments.